STOURBRIDGE GIRLS' HIGH SCHOOL

Stourbridge Girls Secondary School Hockey Team, 1907–08.
Front row l to r: Phyllis Widdowson; Dorothy Wrigley; Dorothy Burton.
Back row l to r: V. Wheelright; F. Durr; Louisa Burgesss; Gladys Price; W. Green; E. Skelding; A. Wright; Alice Ray; M. Porter.

STOURBRIDGE GIRLS' HIGH SCHOOL

a history of girls gone by

MARION BRETTLE

This book is dedicated to:

The 'old girls' and former members of staff of SGSS and SGHS

Non Sibi Sed Omnibus

Copyright © Marion Brettle 2011

The moral rights of the author have been asserted.
All rights reserved. No part of this book may be reprinted or reproduced or utilised in any form or by any electronic, mechanical or other means, now known or hereafter invented, including photocopying and recording, or in any information storage or retrieval system, without the permission in writing from the author.

ISBN 978-0-9563079-7-2

Published by Ellingham Press, 43 High Street, Much Wenlock, Shropshire TF13 6AD
www.ellinghampress.co.uk

Cover design by Goosey Graphics Company
www.gooseygraphics.co.uk

Typesetting by ISB Typesetting, Sheffield

Printed and bound in the UK by MPG Books Group, Bodmin and Kings Lynn

Foreword

I spent most of my teaching career at Dudley Girls' High School. The Sixties and Seventies were a period of great change in educational thinking. When I became head, I was faced with the mammoth task of helping to turn the school into a 'co-ed' comprehensive.

Just after the plan was put into practice I moved to Stourbridge Girls' High School, fully aware that there would be similar difficulties. Fortunately Red Hill School, as it came to be known, has developed over the years into a much sought-after comprehensive specialising in languages and always near the top of the published examination tables.

However, there are many people who still look back with affection on the old High School.

The Old Girls' Association is still flourishing. Every month members and friends meet to listen to a speaker, chat about their memories good and bad, humiliating and triumphant, and to laugh no doubt at the eccentricities of the staff.

Now I, together with Old Girls and many people in and around Stourbridge, look forward to reading this first history of the school, from its early beginning when girls were given a chance to catch up academically with their brothers at the Grammar School, until the time when it changed its name and character.

We are immensely grateful to Marion Brettle for researching and writing it. I am sure it will be a success.

Beryl Fisher

Stourbridge Girls' High School

This 1932 view of the school shows the pond and the gym.

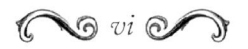

Contents

Foreword		v
Introduction		1
About the Author		5
Chapter One	Early days: Stourbridge Girls' Secondary School and Miss Firth (1905–28)	7
Chapter Two	Stourbridge Girls' High School and Miss Firth (1928–33)	41
Chapter Three	Stourbridge Girls' High School and Miss Dale (1933–50)	55
Chapter Four	Stourbridge Girls' High School and Miss Butler (1950–72)	85
Chapter Five	Stourbridge Girls' High School and Dr Beal (1973–6)	155
Chapter Six	Stourbridge Girls' High School and Miss Fisher (1976)	167
Appendix I	SGHS Old Girls' Association	175
Appendix II	Whatever became of the staff?	191
Appendix III	The 'Old Girls' Remember...	201
Acknowledgement		207
Illustrations		209
Bibliography		211
Index		213

Introduction
why the book had to be written

My personal introduction to Stourbridge Girls' High School was as a very young child, listening to my mother and her old school-friend Ivy Freemantle reminiscing about people called 'Miss Firth', 'Miss Leigh' or 'Miss Sneyd' who appeared to have been teachers there.

My next encounter was when I was taken with my parents (to what I now know to be the High School's junior entrance) to await my oldest sister Pat's appearance after sitting 'the scholarship' (later known as the '11-plus') for entry into the school.

She passed the exam and took up her place at SGHS in September 1947.

The next visit was to see the High School's school play *1066 And All That* which the senior school pupils performed in Pat's first year. My mother wanted to see the play with my middle sister Ann (who was to join the school two years later), but nobody seemed keen to take on the Herculean task of looking after me for the evening. Our father was in the police force and probably on night duty and I was quite a demanding five-year-old for any neighbours to offer. So I went too, with warnings to behave myself 'or else' and 'don't speak a word' during the performance.

As it turned out, these warnings were unnecessary. I was hooked. Hooked on the assembly hall where the play took place and particularly hooked on the play itself and the actors (I think it must have been at this point that my own lifelong interest in the theatre and acting began).

I can still remember being entranced by 'the common man' being wheeled in a wheelbarrow; an insolent Christopher Columbus with an American accent, chewing gum; the chorus of 'Roman soldiers' singing 'We're Going Home'!

I can also remember my mother pointing out certain teachers who had actually taught her when she was a pupil there, and again the name 'Miss Sneyd' comes to mind. I have a vague memory of a small round lady with her hair in a bun smiling kindly as I sat, for once, awestruck on the front row of the audience.

If this was the High School, then I wanted more of it. When both my older sisters were there I was taken along to numerous concerts and plays, and a few momentous occasions to watch a netball match on a Saturday morning when my sisters supported their more sporty friends when they played 'at home'. I was even allowed into the dining-room upstairs where biscuits and orange squash were provided for the teams.

I can remember a very smart PE teacher in divided skirt and Aertex shirt asking, 'when is the little Davies coming here?' (Miss Margot Clark, senior PE teacher at that time.)

The 'little Davies' entered Stourbridge Girls' High School in September 1953 and left in 1960. It would be nice to write that my days there were all halcyon ones. Certainly I had some very happy days there but, as I suspect did most girls, I also had some miserable, tearful ones there, too.

From a wide-eyed, all-admiring little girl of five or six I grew up over the seven years at SGHS to have a slightly rebellious outlook. I felt quite strongly at times that the discipline at the school was more suited to the armed forces than to six hundred or so prepubescent and adolescent girls. I often felt that I was being taught and reprimanded by teachers who, in the main, had been brought up themselves in the late Victorian and early-Edwardian era – the 'spare-the-rod-and-spoil-the-child' syndrome. Many teachers had never married and I thought they lived in a very narrow, school-orientated world.

I resented not being able to defend myself verbally when accused of some wrong-doing. The attitude of many of the staff, I thought, stifled any character and individuality. Life at SGHS was certainly not all *1066 And All That* and scoffing biscuits and orange squash in the dining-room. Certain teachers seemed to have a 'down' on one (I have talked recently to many old school-friends about this and we are all in agreement that this was indeed so). What we didn't appreciate at that time, of course, was that at 12, 13 and 14 years of age, we were probably pretty nasty pieces of work ourselves, so of course teachers had a 'down' on us, especially if we didn't work at their subject.

This, in the main, was all part of 'growing up' and gaining maturity and certainly, by the time I reached the Sixth Form, the staff seemed to me to have mellowed. I had learned a degree of tolerance and appreciation myself, and perhaps it took a questioning, slightly 'anti-establishment' person like me just that bit longer to arrive there!

The days following A levels seemed to be carefree days. Yes, I was looking forward (as were my peers) to a new life and a career, but quite a big part of me was going to miss many aspects of school life. I remember, before we 'broke up' for the last time, a member of my form VI Upper saying that if a job as an SGHS prefect existed then this would be the job for her! Could there be a better legacy for a school than this remark?

I didn't go quite that far myself, but over the years never entirely forgot SGHS. I moved away from Stourbridge for college, university, jobs, subsequent marriage and birth of a daughter, but wherever I lived or travelled to, inevitably an 'old' SGHS girl would appear and we would talk nostalgically about our days there, although generally not entirely through rose-tinted spectacles.

I found that I was very proud to write SGHS on CVs and I was often congratulated on my application forms – a throwback to English lessons? There was a big reunion at the school in 1980 (by now Redhill Comprehensive School) and Miss Butler, my ex-headmistress, now retired of course, was in the vestibule to greet us. Many former members of staff were there, looking older of course, as did we 'girls', and there was much reminiscing and catching up with news.

Time does not of course stand still and gradually over the years news filtered through that such and such a former teacher had died: Miss Butler, Miss Voyce, Miss Sneyd and so forth. And then it seemed I was attending funerals and memorial services for my former school-friends. The good people of Stourbridge were beginning to forget that the High School had ever existed.

I had already developed the research and writing bug and the germ of an idea of writing a book about SGHS slowly formed in my mind. Like all researchers should, I looked around to establish whether or not anything had already been written. Mr Chambers (headmaster of King Edward Grammar School for Boys) had written about *his* school. Other books about the history of Stourbridge only made brief, if any, references to the High School. I found myself slightly enraged about this. Did the

Introduction

High School and its history count for nothing? For decades SGHS girls had been coming down Church Street or the back path into Parkfield, dressed, according to their era, in varying styles of uniform; they and their 'doings' were an integral part of Stourbridge town and its history. I think there is little doubt that, certainly during my era at the school, one considered oneself one of the elite if one was an SGHS girl. This, of course, raises the issue of the unfairness of the 11-plus examination, but this is not to be discussed at this point! Suffice to say that the pupils, the staff and the school itself were and always should be a very important part of Stourbridge history and there seemed to me to be a danger of the High School gradually becoming completely forgotten. By this I don't mean the building, for that, of course, is still standing as Redhill School. However, Stourbridge Girls' High School was fundamentally a different community with its own history from 1905 to 1976, which developed and grew under five headmistresses; its traditions; its school life during two world wars, its rules and regulations, punishments and rewards...

There seemed an urgent need for a book about SGHS.

So,

If it were done when 'tis done, then 'twere well
It were done quickly;

How I remember Miss Pritchard's beautiful speaking voice quoting these lines from Shakespeare's *Macbeth* (Act I Scene VII!).

None of us are getting any younger! Stourbridge 'old girls' are becoming older, but I have been overwhelmed by the interest shown and help given in my writing of the book by them and former members of staff of SGHS, some aged 96 and 97 years of age. And there is much life in us yet! So here is the story of a school and girls gone by and I hope people enjoy reading it as much as I have writing it. It is not an over-sentimental story and I couldn't resist another 'quote' – this one taken from Wordsworth's 'The Prelude, Book I: Childhood and Schooltime' (studied by many of us for A level English and with apologies to Wordsworth and Miss Woodall for changing the personal pronoun!). These lines, to my mind at least, sum up the days as Stourbridge High School girls:

...[we] grew up
Foster'd alike by beauty and by fear...

MARION BRETTLE (née DAVIES)
SGHS 1953–60

About the Author

Marion Brettle studied librarianship at the College of Librarianship, University College Wales, becoming a chartered librarian in due course. She has always had a close affinity to children's literature, in the UK and internationally, and has served on the IBBY British section committee (International Board on Books for Young People). She was also privileged to be on the Carnegie/Greenaway medal award panel (for an outstanding book for children) and her MA degree dissertation in Children's Literature (University of Surrey) was based on Carnegie medal winners as a reflection of changes in society and the concept of childhood. She has reviewed books for both children and adults for the website Write Away (www.justimagineastorycentre.co.uk).

Marion has held a range of professional librarian posts and, in particular, she was YTS Library Course Co-ordinator for Dudley Libraries (based at Stourbridge Library) and job-shared the post of Children's Librarian, again at Stourbridge Library.

Her career changed tack some fourteen years ago, and, after qualifying as an English (EFL/ESOL) teacher, she taught on short contracts abroad and in the UK. She is now an examiner for Trinity College London, travelling extensively in the UK and abroad, mostly in Italy and Spain, to assess foreign students in English Language Speaking and Listening examinations.

Her recent personal experience in researching her own family history led her to write her first book (also published by Ellingham Press) in 2009: *The Old Vicarage Much Wenlock and its families and visitors: chronicles of a Shropshire Market Town*.

Marion is married to Richard, a chartered surveyor and arbitrator, and they have one daughter, Alison, whose work as a broadcast journalist/presenter and occasional teacher of English has taken her to countries such as Qatar, Kuwait, Romania and Equatorial Guinea. The Old Vicarage, Much Wenlock has been the family home since 1999.

Chapter One

Early days: Stourbridge Girls' Secondary School and Miss Firth (1905–28)

In 1902 the benefactor Andrew Carnegie gave Stourbridge Council £3,000 towards a new purpose-designed public library for Stourbridge in Worcestershire. The building was at the junction of Church Road and Hagley Road and its foundation stone was laid on 25 February 1904 by Isaac Nash, an edge tool manufacturer. By 1908[1] it housed an art and technical school on its first floor and a girls' secondary school (Stourbridge Girls' Secondary School) on its upper floor and in its basement.

The school had been opened by the Worcestershire County Council in October 1905 for the purpose of providing secondary education for the urban districts of Stourbridge, Lye and Wollescote, and the parishes of Pedmore, Hagley, Clent and Belbroughton. It was recognised as a secondary school for girls under the Secondary School Regulations from 1 August 1908, having previously been recognised as a pupil teacher centre only.

Thus did begin the history of Stourbridge Girls' Secondary School (SGSS) and, later, the

Stourbridge Girls' Secondary School housed on the upper floor and in the basement of the Art and Technical School and Public Library building, Hagley Road and Church Street, Stourbridge (circa 1919).

County High School for Girls or Stourbridge Girls' High School (SGHS). But it had been a very long and difficult journey before arriving at this stage!

The Education Act of 1870 had made elementary education compulsory but there was no state or public provision for secondary schools for girls. Thus, any parents who wished their daughters to receive secondary education had, in simple terms, to pay. This meant, of course, that any form of higher education for girls was limited to wealthy families and was confined to public, private or endowed schools. It should also be remembered that many parents believed at this time that a 'woman's place was in the home' and that anything more than elementary education was totally unnecessary for girls!

However, in 1902 a highly controversial Education Act (framed by a Mr Balfour (later Lord Balfour) and Sir Robert Morant was passed, as a result of which the country's educational system underwent radical reorganisation. Secondary schools even for girls were to be introduced – the powers that be having recognised at long last that a well-educated mother was likely to be of greater benefit to her family than that of one with a mere smattering of the three Rs. Also, women would be needed increasingly in commerce and the social services, education, health and welfare work.

As might be expected there was long and acrimonious public debate about the establishing of such schools, Stourbridge being no exception. Who was going to pay for one to be built and, equally important, who was to maintain it?

In short, the 1902 Act abolished the existing School Boards in England and Wales, and all elementary schools were placed in the hands of Local Education Authorities (LEAs) under the control of the County and County Borough Councils. The 1902 Act, for the first time, made significant provision for *secondary* and *technical* education and councils were encouraged (although not compelled) to subsidise existing grammar schools and to provide free places for working-class children.

The LEAs were to be in charge of paying teachers, ensuring that the teachers were properly qualified and providing the necessary books and equipment.

Eventually, in accordance with the 1902 Education Act Worcestershire County Council acquired the site[2] of an ancient Dutch-gabled shop property at the junction of Hagley Road and Church Street in Stourbridge and it was decided to build there an art and technical school building which during the daytime would accommodate the Stourbridge Girls' Secondary School and a pupil teacher centre. On the ground floor a much-needed new

Miss Ethel M. Firth (headmistress) sitting at her desk, SGSS, always immaculately dressed!

SGSS badge depicting the Malvern Hills, river and pear tree of Worcestershire.

public library would be created using Andrew Carnegie's initial gift of £3,000, to which he later added a further £700 when it became necessary to extend the building.

The building was designed by Mr Frederick Woodward, surveyor to Stourbridge Council, and cost £9,000. Miss Ethel M. Firth, who had trained at Tottenham Training College, was duly appointed as the first headmistress of Stourbridge Girls' Secondary School. She was young for such a post, being only twenty-nine years of age but she came from a family of educators, which must have been in her favour when appointed.

The school secretary was Mr W. M. Robins, who had been a shorthand teacher at the Technical School, and the fees were £4 a year or £1 6s 8d a term. At the time of its first HMI government inspection in 1909 there were 108 girls in the school and this number included seven bursars and 18 pupil teachers. The school was an immediate success although it soon became apparent that the girls and teachers would have 'outgrown' the accommodation in the not too distant future, because numbers of pupils increased fairly rapidly. Within a few years the pupil teacher centre was closed, but still the accommodation remained cramped and, as we shall read from first-hand accounts, extremely inconvenient for pupils and staff.

Miss Firth and her staff (although perhaps not the pupils) must have felt extremely apprehensive when the very first HMI inspection of the school took place on 8 and 9 June 1909. The report[3] makes very interesting, even at times amusing, reading for a twenty-first century researcher but, sadly for the headmistress and her entourage, was occasionally very damning and critical in its findings.

A view of the corridor at Stourbridge Girls' Secondary School (the girls had to congregate here at breaktime).

Miss E. M. Firth (sitting on chair centre) with members of her staff flanked by Miss Harris (on her left) and Miss Turner (on her right), senior assistant mistresses. The gentleman is probably either the secretary Mr W. Robins or the Art master Mr Cromack.

The Report began by setting out the number of pupils – 104 in 1908 and 108 at the time of the inspection, distributed among seven forms. Of the 108 pupils 35 were scholarship holders and the pupils were drawn from certain 'classes in life'. Twelve were from Professional, Independent; 15 from Merchants, Manufacturers, etc.; 14 from Retail Traders; two from Farmers; 23 from Commercial Managers and 42 from Service (domestic and other); Postmen, etc., and Artisans. There were 18 Pupil Teachers and seven Bursars. Fees were £4 for residents in Worcestershire Administrative County (plus an extra 7s. 6d. charged for stationery). For pupils from other areas the fees were double, i.e. £8 per annum.

Interestingly, only 58 girls came from Stourbridge itself; 42 came from 'other places in Worcestershire' and 8 from Staffordshire, reflecting the absence of similar schools

Form IVb working hard in the school garden.

TIME TABLE 1908-9.

Day	Form	9.30–10	10–11	11.10–11.50	11.50–12.30	2–3	3–3.40	3.50–4.30
Monday	Ib	Scripture	History	Arithmetic	English (Comp.)	English (Lang. & Lit.)	Needlework	Geography
	Ia	"	Arithmetic	Latin	English (Comp.)	Geometry	Science	History
	II	"	English	Geography	Mathematics	Writing / Needlework or Cookery		
	III	"	Mathematics	French	English	History / Science (Pr.)		
	IV	"	English	Geography	Mathematics	Physics (Th.)	French	History
	V	"	English	Geography	Mathematics	Physics (Th.)	Latin	History
Tuesday	Ib	Scripture	Arithmetic	English (W. Dict.)	Geography	French	History	Drill or Games
	Ia	"	Latin	Algebra	French	English	Arithmetic	Drill or Games
	II	"	Science [Th.]	English	French	Mathematics	Geography	Music (Th.)
	III	"	English	Mathematics	History	Latin (or English)	French	Arithmetic
	IV	"	French	English	Mathematics	Mathematics	Drawing	
	V	"	French	English	Latin	Mathematics	Drawing	
Wednesday	Ib	Scripture	Botany	French	Arithmetic	Writing / Needlework or Cookery		
	Ia	"	Botany	Algebra	History	Writing / Needlework or Cookery		
	II	"	Mathematics	Drawing		Latin	Arithmetic	History
	III	"	Latin (or French)	Music (Th.)	French	Geography	Mathematics	Drill or Games
	IV	"	French	Physics (Th.)	History	Mathematics	English	Drill or Games
	V	"	Mathematics	Physics (Th.)	History	French	English	Drill or Games
Thursday	Ib	Scripture	Arithmetic	Geography	Reading	English (W. & Comp.)	History	Drill or Games
	Ia	"	English	Geography	Reading	Science (Pr.)	French	Algebra
	II	"	Latin	History	Reading	Botany	French	Drill or Games
	III	"	French	Mathematics	Needlework	Science (Th.)	Geography	Mathematics
	IV	"	Geography	English	Needlework	French	Mathematics	History
	V	"	Geography	English	Needlework	French	Mathematics	History
Friday	Ib	Scripture	Drawing	Arithmetic	French	English (Read. + Recit.)	Music (Th.)	Music (P.)
	Ia	"	Drawing	Arithmetic	Geography	French	Music (Th.)	Music (P.)
	II	"	Science (Pr.)	English	Arithmetic	French	Mathematics	Music (P.)
	III	"	English	Drawing		Arithmetic	English	Music (P.)
	IV	"	Mathematics	Physics (Pr.)				
	V	"	Mathematics	Physics (Pr.)		Political Economy	Mathematics	Music (P.)

SGSS School Time Table 1908–9, on which HMI Inspectors based their first Report. A busy day!

elsewhere in Worcestershire and surrounding counties. Thus, SGSS was something of a pioneering establishment; in fact it was the first of its kind in the county. There were seven 'regular' assistant teachers and two 'occasional' in addition to Miss Firth.

Of the 35 scholarship holders, 23 held County Council scholarships (three of these obtained their scholarships while already in the school) but the remainder obtained them direct from their public elementary schools. In addition six girls were admitted free in order to satisfy the Board's Secondary School Regulations and six girls had their fees paid for them by Scott's Charity. The pupil teachers and bursars received free education so that 60 out of the 108 girls in the school paid no fees.

Girls could be admitted at the age of ten, and 'it is clear that every effort should be made to encourage parents to send their daughters to the School before they are thirteen, and also at the beginning of the Autumn Term instead of the commencement of the other terms.'

The Report stated that a very large proportion who left took up elementary school teaching as their career, but 'it is noticed however with regret that none of those who left last year proceeded to a Training College, nor in fact did any girls proceed to places of further education.'

The school was governed by a Managing Committee consisting of 20 members and included 'two ladies' – male supremacy still reigned in 1909!

The Report made certain recommendations regarding premises and equipment.

It mentioned that the

> school is housed on the top floor of the Technical School, with the use of the Cookery room on the ground floor and of two rooms in the basement which are used as a dining room and a drill room...It is to be regretted that there is no playground, but this was fully realised by everybody when the arrangements were made. A conveniently situated playing field has been rented on an annual tenancy at £18 a year: some inconvenience has been caused by horses being allowed to graze on the ground...

It stated that although the staircases were very steep, when the top floor was reached, the appearance of the corridor and classrooms was made bright and cheerful by flowers, plants and a few pictures. A few small improvements were suggested:

> a small radiator or stove may be required in the Staff room so as to warm it sufficiently in Winter, some means for drying the girls' cloaks in wet weather might easily be arranged in the cloakroom, and a sofa should be provided in the Headmistress's room (as is usually found in girls' schools) for the use of girls when they are taken ill in School...

(If the girls had been putting on damp, wet clothes, then very likely they *were* taken ill and it was surely not over-indulging the staff to try to warm their room!)

The Report, not surprisingly, investigated in depth and made recommendations regarding staff and curriculum. The following is an extract from the Report (pages 7 and 8) concerning the headmistress, Miss Firth.

STAFF
> The Headmistress was trained at the Tottenham Training College and holds the Government Teachers' Certificate. She possesses no University Degree, but is working to complete her LLA (St Andrews) course, having successfully taken two groups last year. She has held her present position since the inception of the School in the Autumn of 1905. Her teaching experience previously was confined to Higher Grade Schools and Pupil Teacher Centres: this experience has been useful, but it is to be regretted that it has not been wider, and that she has no actual internal knowledge as a Mistress of Girls' Secondary Schools of the grade which this School might reasonably be expected to reach. It is all the more necessary therefore that

> the Staff should include two or three Assistant Mistresses with good academic qualifications and some previous teaching experience in good Secondary Schools for girls...

Thus the Report was rather critical of Miss Firth's lack of a degree and relevant teaching experience. It did concede that it would probably be impossible to attract school mistresses with good academic qualifications on the commencing salaries offered at that time (the Governors' Meeting Minutes 1911 revealed that Miss Firth's salary was £185 p.a. and was later increased to £200).

The Report was equally critical of the other members of staff – mentioning that only one mistress possessed a degree and that there was very little previous teaching experience amongst them. On a better note it praised the fact that the mistresses took considerable interest in Games and that their relations with the headmistress appeared to be cordial!

It dealt with the curriculum, subject by subject; for example, English was praised for its grammar work but in Literature 'somewhat too great a tendency was shown to supply the pupils with readymade opinions and comments rather than to lead them to make their own comments and to form and discuss intelligently their own opinions.'

French written work was creditable but the oral answering was less satisfactory 'and no means should be left untried to correct the fatal habit of indistinct utterance, which made it quite impossible as a rule for the girls at the back of the room to hear what was said in the front benches.'

It was recommended that Latin be postponed until Form II as 'the attempt to master two new languages simultaneously with a total time allowance of four hours is fore-doomed to failure.'

Mathematics, the teaching of which was shared by two mistresses (one apparently better than the other), was painstaking but 'they do not make sufficient appeal to the girls' own powers of thought: they are inclined to do too much work for the girls, and to address their questions only to a few members of the Class, with the result that when questioned most of the girls are singularly incapable of expressing themselves readily or accurately.'

Referring to Science, the Report conceded that owing to the very recent date from which the school had possessed a permanent laboratory it was natural to find that the course of work was not yet fixed and that the standard reached was therefore not very high 'but it is clear that the whole question of Curriculum requires careful consideration.'

It praised the Art teaching, drawing being taught in the School of Art on a lower floor of the Technical School building by the headmaster of that department.

The piano used for Music lessons was considered to be not only of exceedingly poor quality but was so out of tune that its use for the singing lessons was positively harmful!

These are but a few examples from the Report on Curriculum as it would be impossible and unnecessary to include all of its findings. Regarding the corporate life of the school there was praise for the start that had been made towards the development of a really active corporate life. The School was divided into five Clubs or Houses (Blue, Green, Red, Orange and Violet) and there were six prefects appointed by the headmistress who had definite duties and powers.

It was the Conclusion, however, that must have brought some dismay to Miss Firth and her staff (much the same as it would today). It stated that, although the headmistress had done much to develop the corporate life of the school, had influenced the girls for good in the matter of dress and behaviour and had taken pains to make the corridor and classrooms bright and cheerful,

> ...educationally, however, the School falls short of what might reasonably be expected of the Girls' School in Stourbridge. Little of the teaching or of

> the work done rises above mediocrity, and there are few indications that the present Staff are really competent to improve the existing conditions. The teaching is very painstaking and conscientious, but it is not characterised by very much educational intelligence: insufficient appeal is made to the girls' own powers of thought and expression.

The extraordinary indistinctiveness of the girls' answers in class, and the fact that the mistresses made so little effort to obtain either distinct or intelligible answers from them were much commented on during the inspection.

> The future success of the School rests with the Local Education Authority, since it is for that Authority to determine the amount of salaries to be paid to the Staff, and therefore necessarily the type of Mistress to be attracted to the School. It will naturally be some time before the education provided for girls in this School can in any case be compared with that provided for boys in the town at the Grammar School, but if the Local Education Authority and the Managing Committee contemplate the development of such a School it is essential that efforts should be made to attract Mistresses with considerable previous teaching experience in good Secondary Schools for Girls.

One wonders whether Miss Firth *et al.* felt like giving up on the spot. After all, there had not been much opportunity for teachers to actually gain experience in 'good' secondary schools for girls up until the passing of the 1902 Education Act. Women with degrees were in a minority at that time and the old order that supported the view that secondary education was unnecessary for girls was still very prominent in 1909.

However, the headmistress and the teaching staff of Stourbridge Girls' Secondary School were obviously made of stern stuff for they did *not* give up and many of them continued to teach there for a number of years. Day-to-day school life in the 'library' building could not have been easy for them but they had to take the various inconveniences, lack of comfort and space and the unsuitability of the building for a growing school in their stride. Any improvements for their physical comforts must have been welcome!

Subsequent HMI inspection reports bear testament to this whilst remaining critical of some classroom teaching methods. For example in the Report of 28/29 October 1913 Inspection:[4] 'It is satisfactory to find that the few small improvements suggested in the last Full Inspection Report have been carried out' (hot-water pipes in the girls' cloakroom; a radiator in the staff-room; purchase of a sofa). But…

> Three members of staff now possess Degrees…There is, however, no very marked improvement in the methods adapted in the class-rooms. The staff as a whole are thoroughly conscientious, painstaking teachers, but, partly no doubt because of the predominance of this attitude of mind, the excessive seriousness with which the girls are treated in many of the lessons is apt to create an atmosphere of dullness. The development of the girls' own powers of thought and expression should receive much more attention than at present, but it must be remembered that this can only be done if the girls are expected to discuss points much more readily than at present, and, in fact, generally take a much more active part in the lessons than was usual in the days of the Inspection.

The Conclusion praises the fact that the headmistress continued to exert a very good influence over the behaviour of the girls; that the best use was being made of the accommodation with clean, bright rooms and corridors adorned with pictures and flowers. It was also placed on record that the results obtained in the Cambridge Locals Examinations were very creditable to the staff, but

> Educationally, however, the development is scarcely as great as it might have been. The staff work consistently and hard, but the apparent

> limitations in their conception of what is expected of them in the class-rooms is still noticeable; many of the lessons still suggest that the girls are being instructed rather than educated, and much more still remains to be done to overcome the great indistinctiveness of the girls when answering in class...

(How interesting it would have been to be a 'fly on the wall' and witness some of these indistinct answers! Was it because the girls were nervous in front of the Inspectors and mumbled their answers out of shyness or in case they were incorrect, or were they accustomed to listening rather than participating orally in lessons?)

What *is* clear, is that the powers-that-be required high academic standards regarding the qualifications of the staff and their teaching methods to raise the status of Stourbridge Girls' Secondary School to that of a Grammar/High School. It is not unlikely that these requirements brought a certain amount of stress to bear on Miss Firth's shoulders and yet she appears to have been of an indomitable spirit and continued to organise the school and staff, implementing the required changes in addition to teaching, all under extreme difficulties.

She was away from school herself for a whole term in 1911 undergoing an operation and Miss Harris, her first assistant, was put in charge during this time.

The First World War could not have helped matters although the minutes of the Governors' Meetings (beautifully written in copperplate handwriting) do not make a great deal of reference to these years. In October 1914 Miss Firth announced that the prize-winning girls were desirous of foregoing their prizes and donating the money to some war effort relief fund. This was gratefully accepted and the proceeds of their self-denial were given to the Prince of Wales' Fund. Some girls (particularly those who were fee-paying) were taken away from the school during these years as, sadly, their fathers had been killed in action, and times were hard financially for some families.

The school continued to grow, however, in numbers of pupils and by 29 May 1918 a total of 210 girls were in full-time attendance at the beginning of the summer term. For many years the accommodation had been considered inadequate and before the war the seeds were sewn for a new, bigger building but these plans were understandably 'put on hold' during 1914–18.

Chronologically, the next surviving batch of photographs of Stourbridge Girls' Secondary School in the archives date from *circa* 1919 (according to the writing on the netball team photograph). They are of great interest as a record of the girls and staff, of the clothes and uniform, the sport that was played and how the school was organised at that time into forms with form mistresses.

SGSS Netball Team 1919–20 (the Games mistress, seated in basket chair, always wore a tunic too).

Sixth Form SGSS.

Form V Upper with Miss Turner.

Form V Lower with unidentified teacher.

Form 4A with unidentified teacher, but possibly Miss Emms.

Form 4B with Miss Cooke.

Form 3A looking very demure. Teacher unidentified.

Form 3B with an unidentified teacher.

Form 3B hockey team, complete with early-style hockey sticks.

Form 2A.

Form 2B (these forms seem quite large, evidence of a growing school!)

Although the HMI Reports came down heavily on the teaching methods of Miss Firth and her staff, what they failed to reveal was the ingenuity and versatility she had had to employ. In those early days of SGSS her job was no sinecure, as a later article in the Autumn Term 1932 *Pear Tree* school magazine (Vol. 1 No. 4, p. 3) pointed out:

> Miss Firth began her work in Stourbridge in September 1905, with 96 pupils, boys and girls, who were housed in the buildings of the Technical School. For some weeks she coped with these almost alone, helped by a very youthful assistant, and teaching them all subjects of the curriculum from Chemistry to the tonic sol-fa. Her work was made difficult, not only by the immense variety of the subjects she had to undertake, but by the diversity in ages of her pupils and by the lack of sufficient equipment. There were no facilities at all for science teaching, but Miss Firth with surprising ingenuity obtained the services of a local carpenter, who rigged up benches, while she herself supervised the laying of gas pipes to supply the Bunsen Burners, and transformed an ordinary classroom into the semblance of a laboratory...

Miss Firth with members of her staff and pupils – one looking suspiciously like Dorothy N. Sneyd herself, pupil and later a member of staff until 1960, on seat, centre left.

*SGSS: Some of IIIa in the laboratory.
Miss Firth, the headmistress, helped to rig up the apparatus herself.*

*SGSS: The Sixth Form at work with Miss Harris.
(There was a fireplace with a 'real' fire in their form room!)*

Even in those early days 'Colours' were awarded for prowess in games and some of the girls can be seen wearing these in later photographs in the form of a girdle (green, gold and blue) worn low on their hips as was befitting for that time. Tennis and rounders were played during the summer months.

The SGSS governors' minutes 1909–20[5] reveal much of the day-to-day life and business of the school, particularly of problems which needed to be resolved:

> 27th July 1909: An application by Miss Davies, Assistant Mistress asking for an increase in salary was read but Resolved that the application be not considered at the present time. But that she be invited to renew it when she will have been on the staff for two year.

(In fact, there were constant requests for increases in salary by Miss Firth and her staff, but it seemed that these were only granted every two years. There seemed to be a high turnover of staff. Perhaps the Assistant Mistresses thought that their hard work in difficult accommodation was worthy of more money!)

> 30th May 1911: The school was growing and developing to such an extent that it became necessary to separate Forms

V and VI which had been being taught together.

1st March 1916: Total number of pupils was 154. Although there was officially room for 277 there was pressure on the accommodation and Miss Firth therefore requested the use of some of the Art School Rooms. The Headmistress also reported that there were only six classrooms for seven forms and that one class had to be taught in the Lab.

(However, the minutes report that for the time being the Girls' Secondary School should be confined to its rooms on the top floor, the Art College not being keen on giving up any of its accommodation.)

29th May 1918: A total of 210 girls in full-time attendance at the beginning of the Summer Term.

25th September 1918: The Headmistress reported the following results obtained by the school in the July Cambridge Local Examinations:

SENIORS: 32 PRESENTED
2 SECOND CLASS HONOURS
3 THIRD CLASS HONOURS
19 PASSES
4 qualified for entrance to Training College without gaining a certificate
5 failed

JUNIORS: 9 PRESENTED
8 PASSED
1 FAILED

30th October 1918 KITCHEN MAID: It was reported that Miss Chapman, the Kitchen Maid had resigned on September 30th and that MISS ALICE BABBS had been appointed…at the same rate of payment (£20 p.a.) and that she had been promised an extra £5 as from 1st November…in view of the large amount of work required in connection with the provision of dinners for the Secondary School pupils.

The Authority decided that from 1 January 1919 when more than one child from the same family attended (Worcestershire only) a reduction of 10 shillings per term should be granted on fees for such children after the first. Sometimes, girls were ill for the whole of a term and the County Authority kindly remitted payment of the fees.

29th January 1919: Mr. Boyt (Headmaster of King Edward's Grammar School for Boys, Stourbridge) was to present the prizes at the annual prize-giving ceremony for S.G.S.S.

(Mr Boyt, as Headmaster of the 'brother' school, always maintained a close connection with the Girls' School.)

The Headmistress reported that there was difficulty in obtaining a proper supply of coke for the heating apparatus (not because of shortage of coke but that the suppliers were not wanting to deliver it on account of the time and trouble involved in wheeling it round the building through the narrow passage from Church Street).

26th March 1919: The meeting considered a complaint made by the Headmistress with regard to the unsatisfactory state of the playing fields caused through horses and sheep being turned onto the field.

(Bicycles seemed to have been a constant source of trouble)

25th June 1919: The Vice-Chairman submitted a proposal for storing the girls' bicycles at Messrs. Jones's garage opposite the school as an alternative to storing them in the basement of the school premises – many steps etc. It was suggested that a small weekly charge be made to parents of girls storing bicycles.

30th July 1919: Messrs. Jones (garage) were reluctant to send in a tender for storing bikes so no further action at the moment.

The Headmistress had sent a letter to the Director of Education pointing out

> the difficulty that Assistant Mistresses had in obtaining suitable living accommodation in the district and enquiring whether it would be possible for the County Authority to consider the opening of a hostel...the meeting took the view that 'it was not part of their duty to do so'.

(In spite of women's rights beginning to be slowly recognised, society was still uneasy about single women renting accommodation.)

On an even more serious note:

> 29th October 1919: The Chairman reported that as a result of communication made to him by the Headmistress he and the Vice Chairman had met on October 22nd to enquire into a charge of theft on the school premises against three of the SGSS pupils and that charges were established after interviewing their parents...it would be detrimental to the welfare of the school to allow them to remain in attendance...recommended that they therefore request the parents to withdraw the girls, otherwise that they should be expelled...

Following the Education Act of 1918 (drawn up by Herbert Fisher, Liberal MP) education became obligatory for children up to the age of 14. There had already been much discussion amongst the governors of SGSS and Miss Firth regarding the need for new and larger premises and this became more urgent in view of the increase in numbers expected in secondary schools. In view of this and the limited accommodation available to SGSS it was resolved that a new building be erected as soon as possible. The estimated number of places to be provided in the 'new' school was to be 450 and the present fees would be continued until the girls moved up to the new premises when they would be raised.

The greater part of the financial burden of education (some 60 per cent) was to be transferred from local authorities to central government, partly to foster a greater sense of professionalism amongst teachers by allowing them improved salaries and a pension. Obviously great changes were afoot for Stourbridge Girls' Secondary School. Better conditions and accommodation would perhaps attract teachers with degrees, which, in the opinion of the Government Inspectors, would raise the level of education in the school commensurate with 'High School' status.

> 29th October 1919: The Clerk reported that the Board of Education had informed the County Authority that the proposed site in Junction Road appeared to be generally satisfactory and that therefore an advertisement for an Architect be inserted in the 'County Express'; Birmingham Daily Post; and the 'Brierley Hill Advertiser'.

From then on the governors' minutes made constant referral to the 'new school' and the new premises although it was to be many years before the plans came to fruition.

> 28th January 1920: The heating broke down and the girls could not return until Thursday January 29th.
>
> 17th March 1920: Messrs. W. Green & Sons had been instructed to provide and fit 5 new three gallon cast iron tanks for the girls' and mistresses' lavatories at a total cost of £16. 5s the old tanks having become unusable.

And so the school looked forward to its new premises 'up the hill', for Junction Road was not far from their present accommodation – up to the top of Church Street and turn left! The years from 1920–8 (for it was not until 1928 when the move actually took place) must have been full of excited anticipation for pupils and staff.

Meanwhile the school continued to grow and expand in many ways. New staff were recruited, societies formed; the Girl Guide company continued to flourish with a very popular annual camp at Wolverley, near Kidderminster. Horizons for girls were widening slowly.

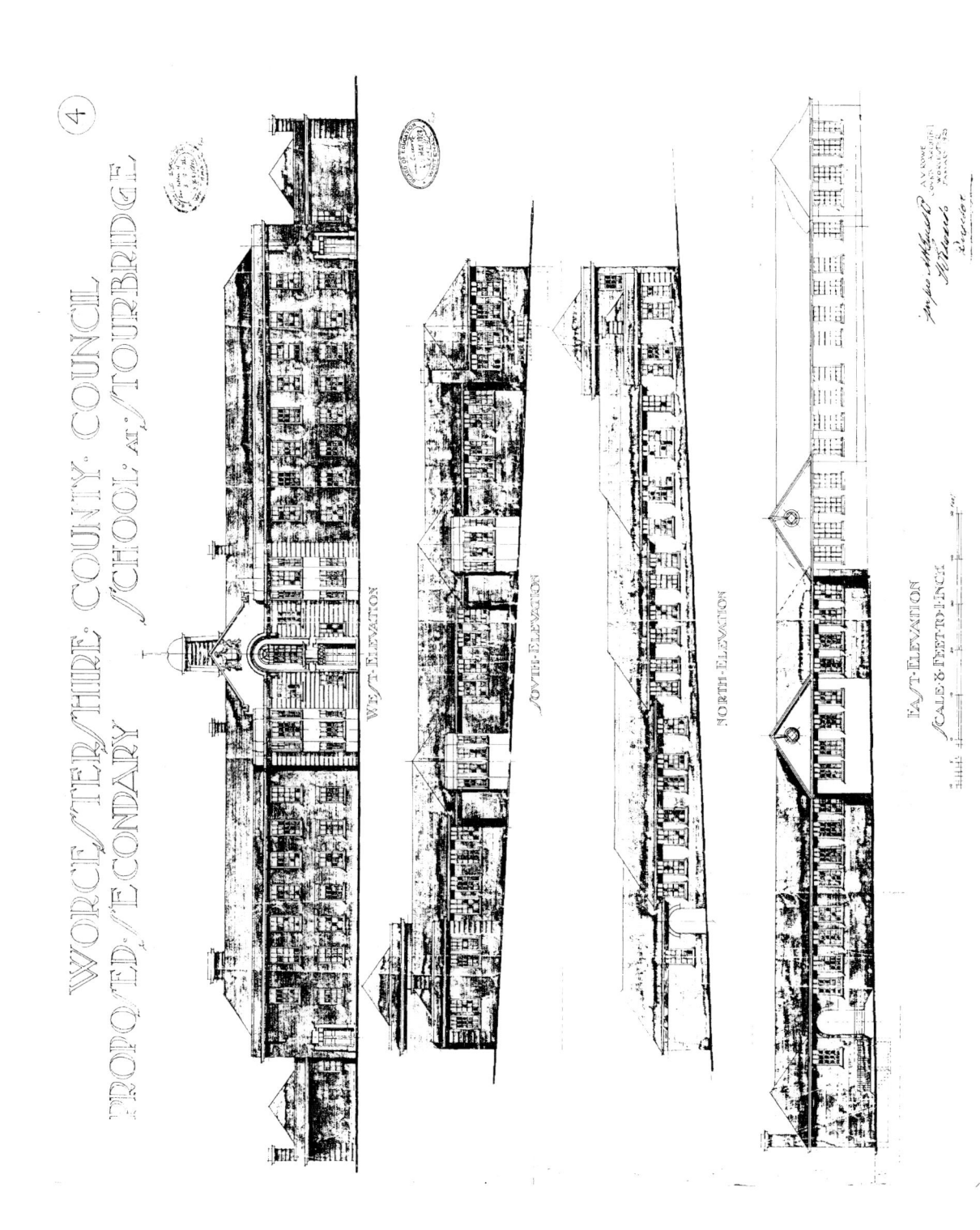

Early days: Stourbridge Girls' Secondary School and Miss Firth (1905–28)

Architect A. Vernon Rowe's vision for SGHS.

SGSS Girl Guides: Dorothy N. Sneyd sitting centre in full Guide regalia.

The archives have revealed a complete 1924 SGSS album of photographs which give a marvellous insight into the school at this time. (It seems that many girls were given, or perhaps their parents had to buy, these albums of school photographs, beautifully mounted with a current photograph of the school at the front. The 1924 album showed the addition of the War Memorial which had been erected in front of the public library building in 1923 in memory of the fallen from the Great War 1914–18.)

In the photographs that follow confirmed names of staff are provided, otherwise a dash.

From these marvellous photographic records we can see that SGSS had taken on much more of a corporate image. The school uniform was established, consisting of butcher-blue blouses (cream silk for special occasions), navy tunics, dark stockings and shoes. Hats still seemed to be the order of the day for some of the mistresses for the photographs taken outside!

Miss Firth and staff, SGSS, 1924.
Standing l to r: Miss Dromgoole; –; Miss Turner; Miss Eastwood; Miss Wells (later Mrs Bache); –.
Sitting l to r: Miss Leigh; Miss Emms; Miss Cooke; Miss Firth; Miss Tilley; Miss Chance;
Miss Edwards; sitting on floor, the Games mistress wearing customary tunic.

Early days: Stourbridge Girls' Secondary School and Miss Firth (1905–28)

Sixth Form and prefects with Miss Turner, SGSS, 1924. Prefects' badges very much in evidence.

Miss Tilley and her class, SGSS, 1924.

Miss Edwards (very properly dressed for the photograph) and her class, SGSS, 1924.

Miss Dromgoole (taught Maths) and her class, SGSS, 1924.

Miss Leigh (taught Geography and was a force to be reckoned with) and her class, SGSS, 1924.

Miss Emms (had a nap at lunchtime with a hanky over her face and often entertained other staff members by mimicking famous people) and her class, SGSS, 1924.

Miss Cooke and her class, SGSS, 1924.

Miss E. Wells (later became Mrs Bache), also helped with the Girl Guides, and her class, SGSS, 1924.

A mistress (name not known) with her form, SGSS, 1924.

Miss Eastwood (Music) and her class, SGSS, 1924.

Group of sixth formers at work with Miss Turner, SGSS, 1924. Girl on extreme right is wearing Barbara Price medal, awarded for Public Spirit in Games.

*Sixth form at work with Miss Turner, SGSS, 1924.
Sitting middle row: second girl from left – Ida Price.*

SGSS netball team, 1923–4.

SGSS hockey team, 1923–4 (games girdles (awarded) very much in evidence!)

SGSS Girl Guide company, 1924.

SGSS Girl Guide company on the march, 1924.

SGSS: 2nd Girl Guides and Brownies (just a little reminiscent of St Trinian's?).

The Girl Guides had continued to flourish and thus the pupils (and staff) under Miss Firth's guiding hand worked hard and played hard with a great deal of social activity and games to break up the monotony of lessons!

It is about this time that I can say I have had absolute first-hand information from two old girls in particular. One was my mother, who was then Marjorie Bird and joined the school as a fee-paying eleven-year-old in September 1926. The other was Ivy Freemantle, a clever scholarship girl who became a pupil of SGSS in September 1925. Ivy remembers that Miss Tilley wrote on her Report Book (stiff black-covered ones in those days) very pointedly 'Worcestershire Free Place'. This did not upset Ivy as she has told me recently that if she hadn't have been a scholarship girl and gone to SGSS and then SGHS, then almost certainly any future career for her would have been in domestic service. (Ivy went on to matriculate, to become a teacher; to lecture at Shenstone Training College and eventually became a principal lecturer at Doncaster College. Her father had been wounded in the First World War and could only get a gardening job on

Stourbridge Secondary School for Girls.

REPORT for Term ending 18th December, 1925.
Name: Ivy May Freemantle
Form: II 6. No. in Form: 17. Average Age: 11 yrs 6 mths
Age: 11 yrs 7 mths Position in Form: 3rd.

EXAMINATIONS

Subject	Marks per cent.	Position in Form	Remarks	Teacher's Initials
Scripture	67	3	Good	DIS
English—Literature	56	5	Fairly good	DIS
Composition	60	3	Good	DE
History	64	3	Good	ErW
Geography	89	2	Good	Gd
Latin				
French	75	3	Good	AET
Art—Imitative	53	8	Ivy works well	PVE
Creative				
Imaginative				
Mathematics—Arithmetic	64	8	} Fairly good	M.R.
Algebra	36	7		
Geometry	48	5		
Trigonometry				

REPORT Continued.

Subject	Marks per cent.	Position in Form	Remarks	Teacher's Initials
Science—Nature Study	56	5	Fairly good	hS
Physics	50	4	Fairly good	E.IO
Chemistry				
Needlework			Fairly good	DIS
Cookery				
Music	84	1	Very good	DIS
Physical Exercise			Very fair	EFW

ORDER MARKS
A — 0
B — 1
C — 1
Conduct: Good.
N.B.—Order Marks are given for (A) Bad Conduct, (B) Disorder, (C) Carelessness.
(Signed) D.P. Eastwood, Form Mistress.

No. of times absent during Term: 0. No. of times late during Term: 0.
Remarks: Ivy is doing good work.
(Signed) Ethel M. Firth, Head Mistress.
Next Term begins 13th January, 1926.
Signature of Parent or Guardian: H. Freemantle
Date: Feb: 1st 1926.

Ivy Freemantle's first school report, SGSS, December 1925.

demobilisation – there were other siblings and the fees could certainly not have been afforded had Ivy failed the scholarship examination). My mother and Ivy are now 96 and 97 years old respectively – thought to be the longest surviving 'old girls' to have attended SGSS and the new High School in Junction Road!

For some reason my mother did *not* keep any of her reports but she would be the first to admit that she was no great academic. She was quite good at French, no good at all at Maths but liked Miss Dromgoole very much. She was also a good pianist and needlewoman but says that when Miss Firth read out marks for each class in order of merit she never even started to listen for her name until past halfway!

She remembers Miss Firth as being quite strict and that she was hauled over the coals once because she went to school in a red dress – her mother (a professional tailor) had not quite finished making my mother's uniform.

She travelled in from Brierley Hill on the bus which stopped right opposite the public library building and had special permission to leave a little early to catch the bus home for lunch. She remembers, as many other old girls do, the flights of stairs down which she had to run. Even in those days there was much camaraderie on the bus going home after school with boys from KEGS.

Meanwhile the 'new' school was progressing in Junction Road and great was the excitement of girls and mistresses as the date for moving approached, but this was not to be until September 1928.

The *Pear Tree* magazine (so familiar to the old girls of both SGSS and later SGHS) has proved invaluable to the research for this book, containing news of the school sports' teams; information regarding names of prefects, head girl, prize winners; House successes, details of

Front cover of first **Pear Tree** *magazine, SGSS, Summer Term 1926.*

outings and societies; news of former staff and old girls, to say nothing of the many poems and articles and sketches penned by the pupils and sometimes by members of staff.

The very first magazine (Volume 1 No. 1) was produced in the summer term of 1926 (and many readers will no doubt recognise the size, format, and colour (sage green) of the cover for it continued in this form until 1967 before any significant changes!).

There are articles on 'A Year's Guiding'; 'The Musical Society'; and from fairly 'new' 'old' girls, 'My First Term At Oxford' (from fresher M. Lavender); 'A Day At Queen's Hospital' (from trainee nurse E. Gittins) and 'Life in a Domestic Science Training College' (from G. A. Sinclair) to mention just a few. I couldn't resist including a poem from IVb about the difficulties of being a 'travelling' form with which many of us would sympathise!

Pear Tree magazines published in later years contain fascinating articles by former

FORM IVB

1. When people want to find IVb,
   They always have to hunt,
   A Form without a room are we,
   From place to place we shunt.

2. And like a straggling flock of sheep
   We wander round the School;
   Tho' order's very hard to keep;
   We keep it, as a rule.

3. Our lockers are our greatest woe,
   We sometimes lose their keys,
   The tall girls get the bottom row,
   And have to use their knees.

4. Yet we are quite a happy crowd,
   Our numbers help in this,
   When fourteen only are allowed,
   Things can't go far amiss.

5. We learn on Tuesday's how to cook,
   A rabbit how to truss,
   Our recipes go in a book,
   Miss Gibson teaches us.

6. And twice a week we go to gym.,
   To make us strong and fit,
   We drill and dance with skill and vim;
   Till we're too stiff to sit.

7. Each Wednesday is our hockey day,
   In one momentous match
   We beat the mighty Form IVa;
   With bump, and bruise, and scratch.

8. We must confess, the steps we climb
   Make harder work and play,
   But still we hope to have in time,
   A grand new School – some day.

Form IVB's poem from the 1926 SGSS **Pear Tree** *Magazine, Vol. 1 No.1, p. 9.*

mistresses and pupils as they looked back on their time at SGSS. What better way to leave Stourbridge Girls' Secondary School before embarking upon the next stage in the saga of Stourbridge Girls' High School than to share some of their memories of this era?

From the 1976 magazine, the very last edition (p. 9,) we hear from Miss D.N. Sneyd who was a pupil 1914–21 and a member of staff 1928–60:

THE FIRST WORLD WAR AND THE 1920s

With a break of seven years, from 1921–28, my time at the High School stretched from 1914 to 1960, a long time of change and growth. In 1914, the school, then called Stourbridge Secondary School for Girls, was housed in the same building as the Public Library and the Art School. The Cloak Room, Gym and Dining Room were in the dark basement, the Cookery Room on the ground floor and all the Form Rooms on the top floor, above the Art School. In spite of the inconveniences of the building we were a very happy school, finding enjoyment in work as well as in games and social activities. We had a flourishing Guide Company and our camp near Wolverley was the highlight of the summer holidays.

The happy atmosphere of school was largely due to the educational outlook of the women who taught us. Miss Firth, our first Headmistress, had a rare gift for choosing cultured women as her colleagues and leaving them unhampered in their work. Her business acumen enabled her to take advantage of coming trends in education. The school was one of the first in the country to introduce Biology and Geography as examination subjects and to create an Upper Sixth Form to enter for the new Higher School Certificate Examinations, the forerunner of A levels. In 1920, one of my contemporaries, Clara Wright, won the School's first State Scholarship.

A new building had been promised before 1914, but the First World War and its aftermath postponed this until after 1928. I joined the staff for the Summer Term of that year and saw what the old school was like from the other side of the counter! We moved to the new but unfinished building in late September.

On page 10: Mrs E. N. Bache (née Wells), a member of staff 1923–8:

It is now fifty-three years since Miss Firth appointed me as the junior history mistress on the strength of my M.A. degree and my willingness to help with the school Guide company, then being very ably run by Miss Wilson, the gym mistress. It was my first and only post, as I left to be married in June, 1928, so I have not found it easy to remember accurately events which took place so long ago in a comparatively short period of my life.

The school was then housed in the red brick Victorian building which we shared with the Art School and Public Library, and since they occupied most of the ground and first floors we had an unenviable climb to the second floor classrooms and descent to the basement dining room. Fresh from even higher climbs up stone stairs in the Edmund Street section of Birmingham University, I was not unduly worried by the stairs, but still have vivid memories of the stress they caused to some of the older staff.

How I disliked dinner duty in that drab basement! I seem to remember it was also used as the gym, and we certainly held the Guide meetings there. The staff dined in the kitchen-cookery room on the ground floor, in the friendly atmosphere engendered by Miss Gibson, the cookery mistress.

Other members of the staff at that time were Misses Chance, Cooke, Dromgoole, Eastwood, Edwards, Emms, Leigh, Tilley and Turner, later to be joined by Miss Hutchins who gave up teaching to become a missionary in Ceylon, and from whom I still hear at Christmas. Our staff room, also used as the 'sick room', a haven for the occasional victim of head-ache or playground accident, was terribly inadequate – small and shabbily furnished. Looking back, they were mostly very happy days: I enjoyed teaching History and some Latin and was fortunate to be considered capable of accompanying on the piano many of Miss Eastwood's singing lessons, which were an inspiration to me.

Comparatively few events stand out in my memory, though our three-day visit to the Empire Exhibition at Wembley, five or six staff in charge of about sixty or seventy girls, was a never-to-be-forgotten occasion.

We were housed in a school building at Acton, all sleeping in one large room, staff on bedsteads, girls on mattresses on the floor, with paper sheets. What a noise they made the first night, as the girls tossed and turned and ripped them into ribbons! (Next morning they had to buy new ones for themselves, and that night was blessedly quiet.)

From Beryl Price (née Thomas) on pages 10 and 11, who was a pupil 1921–8:

In 1921, the 'Secondary School' as it was then called, was partly fee-paying and partly scholarship. Form One consisted of nine- and ten-year-olds, all fee-paying, and the scholarship girls entered at Form Two; taking the scholarship exam was voluntary, and only a small proportion of girls sat for this, the age limits being not less than ten and not more than thirteen at the end of the school year. This resulted in an age range of several years in Form Two, and entailed much sorting out at the end of the year. As I remember, there were less than two hundred pupils in two streams, 'A' and 'B' (the only difference between them seemed to be that A studied Latin, whilst B learned Cookery), and there were five Houses: Green, Orange, Red, Blue, and Violet.

Discipline was strict. Each B order mark carried a period of detention during a free afternoon, and several Cs together earned the same punishment; I think that two A order marks resulted in expulsion from the school. At one time, the periods of detention were spent learning passages from Shakespeare, which has proved very useful for crossword puzzles in later years.

The school, situated in the present Public Library and Art School building, consisted of the top floor and a few rooms on other floors. In the mornings, early arrivers crammed into the small entrance hall and were not allowed upstairs until the bell went.

The many flights of polished stone steps were in constant use and it is amazing that they caused no serious accidents. The banister rail had brass knobs sticking up at frequent intervals to dissuade would-be banister sliders.

There were no grounds attached to the school, and no assembly hall. For morning prayers we packed into the largest classroom, and at break time we filled the corridors. Games periods were spent at the present sports ground, and we entered the field by climbing a stile. The field had no permanent buildings, but there was a wooden shed where we left our outdoor clothes. In the winter terms we played hockey and netball, and in summer rounders and tennis; the tennis courts were marked out for the season on the most level section of the hockey pitch. Once a week during the summer term each form went off to the swimming-baths in town.

The gymnasium was in a part of the basement, and lit only by small, very thick glass windows at the top of the wall. It was a very dismal room, and so was the dining room with its bare wooden tables and benches, which was established in another part of the basement. Most of the dinner girls took sandwiches, but one could have a hot dinner. These were cooked in the cookery room and were very good but rather expensive. After the meal, we were taken for a walk in a straggling 'crocodile'. Passers-by cast shadows through the basement windows; on the Church Street side were the legs of people walking on the pavement, and on the Hagley Road side were people going up and down the steps of the 'Gentlemen's Convenience'.

Prize-giving was held in the town hall, girls occupying one side of the auditorium and parents the other. On the morning of the prize-giving we all filed down to the town hall and were given our places, to which we returned in the afternoon. At one prize-giving a play in Latin was staged, and we (the actresses) thoroughly enjoyed ourselves, prancing round the stage barefoot and dressed in sheets for togas, but I doubt whether many of the audience understood it, or thought it was great entertainment. All the prizes at this period were beautifully bound in leather with the Pear Tree embossed in gold on the front cover; one chose one's own prize, and no matter how modest the book, it was always sent to be re-bound.

People did not travel about much in the Twenties. In my form, I think that only one girl came from a car-owning family, so trips were real adventures, and the great big world started at Snow Hill station. There were no trips abroad from school; our big outing was a trip to Stratford-upon-Avon by train. There, we visited Shakespeare's birthplace (and scratched our initials on the walls amongst thousands of others while Miss Tilley's back was turned), ate our sandwiches in a quiet corner and went to a matinée. We visited the Old Theatre and when that had burned down we went to the plays in a Stratford cinema, which was used before the present theatre was built. Even more adventurous, a small party of us was taken to see an exhibition at Wembley, which was a great show of all the countries in the British Empire.

In the Twenties we sat for the Northern Universities School Certificate at the age of sixteen; the grades were pass, credit and distinction. A minimum of six credits were needed for a matriculation certificate, which was required for application for a place at university; the Higher School Certificate was taken two years later. The Sixth Form was very small, sometimes as few as five, while a class of ten was considered quite large. A small number went on to university; I remember one girl going to Oxford, which was quite an achievement for a girl at that time, and several others went to Birmingham University. No science subjects were taught in the Sixth Form. It was frustrating to find that one's best subjects had disappeared from the curriculum after School Certificate, but with such a small number of staff and pupils, only the most popular subjects, such as History, English and French, were taken; I remember that the upper sixth form room had a grate with a real fire in it.

In 1921, stiff straw hats like men's boaters were worn, and a favourite trick was for someone to come up behind and tip your hat forward smartly, so the hard edge of the brim hit you across the nose; this could be quite painful, and we were pleased to change to a softer hat of navy and white straw. The winter uniform was a hat of soft navy blue felt, like a nurse's cap, a navy blue coat and gym slip, and butcher-blue cotton blouses. The summer uniform was a butcher-blue cotton dress with a navy blue blazer, similar to those worn today. Black stockings were worn all the year round, wool in the winter and lisle in the summer; these were often darned, and C order marks were given for any holes revealed during stocking inspection. Uniform was compulsory, and no one dared to arrive at school without a hat.

There were no married teachers among the staff at that time, and I can remember only two who left to be married. Art was studied with the art master, who was not a member of the staff, but belonged to the Art School in the same building.

The Art School possessed many statues, which were kept in the art room, and also overflowed into many other places. There were some in a corner of the corridor on the first floor, and the space at the back of the desks in the lower sixth form room was crowded with them. The form room just inside the Church Street entrance had a small room attached to it and this also contained statues; when the mistress handed her hat and coat to one of us to hang up in the small room, we would spend as long as we dared trying her 'pudding basin' hat at various angles on all the most unsuitable figures. A very dusty, gloomy part of the basement was another repository, and one crossed this with a feeling of fear, expecting that at any moment the javelin might be hurled and the discus thrown with oneself as target.

Spending five or seven years in the same school gave one a feeling of belonging; there was little change and the continuity supplied a feeling of security. Some of us have been lucky in having our interest continued by seeing our daughters, and even granddaughters pass through the school. For those of us who have remained in the district, or who have returned after periods elsewhere, it is one of the pleasures of life to meet and say, 'Do you remember...?'

From O.M.B. and N.A.P. on pages 11 to 13, pupils from 1922–30:

Having been at Stourbridge Secondary School for Girls from 1922 to 1930 it seems appropriate to reminisce about conditions as they were fifty years ago, especially now that the school is undergoing a change of character.

The first six years there were spent in the old building which is now the Art School. I can remember feeling overwhelmed on my first day by the number of stairs and odd little corners which were used as cloakrooms. To look from the top of the main staircase into the well below was most awe-inspiring and although we did not worry about all those stairs in our youth we have since realised how inconvenient it must have been for staff to maintain control in such an inadequate building. To prevent girls from sliding down the banisters small brass studs had been fixed at intervals to the top of the rails. A book called *Mädchen in Uniform*[6] was published at this time and it described how a girl in Germany, overwhelmed by the excessive discipline in her school, had committed suicide by throwing herself from the top of such a staircase. The image of this terrified us when we looked over the banisters from the upper floor.

(They almost certainly did not realise that it also depicted a lesbian pupil/teacher relationship.)

The basement was used for our gym lessons. Through the thick glass bricks of the ventilators we could see the feet of passers-by...Apparatus was sparse but we had a vaulting-horse, a box, balancing forms, wall ropes and a ladder, and enjoyed our lessons in spite of the limitations. Outdoor games facilities were held on the same field that is now used, and for swimming we walked to the municipal baths.

The dining-room was also in the basement, and those of us who lived at some distance took sandwiches for midday. Our one concession for cooking was a stove on which we made tea and occasionally boiled eggs. After lunch we were either taken or sent for a walk in crocodile formation with prefects. Each mistress on Dinner Duty had a favourite walk, so we knew what to expect. Miss Leigh's was 'Hanbury Hill, Love Lane, Stanley Road and home again'. I think we made it into a refrain.

To find enough cloakroom space for 250 to 300 girls' coat hooks had been fixed under the stairs and in various corners of the basement. It was almost impossible to find one's coat in the gloomy conditions prevailing there, especially on wet days.

The headmistress's room was on the second floor, and also the rest room and the large lecture room with a gallery. This room was used not only as a form room but also as a music room and for assemblies. The back seats were always in demand as one could look from the windows into the Hagley Road. From the rest room was a window through which one could climb onto a small balcony overlooking the war memorial, and some of us were allowed to stand there to take part in Armistice Day ceremonies. In various corners of the corridors there were life-sized statues of classical subjects, including the Discus Thrower and the Venus de Milo. These seemed overpowering to us when we first started school.

Miss Firth was the headmistress during the whole of our schooldays. Our chief

A scene from the film **Mädchen in Uniform,** *1931.*

recollections of her are of carefully coiffeured hair and immaculate clothes, which were particularly smart on speech days. These were held in the town hall, all the girls wearing cream silk blouses and navy tunics, although our usual blouses were of serviceable blue nurse-cloth.

Miss Turner, the chief assistant, taught Latin throughout the school and History to the older girls, by whom she was well liked. I remember being invited by her to join the Dudley Historical Association on a visit to Eastnor Castle, thus probably introducing me to a lifelong interest in historical sites.

Miss Tilley taught English; she was small and vivacious, with fair hair cut short and with a fringe. She could always be guaranteed to reminisce about her days at Oxford and especially how she obtained large books from the Bodleian Library, demonstrating how she hauled them from a low shelf to a high desk. She also told us how she memorised Latin verbs by keeping a list of them pinned over her washstand. She read plays and poems to us in such an eloquent and dramatic manner that they are still vividly remembered.

Some of us were fortunate enough to go to Stratford-upon-Avon with Miss Tilley to stay for a week. While we were there we went to see Shakespearian plays in a cinema as the original theatre had been burnt down. It was a wonderful experience, as different plays were performed each day and, including two matinées, we saw eight different plays during our visit. We also punted on and swam in the river as well as visiting places of local interest and collecting autographs of the actors including Laurier Lister, Wilfred Walter, George Hayes, Eric Lee and Ernest Hare.

Then there was Miss Cooke who taught Mathematics and Scripture. She had long, golden hair which was usually coiled at the nape of her neck. At one time she owned a small rabbit catcher's hut called Samson's Cave near Enville. She invited six of us girls to stay with her there for a weekend. Miss Cooke slept in the cave and we were in a tent nearby. One night we were awakened by her screams; her long plaits had fallen to the floor and a huge, black slug had climbed up one of them and terrified her.

Miss Leigh, the Geography mistress, was also a woman of great character. She made us work very hard and always gave us long holiday tasks. Even so, we admired her intellect in spite of her somewhat eccentric appearance. Her form was 4A and her room was on the ground floor near to the Church Street entrance, with a small adjoining room for storing geography equipment. I can well remember her little bell. Our form had come noisily into the classroom while she was in the preparation room; she appeared at the door, rang her bell and said, 'Girls, I have a headache; I have had one all day; is that enough?' It was; silence prevailed.

Miss Emms taught Botany and Needlework. She took us for rambles to Eymore Woods, Kinver Edge and to study pond life in the pools of Himley Park. Here on one occasion we obtained the autograph of the second son of the Earl of Dudley, the Hon Jeremy J. Ward, who was subsequently accidentally killed in London. Another time my blue-and-white school straw hat blew off into a pool. It was fished out, but so wet that I held it on my lap in the coach. We were not allowed to be hatless and Miss Emms told me to put it on at once. I did and had water dripping down my neck all the way back. During mock examinations prior to matriculation, our form did very badly in Botany, and Miss Emms announced, 'I have taught you everything I know, and now you know nothing.' She appeared surprised when we giggled, and actually most of us did well in her subject eventually.

Miss Eastwood taught music in an imaginative way and inspired even the less musical amongst us to appreciate it. Other teachers at that time were Miss Wilson and Miss Soper who taught gym and always wore gym slips; Miss Dromgoole, short and dark-haired who taught Mathematics most efficiently; Miss Chance whose subject was Science; two men, Mr Cromarch and Mr Vidgen-Jenks, taught Art, and Miss Edwards and Miss Ashworth endeavoured to make us proficient in French. There were also Miss Wells who taught History, Miss Gibson whose subject was Cookery and Miss Hutchinson who taught English; other names have been forgotten over the years.

From F. Barlow (née Hughes) on page 13, a pupil from 1926–31:

I began school in the old Art School building at the age of twelve. We had to climb seventy-two steps up to our form room, IIA. Our first form mistress was Miss Dromgoole, who took us for Maths. Miss E. M. Firth, the headmistress, had prayers every morning in the lecture room, with seats going up in tiers. Her office was next door.

We wore navy blue tunics, blue blouses, and long black woollen stockings, of which I had two pairs each term. We wore little cloth caps and navy blue coats out-of-doors, and we always had to wear navy blue gloves; in fact we had them on so much that I seemed nearly to go to bed in mine.

I remember a number of our mistresses, including Miss Chance, Miss Leigh, Miss Emms, Miss Eastwood, Miss Tilley, Miss Gibson and Miss Ashworth. Art was taken by Mr Jenks downstairs in the art school. We had three subjects for homework every night, and these had to be entered in a book called our homework timetable, together with the time spent on each subject. We also had to fill in what time we went to bed, and have the entry signed by our parents. We handed in our timetable each morning at school.

On Tuesday afternoons, we went up to the field in Junction Road, the present playing fields, for games. I always remember how the hockey pitch sloped on one side, which meant that the balls rolled downhill quite quickly from that side, so that one was lucky to receive a ball from that direction when playing centre.

I remember how we used to talk of 'the new school' and how we thought we were in heaven when we moved into it. I also remember having to carry up books from the old school to the new one. When we were in, it seemed too wonderful for words. It was so spacious after the old school and so convenient in every way. We loved being able to go outside into the quadrangle.

The uniform was changed. We had green blouses and in the summer green Tobralco dresses; but we still had black stockings, even in summer. (In winter, we wore navy blue felt hats and in summer panamas.) The name of the school was changed too: we became the County High School.

I enjoyed my schooldays, and even now I like to go back as a member of the Old Girls' Association. I am happy to meet old friends from school there and to see some of my own former pupils.

The *Pear Tree* magazine Spring Term 1962 contains an enthralling account from Miss Tilley (pp. 9-10), the magazine's first editor, where she recalls 'Some Memories of the Girls' Secondary School, Stourbridge 1921–':

> Though it is forty-one years ago that I came to Stourbridge, I can remember my first day at school very clearly. Entering by a door in Church Street I climbed many stairs to the Assembly Room, which was quaint with many steps leading to the back wall; on these were benches between which girls crowded. Miss Emms once counted the stairs and found them eighty-nine, I think. There were in addition fifteen to twenty stone steps leading to the basement, one room of which, lighted by two naked gas jets, served as the dining-room. Another, lighted dimly by windows above the pavement, was the gymnasium; and one day a week I took a sixth form lesson there sitting on the forms that surrounded the walls. Another of these basements was used as a cloakroom. There were pegs on which coats were hung but no lockers for keeping shoes. The girls cheerfully mounted to the form rooms in their outside gear, to my astonishment, brought up on parquet floors and slippers. In addition to the door on Church Street was another, by which half the school entered, giving on to Hagley Road, and when a delinquent was being pursued she might escape in that direction.
>
> In the Assembly Room the staff with Miss Firth in the middle stood in a row facing the girls. There were Miss Harris, Senior Mistress, in charge of English, helped by Miss Emms and me and Miss Smith. Miss Emms was a great asset. During the dinner hour she would often amuse us by her mimicry of well-known people, until we assured her she was more fit for the music-hall stage than for a school-marm. Miss Turner was a classical scholar. She hired a plan to scale of a Roman villa with its atrium and rooms, kept on the sixth form table for weeks for us to learn the appearance of a Roman house. Miss Edwards, a most generous personality, whose £100 bequest founded the school fund, had a French accent that was so true that the French diction of the school was said to be the best in the county. Miss Cooke, who often took girls camping at Samson's Cave for the week-end. Miss Eastwood, the skilled music mistress whose songs are still remembered with joy by old girls. Miss Dromgoole, whose quiet, clear exposition of mathematical problems inspired her girls. Miss Chance, who did wonderful work in Biology considering the lack of a proper laboratory. Miss Wilson, a greatly loved Gymnastics mistress. Miss Marks, who endeared herself to all by allowing us to come to her evening classes and make scrumptious Christmas cakes. Miss Leigh, a very expert Geography mistress who made Geography a real science to the children and who took a bevy of girls to high ground at 6 a.m. on the day of the sun's eclipse in 1927. We had no Art Mistress; we shared Mr Cromack, Art master to the Art School.
>
> After Assembly I was taken to a room on the top floor facing New Road. It was divided from the next room by sliding screens between whose wings the wind whistled and which Miss Evans, who was always ready with an apposite title, called the 'chamber of winds'. Here I was shown a bevy of thirty girls, IVA, and asked to give them a lesson. There were no desks or chairs in the room – I don't know why – except a chair for me on the dais. In trepidation, I asked them to sit on the floor. I had always been accustomed to country children

and had been warned to be careful with children of industrial areas. But they did not hurl their shoes at me in lieu of inkpots. Indeed, these children have always been friendly and kind, and at the end of the day one insisted on blowing up my flat bicycle tyre. There were no books so I read them 'The Lady of Shalott'. Fortunately they had not read it before and were quite pleased to give intelligent answers to my questions.

At eleven o'clock there were cups of tea in the sixth form room on the second floor. The girls were turned out to wander the corridors.

Dinner was eaten in the kitchen on the ground floor. The windows were high up and rows of benches filled most of the space in addition to a long table in front of the range. The girls came and carried their dinner on two plates to the basement, one the first course, the other the sweet. The dinners could not have been exactly hot after journeying down those many steps. Some girls brought their own cold lunch paying two pence a week for the use of a plate. The basement was a most deplorable place for a meal but there was no help for it. The Great War had stopped the building of a new school, though the land was already acquired. But the children, as children always are, were cheerful and happy in spite of their surroundings. The staff took it in rotation to shepherd the flock, one of whom carried her first course down to her though she rose to the kitchen for her pudding.

During the interval before afternoon school the girls were sent to the field in summer, but at other times were enjoined to walk towards St Mary's Church, Oldswinford, and not to form threes on the pavement.

Meanwhile the staff sat drinking tea round the kitchen fire. Later, they sought refuge in their form rooms, except Miss Emms who went to the staffroom. This was a small room on the top floor, the width of the sofa covered in green baize to match the tablecloth. Miss Emms folded her handkerchief, put it firmly across her eyes and lay down to get some rest before 1.55. Just outside in the corridor was a locked bookcase, the school library, opened on Fridays.

In 1925 we suffered a full inspection. The inspectors complimented us on the work we were doing, considering the difficulties under which we toiled.

Notes

1. Haden, H. J., *Stourbridge in Times Past*, Chorley, Lancs., Countryside Publications Ltd, 1980, p. 13
2. *County Express*, 1980 (OGA Archives)
3. Board of Education, Whitehall, London, *Report of First Inspection of the Secondary School for Girls Stourbridge held on the 8th and 9th June 1909*, p. 3 (OGA Archives)
4. Board of Education, Whitehall, London, *Report of Inspection of Stourbridge Secondary School for Girls held on 28th and 29th October 1913*, (OGA Archives)
5. Government Minutes (1909–20) Stourbridge Secondary School for Girls (Ref. BA 1017/15 Worcs. County Record Office)
6. Winsloe, Christa, *Das Mädchen Manuela* (novel, Germany 1929); *Gestern und heute* (Germany, play); *Mädchen in Uniform* (Germany, film 1931); *(The Child Manuela*, novel of above, Eng. version: Virago Press Ltd, 1994).

Chapter Two
Stourbridge Girls' High School and Miss Firth (1928–33)

Sketch of SGHS drawn by Mr Vidgen-Jenks (Art master circa 1928).

The pupils and staff moved up to the new building (now known as The County High School for Girls and later simply Stourbridge Girls' High School) in September 1928 in excited anticipation. The architect who had designed the building was A. Vernon Rowe, the Worcestershire County Architect, and the new school could not have been more different from the Public Library/Art School building. There was accommodation for 400 girls although there were only 258 that September 1928 – ample space in which to grow! The quantity surveyor was Mr A. W. Baylis of Birmingham and Worcester and the clerk of works was a Mr W. J. Kerrod. The building contractors were Messrs A. H. Guest Ltd of Stourbridge and the building contract amounted to £28,400, including caretaker's house. The heating of the building was carried out by Messrs Henry Hope and Sons Ltd of Birmingham and the fitting of the laboratories by the Educational Supply Association Ltd of London, the total cost of the work being £1,270.[1]

The school site (including the playing field site opposite the school) contained about 10 acres and cost £2,369. A scheme for the layout of the playing field site would shortly be taken in hand and the laying-out of the school grounds had been carried out by Messrs Godfrey, Stourbridge.

As Dorothy Sneyd mentioned in her memoirs in the previous chapter, although the girls and mistresses moved in for that autumn term, in actual fact the school building was not quite finished, but nevertheless must have been a source of wonder and delight to them all after the cramped, dingy premises in Hagley Road/Church Street.

The *County Express* newspaper[2] gave details of the facilities at the 'new' school.

> ...The new school contains 15 classrooms, including VIth form room, laboratories for Physics, Chemistry, Biology, Botany and Zoology; also Art Room, Cookery and Laundry room, Assembly Hall, Dining Room with Kitchen and Servery, Cloak Rooms' Lavatory accommodation; there are four hard tennis courts and a detached gymnasium is also provided. Space has also been reserved for the construction of an open-air swimming bath.
>
> The school is a one-storeyed building (with the exception of the principal block facing west, which is two storeys high) and is formed round two quadrangles. The open space on the west side is laid out with lawns, shrubberies and ornamental pool. The open space on the south side has been prepared for physical training, etc.
>
> The central feature of the principal elevation is a classic stone porch with the County Coat of Arms carved in the pediment over the entrance.

Close-up detail of the County Coat of Arms incorporated into the school badge.

The school was officially opened by the Duchess of Atholl on Thursday, 14 March 1929. This was reported upon at considerable length in the *County Express* newspaper.[3] An impressive number of people attended, and it was found necessary to confine the invitations largely to members of public bodies and to parents.

Suffice to say that 'anyone who was anyone' in Stourbridge, and particularly those members of the hierarchy connected with the school and education, wanted to attend such an auspicious occasion. Her Grace the Duchess arrived at the school, greeted by a semi-circle of pupils outside the main gates

Library in the 'new' school, SGHS, 1928.

Dining-room in the 'new' school SGHS. Were the tablecloths and flowers only there for the photograph?

with nearly an hour to spare before the proceedings officially began and she 'passed the interim in making a very careful inspection of the whole of the building and its equipment, and, at the close of the inspection she addressed the scholars. Immediately prior to entering the assembly hall Her Grace received a beautiful bouquet of red carnations, presented to her, on behalf of the school, by Leila Woodall, and buttonholes were presented by Mary Wyld to Mr G. S. Albright [Chairman of the Higher Education Subcommittee of the Worcestershire Education Committee]; Mr A. Weston Priestley [Director of Education] and Mr J. E. Boyt [chairman of the governors of Stourbridge Girls' High School and also headmaster of King Edward's Grammar School for Boys Stourbridge].'

The proceedings began with the singing of the hymn 'Pray That Jerusalem' by the pupils and the offering of the dedicatory prayer was by the Reverend W. J. North, vicar of St John's parish.

The Duchess then gave a stirring speech emphasising that the pupils at SGHS had the advantage of a much longer school life than those who only attended elementary schools and that the country 'looked to the boys and girls coming out of secondary schools as people who would have clear standards of right and wrong...the school...also helped them to a new enrichment of life through all the intellectual interests to which they were introduced – enrichments that came from some understanding and knowledge of the great thoughts of the great writers of our land and other countries.' (One of these being Ruskin whose understanding of true education was to make people not merely do the right thing but to enjoy the right thing; not merely to be industrious but to love industry; not merely to learn but to love knowledge.)

The Duchess envied the girls 'more than she could say' the possession of their biological library with the opportunities it gave them to study Botany: 'Studies of that kind were like giving them a golden key that was going to unlock the door into a kingdom of never-failing wonder and delight...'

She was very glad also to see the charming school library and to know that it was well used and that one could have no better life companion than a good book or a library of good books.

It would have been difficult to find a more inspiring role model for the SGHS girls at the opening ceremony than the Duchess of Atholl. Born Katharine Ramsay in 1874, the eldest daughter of Sir James Ramsay, she married John Stewart-Murray, the eldest son of the 7th Duke of Atholl who succeeded to the title in 1917. The Duchess was elected to the

House of Commons to represent Kinross and West Perthshire in 1923. She thus became the first woman in Scotland to be elected to Parliament and in 1924 Stanley Baldwin appointed her as parliamentary secretary to the Board of Education. After losing office in 1929 she concentrated on campaigning against many issues such as oppression in the Soviet Union and female circumcision in Africa, and she took a very keen interest in foreign policy. She published several books. It must have been quite a coup to secure her presence at the official opening of the school and really illustrates the status of SGHS at that time.

The Duchess of Atholl.

My mother remembers the opening ceremony very clearly and also the fact that Miss Firth was extremely smartly dressed as was befitting for such an auspicious occasion! She and Ivy Freemantle and countless other SGHS pupils remember with a vengeance that the glass-roofed corridors opening onto the quadrangle had no sides to them at this point in time (although they were later covered in 1936 to prevent snow banking up against the form rooms!).

And so the girls and staff settled down to their brand new building, reaping the benefits of the spacious and light accommodation. Sadly a few members of staff had not been able to join them. Miss Harris, senior mistress from 1906 to 1923, had died in May 1927 'after a long and lingering illness'. Miss Wilson, who had been Games and Gymnastics mistress from January 1922 until April 1928, had left to get married. Miss Hutchins, junior English mistress from January 1924 until August 1926, left to enter training to become a missionary and went on to teach at a girls' college in Chunduki, Jaffna. (The girls looked forward to her letters full of unusual and interesting news on the Tamils.)

However, new members of staff were recruited, amongst them a Miss Soper, 'who had already won the hearts of the girls by the energetic interest she shows in all appertaining to their physical development...'

Miss Gibson, who had been responsible for Domestic Science and for the kitchen and dining facilities at the 'old' school, was away long term with rheumatism which necessitated a period of rest in a nursing home. It was hoped that the unhealthy atmosphere of the 'old' school kitchen need not be held responsible for her severe illness at the end of the previous term. Obviously, better accommodation and facilities were long overdue! (The *Pear Tree* magazines frequently report on long-term illnesses and deaths of girls and staff, reflecting the poorer state of health and medicine of that era.)

Increasingly, members of staff with university degrees were recruited, and by 1932 Miss Davies, Miss Fanthorpe, Miss McDonald, Miss Voyce, Miss Sneyd, Miss Wells (known to many of us later pupils!), Miss Hampson and Miss Hill had joined the ranks of SGHS teaching staff. (Miss Wells taught French; Miss Voyce, History; Miss McDonald, PE; Miss Sneyd, History; Miss Eastwood, Music; Miss Dromgoole, Maths, Miss Cooke, Science and Maths; Miss Tilley, English; Miss Edwards, French; Miss Chance, Science.)

Once again the *Pear Tree* magazine, and particularly the 1932 edition, was invaluable in providing an insight to the school year. Results were given of the July 1932 Higher School Certificate; Matriculation and School Certificate and School Certificate examination results. There is a report from each House Captain – Blue House (M. Plimmer); Green House

Members of Staff, SGHS, 1932.
Standing l to r.: –; Miss Wells; –; Miss Voyce; Miss Fanshaw; Miss McDonald.
Sitting l to r: Miss Sneyd; Miss Eastwood; Miss Dromgoole; Miss Cooke; Miss Firth, headmistress; Miss Tilley; Miss Edwards; Miss Chance; –.

(Muriel Telford); Orange House (D. V. Blakeway); Red House (Ivy Freemantle) and Violet House (C.M. Bridge).

There was news of various societies and clubs – Art Club; Dramatic Society; Historical Society; Musical Society; the Choir (who amongst other things had visited Sandfield House and sung carols to the 'inmates'). There was a Scientific and Geographical Society whose members had visited Messrs Ashford's dairy, Stourbridge; Baggeridge Colliery, Dudley; Birmingham Midland Dairy to see milk-grading and egg-testing and the Telephone Exchange, Dudley. Also a joint Historical and Scientific and Geographical Society outing was arranged to Ludlow where 'a most happy day was spent, the members enjoying the picturesque journey, the tour of the castle ruins and the picnic on the riverside'.

Sport was featured – Hockey, Netball, Rounders, Tennis, Swimming, and Cricket, a new addition in 1931. Ivy Freemantle had won both the Albright Medal and the Barbara Price Medal but as she had held the former for the last two years in succession, 'she begged that it might be passed on to the next girl on the list. This was Olive Case.'

During the Shakespeare Summer Festival of 1931, 12 girls spent a week in Stratford under the care of Miss Voyce and during the Birthday Festival 41 girls were taken to see *King Lear, Julius Caesar* and *As You Like It.*

In addition to singing carols to the 'inmates' of Sandford House, VI Lower visited and took with them 400 eggs and some sweets and tobacco. (Good works for the community had started!)

It is obvious from the articles in the *Pear Tree* that the High School was growing and that the girls were widening their horizons, both educationally and culturally. Prior to the outings and visits to places described so avidly by some of the girls in the magazine, travel would have been very restricted to the wealthier few. In the following photographs the girls look very neat and confident in their uniform and it may be observed that they now display a SGHS badge sewn on to the front of their gym slips/tunics. The SGHS pupils must have become a very familiar sight going up and down the hill, via the back and front entrances of the school, and into the town of Stourbridge.

My mother confesses to the occasional forbidden visit into 'Gougs', the Italian coffee and

Sixth Form and Prefects, SGHS 1932, with Miss Tilley.
Standing l to r: Ivy Freemantle; Marjorie Plimmer; –; Muriel Telford; Edna Southall (Ivy Freemantle is wearing the Barbara Price medal).
Sitting l to r: Barbara Hill; Catherine Bridge; Miss Tilley; Cissy Davies; –.

Two mistresses try out the new tennis courts at SGHS.

The girls try out the new tennis courts. Note the gymnasium in the background.

The girls enjoyed using the new gym and equipment.

Hockey team SGHS 1931–2.
Standing l to r: –; Nellie Uglow; May Brown; Olive Case; –; –.
Sitting l to r: –; Josephine Corcoran; Audrey Dodd; Ivy Freemantle; –.

ice-cream café (as did her youngest daughter some 25 years later!). The café then was down lower High Street past the boys' grammar school and then moved to its eventual position on the corner of Coventry Street. Gougs' Italian-style ice-cream with flavoured syrups on top was the order of the day for my mother and her friends. Sadly, my mother had to leave the High School at the age of 15 to keep house for her father and older brother because her own mother died. Her friend, Ivy Freemantle, however, stayed on into the Sixth Form and covered herself with glory in all directions – Prefect, Head Girl, Red House Captain, Games Captain, excelling in all games and swimming and winning the coveted games girdle and colours which were awarded to those who deserved them. She also excelled academically and went on to Shenstone Teacher Training College, teaching in schools for a while before becoming a lecturer there and eventually at High Melton Hall College, Doncaster:

PRINCIPAL SUBJECT.
ENGLISH LITERATURE. PAPER II.
PRESCRIBED BOOKS.
GROUP II.

UNIVERSITIES OF MANCHESTER, LIVERPOOL, LEEDS, SHEFFIELD AND BIRMINGHAM.

HIGHER SCHOOL CERTIFICATE EXAMINATION.

THURSDAY, JULY 6th, 1933. 2—5.

Candidates may answer **ANY** *five questions.*

Begin each question on a fresh page.

Chaucer: Prologue to the Canterbury Tales.

1. **Either** (*a*) Describe as fully as you can the dress worn by **three** of the pilgrims, and use your description as a basis to discuss the use Chaucer makes of dress in depicting the personality of his pilgrims.

   Or (*b*) To what extent does Chaucer sympathise with, and to what extent does he criticise, the manners and the life of his more aristocratic pilgrims?

Spenser: Faerie Queene I.

2. **Either** (*a*) "The formidable dragon against which the Red Cross Knight has to fight is, in a way, a mere pasteboard monster, one to frighten little children, but it has been transformed into a thing of art by a great master of painting." Describe in detail Spenser's picture of this dragon (**or** of any other monster in *Book I*), and comment on it in the light of the above criticism.

   Or (*b*) Write on Spenser's similes with special reference to (i) the sources from which they are drawn, (ii) the detail with which they are elaborated, (iii) the use Spenser has for them in the poem.

Milton: Samson Agonistes.

3. **Either** (*a*) "*Samson Agonistes* shows that Milton had a Puritan's belief in the moral worth of temptation." Discuss this.

   Or (*b*) Name **three** characteristics in which *Samson Agonistes* as a "classical" drama differs from the usual English play, and say what Milton's drama gains and loses by each of these three characteristics.

Palgrave: Golden Treasury, Books I and II.

4. **Either** (*a*) Describe, with critical comments, the types and estimate the poetic worth of **either** the religious **or** the pastoral poetry in Books I and II of the *Golden Treasury*.

   Or (*b*) Relying on poems in Books I and II of the *Golden Treasury*, point out and illustrate what **either** Spenser **or** Shakespeare **or** Milton **or** Dryden has in common with other poets of his day and how far he differs from them.

Browne: Religio Medici.

5. **Either** (*a*) Write a short essay on **one** of the following: (i) the spirit of tolerance in Browne, (ii) Browne's attitude to death, (iii) Browne's idea of science.

   Or (*b*) Describe Browne's style with special reference to (i) its vocabulary, (ii) its syntax, (iii) its appropriateness to his theme.

Gibbon: Autobiography.

6. **Either** (*a*) "Alike in its proportion and its style, in its confidences and its reserves, the *Autobiography* is a masterpiece." Illustrate and discuss.

   Or (*b*) Show how Gibbon's life was influenced by any **two** of the following: (i) his education, (ii) his familiarity with foreign countries, (iii) his knowledge of **either** Hume **or** Voltaire.

Pope: Satires and Epistles.

7. **Either** (*a*)

   "Curst be the verse, how well soe'er it flow,
   That tends to make one worthy man my foe,
   Give virtue scandal, innocence a fear,
   Or from the soft-ey'd virgin steal a tear."

   How far, in the *Satires and Epistles*, is Pope innocent of such faults?

   Or (*b*) Analyse **two** of Pope's satiric portraits to bring out (i) his method of portraiture, and (ii) the suitability of his style for satiric painting.

a superb example of reaping the benefits of a free place and more than paying back her own contribution to the school. As in later years two medals were awarded annually at prize-giving ceremonies – the Albright Medal for the girl who in the opinion of her schoolfellows has done the most for the school during the past year and the Barbara Price Medal for the girl who has played the most unselfish part in school games during the year. Ivy won both.

Her one 'gripe' was that Maths and Science subjects were not on offer for the Higher School Certificate as she actually preferred these to Arts subjects, but she succeeded nevertheless. Opposite is a copy of the English Literature Paper II which she took and passed in 1933 – not perhaps that dissimilar to the A level GCEs that many of us sat in later years – not a coursework assessment in sight but 'exam only' on one particular day!

The 1932 *Pear Tree* magazine was something of a bombshell regarding SGHS news. Firstly it gave a sad report on the death of Miss Turner (senior Classics and History mistress) on 9 October 1930 who had taught at the school from 1911 to 1930.

> We have to record another sad loss the School has sustained. On October 9th, 1930, Miss Turner, our Senior Classics and History Mistress, died. Her heart was closely bound up with the School which had formed her greatest interest for nineteen years.
>
> We missed, and still miss her, her sympathetic kindness, especially to others in distress; her ability to see both sides of a question, due, perhaps to her wide scholarship and her sense of fair play; her spirit of impartiality and her courage. Perhaps even more do we miss her keen sense of humour with the tolerance with which she regarded all kinds of human frailty, growing out of her own wide understanding; the zest with which she entered into, and helped to contribute to, the joys of other people. It was a sad day when we saw Miss Turner for the last time, though her spirit and her memory still live in the hearts of the Staff and of the Old Girls who were happy enough to come into close contact with her.
>
> (*Tribute to Miss Turner, the* Pear Tree, *Autumn Term 1932 Vol. 1 No. 4, p. 4*)

Miss Turner and Miss Harris (who had died in 1928) had supported Miss Firth like staunch 'henchmen', especially when Miss Firth had been away ill or having serious operations. She must have felt their loss keenly and it is not surprising to read in the *County Express* of Saturday 28 May 1932 that she was planning to provide a stained glass window memorial to these two teachers. She had received a number of designs and had herself wanted the arms of their university (London) to be incorporated but exception was taken to this by some of the school governors. There was a later suggestion of symbolical figures with small panels with the top of the window reserved for the arms of the counties of Worcestershire and Staffordshire and those of the Borough of Stourbridge.

Miss Firth had apparently more recently discussed the matter with the Art mistress Miss Davies and current Art master Mr Vidgen-Jenks, and the latter had suggested a prize of £5 5s for the College of Art students to submit a suitable design. Miss Firth had received eight or nine such designs but only one appeared to be suitable or appropriate. Consequently the Old Girls' Association had held a garden party in June 1932 and two possible designs were put on display there. Eventually a decision was made and the windows were ordered to be made in London.

But the 1932 magazine contained even more news about the headmistress, Miss Firth, herself. Whether due to ill-health (the reason officially given) or possibly worn out by running the school and the possible veiled hints/comments from the governors at her lack of a university degree, Miss Firth had decided to resign. She had certainly been away from school a great deal and for a long time pupils' reports were stamped with her signature, and other teachers had been standing in as temporary/

THE :: PEAR :: TREE

THE MAGAZINE OF THE STOURBRIDGE COUNTY HIGH SCHOOL FOR GIRLS.

Editor: A. E. TILLEY.   Sub-Editor: C. J. VOYCE.

Committee:
D. Blakeway, C. Bridge, I. Freemantle, B. Hill, R. Phillips, M. Plimmer, E. Roach, M. Telford, M. Wooldridge.

Vol. 1. No. 4.   Autumn Term, 1932.

SCHOOL NEWS.

Our first announcement is a sad one—that of the resignation of our Headmistress. We talk of this more fully in "Personalia."

On Monday, October 31st, the whole School assembled at 11 a.m. when Miss Emms, on behalf of the Staff and the School, begged Miss Firth to accept a gold necklet with two pendant black opals, as a token of their affection for her and the regret they felt at her leaving.

Miss Firth has very kindly presented the School with a silver cup to be held by the House with the foremost place in School Records. Miss Cooke is Acting Headmistress until next term.

Parents' Days. On the afternoon of June 21st, the School was thrown open to parents. We hear that they much appreciated this and were glad to realise the congenial conditions under which their children worked. Happily the sun shone on them and made tea in the quadrangle a very pleasant affair.

On October 18th, the parents of girls in the Upper School, and on October 19th, the parents of those in the Lower and Middle Schools, were invited to spend an afternoon with us, as Miss Firth felt she would like to have them again before she left. As on the previous occasion, they very much enjoyed the girls' singing in the Assembly Hall, but owing to the season, they had tea this time in the Dining Hall.

In addition to this, there were three farewell parties for the children. On each occasion girls expressed the sorrow they felt at Miss Firth's leaving them and their gratitude for what she had done for them. At the same time we confess they enjoyed the parties.

SCHOOL NEWS: *The* **Pear Tree,** *Autumn Term 1932, p. 1.*

acting heads. Perhaps she felt her position had become untenable with the recruiting of new members of staff with degrees and that she might have lost status had she stayed. This seems a possibility, especially as she actually lived on until 1965. She would also have missed her staunch allies, the Misses Turner and Harris.

Whatever the reason, she was going and going quickly, but we are left in little doubt that she had been a popular and respected headmistress of SGHS.

The 'Personalia' section of the magazine was something of a tribute to Miss Firth.

> It is with great regret that we have to mention that Miss Firth left us at the end of October. She has been in indifferent health for some time, and in the autumn of last year had to undergo a serious operation. Since then she has realised that she lacked sufficient physical energy to carry on the organisation of a large school and, with great reluctance, she felt obliged to resign her headship.
>
> During all these years the scope of the School has widened steadily, offering the girls of the town and the neighbourhood a liberal education, aiming at fitting them to take their positions as reliable citizens, and, until 1928, when it was moved to the new buildings which it now occupies, all this against great disabilities.
>
> In carrying out her ideas, Miss Firth has always considered very carefully, not only the well-being of her girls, but of her Staff, who have always felt behind them a generous and broad-minded support. While the same generosity of spirit was shown in the special help she would seek for, and give to, pupils who were struggling under financial stress.
>
> Miss Firth may well feel proud of her efforts, when she contemplates the school she has built up and the satisfactory work that many of her old girls are doing, and looks back on the small numbers with which she started and the difficulties with which she had to contend.
>
> It is with very great regret that we say Goodbye to Miss Firth as our Headmistress, though we hope to see her often at our gatherings, as she herself confesses that so many Old Girls around keep alive her interest in the School, amongst whose numbers are found the daughters of several she taught in earlier years.

(PERSONALIA: The Pear Tree, *Autumn Term 1932, pp. 3 & 4)*

Thus, Miss Firth's era came to an end. A new headmistress had been appointed and the girls and staff waited (probably with baited breath) to see who she was to be, and what she was to be like. But before entering this next phase in the story of SGHS it is interesting and revealing to read about the memories of those who experienced the 'new' premises first-hand during Miss Firth's High School reign.

On pages 13 to 16 of *Pear Tree* magazine, Summer Term 1976, from Dorothy Myatt, pupil 1929–36:

THE HIGH SCHOOL IN THE 1930s

In mid-September, 1929, I made my way up Church Street to join The High School for Girls – a connection with secondary schools which has continued, with only a short break for further study to the present day. An invitation to write about the School in the nineteen thirties brings all kinds of memories to mind: most of them centre upon people. Walking just in front of me was Miss Wells: it was her first day as a member of staff and she was to be my form mistress in that first year. We were in the new school: the building in Junction Road had been completed in 1928 and staff and pupils had removed from the building which survived as the library, on the corner of Church Street and Hagley Road. There were less than three hundred pupils and a staff of thirteen – numbers were to grow to three hundred and fifty before I left. There were two forms in each year, each with about twenty-six pupils. A few girls had 'won the scholarship' but most were fee-payers. If I remember aright, the fees were three pounds ten shillings a term.

Miss Eastwood taught us Art and Music in that first year. I recall my pathetic attempts to draw a sponge and to join in singing 'Who is Sylvia?' and 'The Gentle Maiden'. We had Chemistry in the laboratory upstairs with Miss Oxford. She habitually kept the class in for three – or was it five? – minutes for noisy behaviour. We were summoned to a Green House meeting. No one explained the house system to us; some of us thought it had something to do with plants and Biology. Only later did we realise that there were five houses, each bearing the name of a colour.

The dining-room was also on the first floor. Did we really have white linen cloths on our tables? I suppose sixty or eighty girls stayed for dinner. If one wanted a school dinner, one had to sign a sheet in the form room before prayers. The numbers were checked in the dining-room and had to agree with the lists. What shame and disgrace awaited the unfortunate girl who was left standing when all the other names had been called! Some Sixth Form pupils sat at the tables. They seemed so grown-up in their cream silk blouses with the silver badge of House Captain or School Prefect dangling at the end of a piece of coloured ribbon.

Miss Leigh reigned in the Geography room in the corner overlooking Junction Road. Most of us were frightened by her rigid discipline and unconventional punishments. I think it was Peggy who, caught trying to tie her legs together with a handkerchief during a lesson, was condemned to enter the room with her legs so tied for many a week. However, good behaviour was rewarded by talks about life in Constantinople as Miss Leigh had known it. There must have been much good teaching too, for I remember a great deal of those Geography lessons and it was in that first year that I began writing a book on Africa! Did Miss Leigh ever use any other comment but 'satisfactory' on school reports?

My second year saw the arrival of Miss Voyce who taught us both French and History. Of the History, I remember nothing, but we did 'do' reflexive verbs and for long afterwards I was bewildered by the existence of that second pronoun.

Miss Cooke taught us Mathematics and we all worked at the speed of Winnie Watkins – a mathematical genius in my eyes – who sat in the back corner. Our progress was somewhat impeded by Miss Cooke's other interests. Her enthusiasm for bee-keeping and gardening prompted her to throw open the window in the middle of a lesson to discuss these matters with Bateman, the groundsman. A brilliant mathematician herself, Miss Cooke found it hard to understand the limitations of her pupils and we envied the girls who were fortunate enough to enjoy the more logical methods of Miss Dromgoole.

The agony of swimming lessons remains the dominant memory of my third year – not the swimming itself; that I enjoyed – but the headlong dash to the baths in Bath Road and the equally frantic rush to dry and dress oneself to return to School, walking both ways, made me loathe Thursday mornings. We read *Treasure Island* with Miss Emms before setting off for the baths and I have never overcome my distaste for the book…

On page 16 from Olive Barritt (née Clare), pupil at SGHS, 1930–7:

It is more than forty years since I first walked through the High School gates, yet I can clearly recall the feelings of excitement which were aroused in me by the sight of the attractive gardens and smart modern building, a contrast to the utilitarian primary school, with its Victorian atmosphere. But before I could be sure of gaining the Scholarship which would ensure the privilege of continuing my education in those pleasant surroundings, I had to face the ordeal of an interview with the headmistress. Could I convince her that a thin little girl of ten was suitable for her fine school? An interview with Miss Firth was as awe-inspiring as with the Queen, and it was common knowledge that one needed more than success in the written examination to convince this impressive lady of one's suitability. I must have been able to answer her questions with enough common sense or charm, as a week or so later we received the good news that I had been awarded the coveted scholarship. The next excitement was to wear the new uniform, black stockings, velour hat, and all – with great pride to be visibly a High School Girl.

I could now feel I was being really educated, with specialist teachers for each subject, maths instead of mere arithmetic, and with the addition of glamorous periods of Chemistry and Biology to stimulate our thirst for knowledge. I think we even enjoyed having homework, while protesting that it took far longer than teachers imagined, for did not a bulging satchel mark us out from the common herd?

We enjoyed new lessons, made new friends, had higher status – but also had to face new methods of discipline. We soon realised which teachers had the power to ruin our end-of-term Conduct reports. At first it was difficult and embarrassing to have to explain to anxious parents that all those C order marks meant only trifling errors or forgetfulness.

A view of the 'new' school by the editor of the 1929 *Pear Tree* magazine (sadly not available in the OGA archives) but reproduced (extract only) in the 1976 magazine on page 13 has a poignant message:

The Speech Day joke could be a joke no more – Stourbridge High School had really come into being…I came to see it occupied and my admiration grew and grew as its wonders were pointed out to me.

First of all, there was the wonderful Hall. Speechless I stood at the entrance…and tried to imagine how it would feel to assemble there for Morning Prayers. In the old school, the whole school was packed into the largest classroom where there was only standing room for everyone including the staff. At every step I found myself contrasting the new with the old; classrooms all on the same level instead of the old interminable stairs; a wonderful Art Room all our own; three laboratories instead of the one small one we were used to…Then I was immensely struck by the kitchen and dining-room – I blessed the passing of the old gloomy dungeon which had functioned as a dining room… Quite one of the chief wonders was the gymnasium…Everything struck me as artistically satisfying…but another thought came to me, and this I would add. Whatever the old school lacked, it was our school, and we do not want to forget some of the things which present members of the school would deride.

Notes

1. *County Express* 1980 (OGA Archives)
2. *County Express* 9 March 1929 (Stourbridge Local History Library, microfilm)
3. *County Express* 16 March 1929, p. 7 (Stourbridge Local History Library, microfilm)

Chapter Three

Stourbridge Girls' High School and Miss Dale (1933–50)

Miss Beatrice M. Dale took over the reins of running SGHS in the Spring Term of 1933. No doubt Miss Cooke, who had been acting head after Miss Firth had retired, handed them over with some relief. The new headmistress brought no 'baggage' with her concerning the lack of a university degree and was, in fact, a Cambridge graduate holding an MA in Classics! No mean feat for an Edwardian girl.

By all accounts she had a very forthright manner, which some girls and mistresses found intimidating, and I must admit that the school photographs of Miss Dale certainly portray her as being rather stern. However, according to Miss Voyce, she ran Stourbridge High School efficiently for twenty years *without* secretarial staff of any kind and 'essentially, she was certain that the purpose of such a school was to imbue its pupils with standards of absolute honesty, good manners and taste, diligence, and consideration for others, rather than to point them to the higher academic peaks.'[1]

Miss Dale involved herself readily in the musical and artistic activities of the school. She also kept goal for the staff hockey team, successfully intimidating the school forwards – a force to be reckoned with in more ways than one!

The 'Personalia' section of the Autumn Term 1933 *Pear Tree* magazine (p. 2) welcomed Miss Dale officially to the school. Apparently one young pupil had seen Miss Dale near her study, dressed to go out one day, and asked her with the confidence of the young where she was going to. When Miss Dale replied, 'To a party,' the child had exclaimed that Miss Dale 'was a lucky dog', so one feels that Miss Dale was not *so* intimidating! Whoever wrote the welcoming words to Miss Dale in the magazine refers to this incident (which must have spread around the school) and added, 'We have decided that we are the lucky dogs to be able to welcome a Headmistress who is so pleasant, friendly and kind.'

Once she had settled in, Miss Dale introduced several changes for the school.

Under Miss Firth's recent headship, presumably when she had been off sick, the school reports, still written in hard-covered black books were signed with a rubber stamp. Miss Dale actually *wrote* a comment herself and signed the report. She introduced green cotton blouses for winter uniform and in summer dresses in two shades of plain green (Tobralco material) with white piqué collars which replaced the cream shantung ones. Better still, fawn lisle stockings could be worn instead of the black woollen ones for Seniors in the summer and white ankle socks for the Juniors. Panamas were also summer headgear. The winter uniform, for all pupils including the sixth form, was still a three-pleated heavy serge tunic with a belt of the same material fastened with buttons. No school ties at this point in time!

Miss Dale also abolished the 'homework book' and the nightly hand-writing practice. In

SGHS, March 1936. Miss Dale with some staff and pupils.

Staff l to r: Miss Voyce; –; –; Miss Eastwood; Miss Tilley; Miss Edwards; Miss Leigh; Miss Dale; –; Miss Sneyd.

Miss Dale with some staff and pupils, SGHS March 1936.

L to r: Miss Edwards; Miss Leigh; Miss Dale; –; Miss Sneyd; Miss Dromgoole; Miss Wells; Miss Cooke; Miss Lewis (later Mrs Payton – first appearance (known to many of us later pupils)).

Sixth Forms (upper and lower), SGHS 1934.
Standing l to r: M. Bridge; F. Hand; M. Rowberry; J. Strangwood.
Sitting l to r: M. R. Killon; R. Jones; O. Case; E. Reynolds; I. Jeavons; J. Allen; I. Dutton; B. Brazier; K. Mills.

Junior girls, SGHS 1934 (were allowed to wear white ankle socks!).

Senior netball team, SGHS 1934.
SGHS was beginning to be embroidered onto the tunics.

The Importance of Being Earnest *1933 SGHS staff performance.*
Seated centre: Miss Dale (Lady Bracknell); behind her: Miss Tilley (Miss Prism); tall 'masculine' figure in suit, collar and tie with hand in pocket is Miss Voyce!

Miss Firth's era the girls had to enter in their homework book what time they began and finished each piece of work and what time they went to bed. The book was then supposed to be signed by parents and handed in next morning at school. There was trouble in school if anyone went late to bed, so it was very likely that the bedtimes entered were not absolutely accurate! Miss Dale probably saw through this nightly ritual and decided to discontinue it.

She still kept the rule, however, which forbade girls to go down Stourbridge High Street after school, and shopping in Woolworth's was not allowed.

The years following Miss Dale's arrival were quite eventful for the school and some of these events were memorable, particularly for the girls.

The staffroom in the 'new' building was rather dark and Miss Dale and the mistresses had asked for and received two new windows built in its west wall. In a valiant attempt to help defray the cost some members of staff gave a play – Oscar Wilde's *The Importance of Being Earnest*, thus hoping to raise some money by selling tickets for several performances. The school was agog at the thought of their teachers (including Miss Dale as Lady Bracknell and Miss Voyce as one of the central *male* characters) 'treading the boards'. Miss Tilley seems to have been Miss Prism and Mrs Gibson, Miss Chance, Miss McDonald and Miss Fanthorpe took other parts. A few snapshots have miraculously survived recording the event!

Miss Voyce and two of her 'masculine' fellow actors – did they have their hair cut or did they wear wigs?

Cecily: 'Uncle Jack, if you don't shake hands with Ernest I will never forgive you.'

A 'mixed' foursome poses on the school lawn.

The Ladies: Lady Bracknell (alias Miss Dale) and Miss Prism (alias Miss Tilley) centre.

It's easy to imagine how much the girls would have enjoyed *The Importance Of Being Earnest* and the effect of Miss Dale/Lady Bracknell's 'A *handbag*?' resounding around the assembly hall!

There was another memorable evening for the school on 19 July 1933 when the two beautiful windows (made by Miss Grant of London) in memory of Miss Harris and Miss Turner were finally erected. St Cecilia was chosen for Miss Harris because of her love of music and her desire to instil such a love in the girls. St Ursula, the patron saint of schoolmistresses, was aptly chosen for Miss Turner. The windows were unveiled, appropriately, by Miss Firth after a simple service led by Miss Dale.

It must have been a very moving ceremony, especially for those who had known the Misses Harris and Turner. The hymn 'For all the saints who from their labours rest' was sung.

Miss Harris was senior mistress at SGSS from 1906 to 1923 and Miss Turner was senior Classics and History mistress at SGSS and SGHS from 1911 to 1930.

(It was impossible to do the windows justice in a black-and-white photograph, but they are situated still at the back of the assembly hall of Redhill School in beautiful vibrant colours with simple plaques underneath.)

It is impossible to include all articles/poems, etc. from the *Pear Tree* but one imaginative child from Form IVA envisaged the year 2000 and wrote an article entitled 'A Day At School in 2,000 A.D.' which I felt must be included. What a long way away that year must have seen to the children of 1933! (NB. The author was not my relation.)

A DAY AT SCHOOL IN 2,000 A.D.

!!!!!!!!
Eight o'clock.

Alice awoke, yawned, and jumped out of her chromium-plated bed in her room on the eighth floor of a Stourbridge block of flats. Dressing quickly she ran along the corridor to breakfast, which consisted of five pellets containing vitamins A, B, C, D and E.

Alice flew to school in her aerocar, a birthday present, accomplishing a journey of 10 miles in one minute. Her first lesson was political economy, when various methods for obviating unemployment were discussed. This great evil was practically extinct, and very few people were without work. The problem had been partially solved by reducing wages and working hours, after the cost of living had been greatly lessened by the universal free trade which followed the Industrial Peace Pact of 1940.

The next period was Science, including an explanation of the X, Y + Z ray processes with demonstrations. The science mistress announced that the following Thursday the Scientific Society would go for a half-day excursion to see a platinum mine in the Ural Mountains by express Zeppelin, calling at Tokyo for tea.

At recreation, Alice quickly made her way to the refreshment stall and proffering a teeny (a coin universally used, about the value of a halfpenny) received a glass of liquefied air flavoured with lime juice.

Then she went to an Esperanto lesson; this was taught instead of English, and was used throughout the universe. English was taught as a classic and no other language was learnt.

Although some countries of the earth still used their own language conversationally, nothing but Esperanto was taught on other planets, therefore Alice, who was going to Jupiter for her holidays, paid unusual attention to the lesson. Jupiter was reached in twelve hours by an express stratoplane.

English Literature was the next subject and Alice won praise for her knowledge of ancient poetry, including the works of Kipling and John Masefield.

For lunch Alice merely had a glass of a pleasant tasting drink, comprising all the food values of meat and vegetables.

After lunch she flew over to Germany for a dip in the Danube returning in time for her geometry lesson.

The fourth dimension had recently been discovered and this was discussed in great detail. Later followed a theoretical exercise on circular parallelism, rather difficult but nevertheless interesting.

At 3 p.m. Alice went to a games lesson, returning home at 4 p.m. in time for tea, an all-fruit meal.

After tea she took a friend for an aerocar ride, arriving home rather late owing to an air-traffic jam over the Sahara Desert.

M. DAVIS, IVA

Article from Autumn Term 1933 **Pear Tree** *magazine (pp. 17-18)*
(Well, there are some multi-storey flats in Stourbridge!)

The building was completely repainted during 1935/6 in yellow, green and two shades of cream and during 1936/7 the corridors around some of the quadrangle were covered (preventing snow banking up against the form rooms) – much to everyone's relief!

Members of staff came and went – some to get married, some to take up posts at other schools. The Autumn Term 1937 *Pear Tree* magazine welcomed a Miss L. Woodall to the English staff who will be familiar to many of us later pupils. She quickly became involved in the magazine as a sub-editor.

The year 1937 brought the Coronation of His Majesty King George VI and 'in the bright sunshine of the afternoon of March 22nd, the whole school together with the Governors and the Staff, assembled in front of the school-buildings, for a ceremony of tree-planting'.

The National Anthem was sung heartily and the school then 'turned right and marched to the tennis court, south of the gymnasium; from here they watched the majority of the twenty-two trees being planted. Mr Boyt commenced by planting a Laburnum, followed by Miss Dale (for Alderman Mrs Francis) who planted a pyrus, Mrs H. Watts a prunus and Miss Dale a cotoneaster. Then seven Governors and Miss Emms planted silver birches. In a line with these, west of the gymnasium were placed five more silver birches by the Captains of the School Houses and the Head Girl. The rest of the trees – six beeches – were planted beyond the lower tennis courts by the Governors and the Clerk to the Governors.'[2]

This was not all. On Thursday 6 May the school assembled in the hall for the presentation of souvenir copies (one for each girl) of Arthur Mee's *Salute the King* by the Mayoress, Mrs Eveson. She said that it gave her very great pleasure to do this, specially as some years ago she herself had been a member of the school and was always happy to return. The chairman of the Governors, Mr Boyt, spoke to the girls telling them that although he was not old enough to remember Queen Victoria's coronation he certainly did remember those of Edward VII and George V and that he very much regretted that there was no idea of souvenir gifts in those days. He trusted that the girls would therefore treasure theirs and would be able to show them to their own grandchildren in time!

Miss Dale seconded his vote of thanks and thanked the Borough for the gift of the books. The school also expressed its thanks and sang 'God Save the King' 'with which the simple ceremony came to a close'.

Even then there must have been talk of the rumblings of coming war and it seems appropriate to include here a short poem from the *Pear Tree* (Autumn Term 1937, p. 19) by H. Hunter, a sixth-form pupil:

SUMMER 1937

A Gentle breeze disturbs the summer air;
The sunlight, pouring from a cloudless sky,
Deepens the hue of tired flowers that lie,
Their beauty left, by summer's heat, less fair.

The happy children hurry out to play,
And frolic, chattering, across the fields;
They feel the joy that summer's beauty yields

From dawn till rest comes at the close of day.
At sunset, when the cool sea-breeze creep,
Inward across the misty twilit land,
Then darkness over England takes command,
And veils her beauty, while in peace we sleep.
But what beyond this country's beauty rare?
Not peace, but iron and death – stupid warfare!

H. HUNTER, VI Upper

There is a very meaningful 'Foreword' from Miss Dale at the beginning of the Autumn Term 1938 *Pear Tree* (p. 1) with a very strong message behind it:

> This year is the tenth anniversary of the migration of the School into its new building. It is a moment to pause, look back, and ask whether the material advantages gained by this change have shown a like gain in spiritual and intellectual growth; for sometimes it seems that the school which has to struggle with material difficulties achieves greater unity in its life, and a more real appreciation of the things that have a permanent value, than the school which enjoys easier circumstances...
>
> ...This is also a time at which to look forward. We have reached a point in the history of the world when we must ask, what is to be the future of England and English institutions? It is said that Democracy does not capture the imagination and enthusiasm of youth in England as does Fascism in other countries. Fascism, an ideal which subordinates the individual, body and soul, to the state, and demands a blind patriotism wherein individual freedom of mind and spirit cannot live. If this School is to play its part in our fight for the Democratic ideal, it must foster in all its members a consciousness of the advantages they enjoy, the love of truth, the power to weigh facts and make decisions, a desire in their turn to serve others, a willingness to take their share of burdens and responsibilities not only in their homes but in their civic life. Then our democracy will become a vital force; the interests of the State will be the interests of the Citizen, and our patriotism will be not blindfold submission, but the active co-operation of unshackled minds.

A clarion call indeed, with the country on the brink of war.

But, as yet, all was not gloom and doom that year for the school. After all, war *might* be avoided. The autumn 1938 magazine (pp. 4-5) also describes how a party of twelve girls were invited by the headmaster of the Boys' Grammar School to their performance of *A Midsummer Night's Dream*:

> It was an excellent production. Enjoyment largely arose from the charm of the boys as fairies, and from the sweetness of their voices in the songs. The acting of the 'base mechanicals' was especially noteworthy. The dance between Bottom and Snout aroused not only our admiration but also our sense of humour.

On the preceding day another party of girls accompanied by a mistress also went to the grammar school to hear Professor Newall in an informal talk on Anglo-American relationships. The barrier between girls' and boys' schools was slowly being broken down and there would have been stiff competition for a place in the parties of girls!

A party of Rangers (older Girl Guides) went on a twelve-day visit to the Guide International Chalet, Adelboden, Switzerland. They shared work and play with 50 sister guides from twelve different countries and had a wonderful time, ending on the final evening with the singing of 'Auld Lang Syne' (p. 33).

> With many good-byes, we left this Utopia, where newspapers and motor cars are a rarity, where Guiding is proving what a very real force it is for international peace and good-will.
>
> (D. Myatt)

A Joan Sheppard writes entertainingly about her time as an au pair in France. (She came back to SGHS some years later to teach as a French mistress – known to many of us!)

Section of SGHS photograph, circa 1939.

Staff l to r: *Miss Lewis (later Mrs Payton); –; Miss Voyce; –; Miss Edwards; Miss Tilley; Miss Sneyd; Miss Leigh; Miss Dale; –; Miss Wells; Miss Cooke.*
(*Miss Edwards is looking older and had, in fact, been away from school with a serious illness.*)

Section of SGHS photograph, circa 1939.

Staff l to r: Miss Sneyd; Miss Leigh; Miss Dale; –; Miss Wells; Miss Cooke; Miss Emms; Miss Dromgoole; Miss Woodall –; Miss Eastwood.

(First appearance of Miss Woodall, and doesn't Miss Sneyd look slim?)

And so, on to 1939 and the outbreak of World War II. There were 360 pupils by this time at SGHS and there had to be much adjustment regarding holiday and lesson times. War work as well as school work were on the agenda for pupils and staff alike. Possibly in a fit of patriotism Miss Dale changed the names of the school Houses. Instead of dividing the school into six Houses named after colours (introduced by Miss Firth in the early days) Miss Dale created Stuart, Tudor, Windsor and York and pupils and staff were organised into these four Houses. Siblings were allowed to be in the same one and colours were assigned to each House. Stuart was blue, York yellow, Tudor green and Windsor red.

Perhaps she also realised that for some time to come there would be no opportunity for regular school photographs as the previous photograph seems to be *circa* 1939 – a last effort to photograph the school together before…

As might be expected, the Autumn Term 1940 *Pear Tree* opens with: 'Our Social Activities have been many fewer this year: all spare energy has been directed towards winning the war; also it is impossible to hold meetings after dark under "Black-Out" conditions.'

Miss Bogue, organiser of Dr Barnardo's Homes, came to talk to Forms IIA and IIB, IIL and I, fostering an interest in orphan boys. (The school always remained supportive of Dr Barnardo's – many of us will remember those lovely collecting boxes in the shape of a house in later years and Miss Woodall's involvement).

Articles and poems in the *Pear Tree* magazines feature air-raids and the trappings of war. We read that the school made contributions to the Red Cross Fund and that during 'Wings for Victory' Week, with enthusiasm and hard work by staff and pupils alike, £1,600 was collected – nearly five times the target aimed at.

Collections were made for the Prisoners of War Fund by the sixth and fifth forms who had acted scenes from various plays before the school. The staff gave a fine performance of George Bernard Shaw's *Pygmalion* in 1943 – sadly no photographs this time. Stirring performances were given by 'Miss Sharp as Eliza Doolittle; Miss Voyce as the difficult and moody Professor Higgins and…Miss Grimwood and Miss Woodall, with their super-masculine manner…Miss Tilley was perfectly cast as Mrs Pearce and…Miss Sharp's cockney accent was so realistic and delightful…'[3] (The money raised was put to Miss Edwards's fund for university students. She had retired in 1942 and a fund to help students go to university had been set up with her generous gift of £100.)

The list of war efforts by the school is endless. During the Christmas holidays Form VI helped the Post Office by sorting and delivering letters and parcels. Many girls from Form IV and upwards went, in the summer, to help Mr Pheysey, of Broome, with beet-singling. Large quantities of rosehips, foxgloves and dried nettle leaves were collected and sent to the medical section of the Ministry of Supply as requested: nettles for chlorophyll, foxglove leaves for digitalis and rosehips for Vitamin C. Vegetables were being grown and eaten in the school garden and Miss Wells had given prizes for the best garden in the Senior and Junior School. During the Easter holidays the senior girls had cut the school field while the Rangers cleaned all the windows on the outside of the school and those in the corridors.

The school also prepared itself to be a rest centre for evacuees. In addition to the great number of blankets and mattresses stored for such an emergency there was also a field oven and three huge boilers. Some pupils helped out at the Corbett Hospital and although not allowed to go into the wards they occupied themselves in rolling and cutting bandages in the out-patients' ward. This help was much appreciated by Matron and the nurses. Knitting for the troops, etc. was ongoing throughout the war years.

The school saved paper by writing on both sides of every available scrap and then collected the bits and presented them, at a rate of two sacks a week to the Mayor of Stourbridge.

Some poignant memories of those war years at SGHS are recorded in *Pear Tree* magazines.
(From the Editor: Autumn Term 1940 pp. 2-3)

> The girls have made cheerful and strenuous efforts to help their country. They are always knitting, whether walking, sitting or standing. Lessons have hardly stopped when their needles start clicking…Miss Dromgoole is continually buying wool, distributing it and collecting finished articles… Many parcels of toys, books and clothes have been sent to…different parties of evacuees…Part of the school field has been dug up under the direction of Miss Wells and planted with cabbages and potatoes, which have been harvested and eaten.

From Elizabeth Coghlan (née Fletcher 1933–41) (*Pear Tree* Summer Term 1976, p. 17)

> The early years of the war made little impact on us. A few girls arrived from Birmingham schools, and we had our air-raid drills, carrying our gas-masks everywhere. We knitted mittens and socks for the sailors of HMS Hood and many squares to be made up into blankets for evacuees.

From Miss D N Sneyd (pp. 9-10)

> …we had to adapt ourselves to war conditions, including fire watching. Each night two members of staff and either two Sixth Formers or two Old Girls slept in the building. When I think of it, I can still smell the fish and chips which the girls insisted on bringing for their supper. Miss Cooke spent three Christmas nights on duty alone, and, as my home was also in the neighbourhood, Boxing Night duty fell to me, providing an excellent opportunity to get thank-you letters written early.

And so the war years dragged on. One can almost imagine that there was an air of excitement and purpose for the pupils at that time but, on the negative side, some would certainly have lost relatives in the war.

Sadly, in 1944 Miss Edwards died. She had taught at SGSS and then SGHS from 1920 to 1942 when she retired due to ill health and what changes she would have experienced in the life of the school. She came as Senior French Mistress holding a degree from the University of Wales and had attended the University of Berlin for a year as a student. She had also taught at Le Havre and Weimar. Although Welsh-born she was said to have had the French accent of a native speaker that she tried to cultivate in her pupils with a 'marked' degree of success!

Miss Dale pays tribute to her in the Spring Term 1945 (p. 1) magazine:

> Miss Edwards was essentially a scholar; the drudgery of school life was never allowed to dull the interest of her subject. She fixed her standards and would not deviate from them. She could disagree, unalterably but without bitterness, and we all respected her detachment and the independence of her judgment…
>
> Ill-health caused Miss Edwards to resign her post in 1942; a serious operation a couple of years earlier and the rigours of war-time had made life hard going for her, but she refused to give up her work until her strength failed her. I cannot remember ever hearing her speak a word of self pity, and her sister confirmed this in a letter written after her death in September last. She says, '…She was seriously ill for most of the two years of her retirement, but she never complained and was usually more cheerful than the people who called to see her.'
>
> A school is fortunate which has such servants.

The School Training Fund which Miss Edwards had set up with her own money had allowed a girl to go to Oxford University to study French who would otherwise not have been able to continue into higher education, so a fitting epitaph.

By 1945 Miss Cooke had also died and a birdbath in her memory had been set up on the south lawn.

Miss Sneyd (with her Girl Guide interests)

also wrote (p. 4) about the death of Miss Brander in 1944 who had been a French mistress in the *very* early days of 1916–20. She had inaugurated and was the first Captain of the School Guide Company, with Miss Turner and Miss Cooke as her lieutenants: 'How we enjoyed the Friday evening Guide meetings and the glorious summer camps at Wolverley!'

Both Miss Dromgoole and Miss Woodall had had serious illnesses but were back in harness by 1945, and Miss Presley (remember those lessons in the Chemistry Lab?) was welcomed as a new member of staff!

In the spring 1945 magazine (pp. 6-7) Miss Wells, French mistress, not surprisingly, especially for those of us who knew her, wrote a stirring article about the liberation of France (too lengthy to include in its entirety but the message comes over loud and clear):

> After four years of torturing occupation by the Nazis, France is once more free. We rejoice with her and with all the peoples of the occupied countries as one by one they are freed from the same agony…In order to promote understanding between the young people of France and Britain – an understanding which is indispensable to the future peace of Europe – the Birmingham representatives of the French Provisional Government, together with the Birmingham University authorities, have arranged monthly meetings and holiday 'French weeks' for senior pupils of sixty of the local secondary schools…we have been privileged to send five or six girls. …The poster designed by M. Cox and E. Neill was copied and printed in *Entente*, a magazine of Free France… More recently the school has made an admiral response to the appeal for second-hand clothing for France. In short, for all of us who are interested in France and things French, this has been a memorable year.

The signed minutes of the Worcestershire Education Committee for some of these war years, which have survived (1941–5) thanks to Worcester County Archives,[4] make interesting

Miss E. Wells: 'France is once more free!'

and relevant reading for the continuing saga of SGHS. Ms Emily Francis was in the chair (there was a school prize given in her name in later years) and she signed the minutes. Here are a few examples:

> 28th May 1941: Causes of Premature withdrawal:
>
> Margaret Freeman born 7th April 1924 had secured a suitable post in the Brierley Hill Library – had obtained the School Certificate and was more than 17 therefore Miss Dale allowed her to leave school on 23rd May.
>
> Doreen Newey born 1st October 1926 had been offered a post in the office of Cradley Boiler Works if taken up at once and because of these special circumstances her withdrawal was permitted without payment of charges.
>
> (But, if other cases of withdrawal arise – parents should be reminded of the terms of agreement into which they had entered).
>
> 2nd July 1941:
> The applications of Miss J. Makin and Miss M. Grimwood be passed round the table. [Many of us will remember Miss Makin's rule over the Geography Room!]

24th Sept. 1941:
KNOTT, Winifred – request for withdrawal. She is in receipt of £3 p.a. maintenance from the County Authority but has 'no stamina' although did fairly well for 2 years. Father in army. Withdrawal approved.

Betty Morris's parents find it impossible to meet the school fees as the War has affected his business very much and also doesn't think the girl will give her mind to the school work as she is not doing School Certificate. [There were numerous requests for withdrawal of pupils because of an inability by parents to pay the fees.]

In 1941 there were 357 pupils and the collection of fees for Summer Term 1941 were all collected in except in 1 or 2 cases which were special circumstances.

SCHOOL CLEANERS: The Clerk reported that the County Authority had agreed to the employment of a 'strong woman' during the holiday. [Presumably all the strong men had gone to war!]

26th November 1941: Resolved that the School Attendance Officer make enquiries about absent girls.

27th May 1942: Appointment of a Physical Training teacher – Miss Kathleen Sharp's application passed round and officially approved.

WAR EFFORTS/IRON: the school eventually surrendered the boundary railings fronting Junction Road but not the entrance gates.

29th March 1944: Miss Dromgoole had been absent from duty since 3rd February. Also Miss Dale reported that Miss Woodall was to be absent for part of next Term and that a temporary Mistress should be appointed to fill the gap.

31st May 1944: All of the fees from Spring Term had been collected £1,137 6s 8d. [By 1944 the numbers of pupils at SGHS had reached 435 – considered to be in excess of the estimated capacity of the building. SGHS had outgrown itself again.]

The next entry is profoundly significant not only for SGHS but for the country as a whole.

> The Committee met to receive circular letters dated 9th November from the Director of Education with regard to an Admission Examination for Grammar and High Schools from 1945...

Whilst the war had been raging the powers that be who were concerned with the education of children had been hard at work in another 'direction', culminating in the Education Act of 1944. This was to bring about drastic changes for schools, especially grammar and high schools. Entry was to be via an examination, sometimes referred to as 'the scholarship', later the 11-plus, but education was to be free! No more fees for SGHS, but to become an SGHS pupil, girls had to pass an examination taken on one specific day!

The words 'every Worcestershire child wishing to enter a Grammar or High School in 1945 should be made aware of sitting an entrance exam next March' brought good news and bad, according to opinion: good that bright children from poorer families could sit the exam to attend a grammar or high school and could then attend free of charge; bad that on one day a child's educational future and probably their future and career prospects might be decided for him/her according to performance.

The 1944 Education Act (often referred to as the Butler Act after R. A. Butler, the politician responsible) introduced the tripartite system of secondary education and made secondary education free for all pupils. There were to be grammar/high schools, secondary technical and secondary modern schools, and pupils were to be placed into one of these three which was best suited to their abilities and aptitude, based on their performance in an entrance exam. This of course was groundbreaking in that it opened up grammar and high schools to the 'working class' for the first time but restricted the type of education and curriculum offered to a child if he/she failed the entrance examination.

The Act also brought in compulsory prayer to schools, whether in classroom or assembly (no hardship for SGHS which had always included this in the school day) and, seemingly, shorter school holidays.

The editorial (probably written by Miss Tilley/Miss Dale) in the 1946 *Pear Tree* magazine, p. 1 is poignant:

> This year has not been quite so hard for everybody as the five years before, as we have not had to fire-watch. At the same time we have been busier owing to the increase in numbers, and we have to look forward to shorter holidays under the new Education Act. How will this react on children in the School Certificate and the Higher Certificate forms? They are already under a severe strain of strenuous days and heavy home-work – often till 10 p.m. – followed by weekends of hard reading. Their holidays served to recuperate them, allowed them time to read books not directly connected with school work, or to do interesting and useful things, such as amusing and occupying children of the elementary schools, helping in farm camps, studying a foreign language abroad…
>
> And what of the Staff? Many mothers of one or two children find themselves worn out after a week's school holiday, when they have to occupy their children in addition to doing the housework. But a teacher has to occupy different sets of thirty or more children at a time, has to subordinate self completely, to project herself into that of others during a whole day – a day that is completed by an arduous evening of marking papers and preparing future lessons, generally followed by a week-end of the same kind of work. At the end of a term, her (his) energy is completely drained, so great has been the spiritual and physical strain. The holidays used to restore the balance…
>
> However, we welcome the Act, in that it offers Secondary and University Education to all those able to profit by it.

In spite of the forthcoming changes ahead SGHS seemed to return to 'normal' quite quickly, following the war years. Miss Eileen Moody (one of the governors, who will be remembered by many of us from prize-giving days) generously gave a prize of two and a half guineas, to be spent, of course, at Messrs Mark and Moody, for the best essay on the subject: 'The cultural activities of the district where I live, with suggestions for their extension or improvement.'

The prize in 1946 was won by Barbara Price and the books she chose with her prize money were: Graham's *History of English Philosophy;* Macdonald's *Mediterranean Problems;* Plato's *Republic* (a translation); Fischauer's *Garibaldi;* Maugham's *The Moon and Sixpence*; Holtby's *South Riding*. (Quite a mixed bag, but good value for money!)

There was a Stourbridge 'Book Week' (April 21-6) and parties of SGHS girls numbering about 400 went to the lectures. One evening several of the older girls heard Miss Noel Streatfeild speak on 'Children and Books' and fully realised their expectations raised by reading her books *Ballet Shoes* and *The Circus is Coming*. (It must have been quite a coup to secure Miss Streatfeild as a speaker.)

There were several staff changes and some sad news about former mistresses.

Miss Chance left, reluctantly, after finding a house for herself and her mother in Stafford which also enabled her to fill a post as Biology mistress at the High School there. (So many teachers were in the position of having to earn a living and care for widowed mothers then.) Miss Williams left to take a post as French mistress at the Redland School, Bristol, but the following new members of staff were welcomed: Miss Brent, Miss Jago, Miss Morris (who had been at SGHS as a French and English student a few years previously) and Miss Jones. There were a number of teachers then (and in the future) who had attended SGHS as pupils and then returned as members of staff.

Miss L. M. Emms, who featured regularly

on earlier school photographs from 1908 and in the life of the school, had retired in 1940 and sadly died on 28 September 1947. She had taught at SGSS and SGHS for thirty-two years and Miss Sneyd, as a former pupil and teaching colleague, wrote a poignant obituary in the 1948 Spring Term *Pear Tree* (p. 8):

> Generations of school girls pass so quickly that very few still at School remember Miss Emms; their mothers, aunts and elder sisters will never forget her. One needed to grow up a little to appreciate Miss Emms, for to a newcomer in the Second Form there seemed so many ways of meeting her stern discipline. Too many mistakes in the weekly analysis and parsing, omission of the daily line of copywriting, failure to produce specimens for the Nature Study lesson, and the penknife, lens and two botany needles requisite for dealing with them (no borrowing allowed!) or forgetting to bring one's bean in a bottle or peas on flannel for their growth to be inspected – any of these called down swift Nemesis.
>
> As we grew older these terrors were left behind and we learnt to appreciate Miss Emms' sound learning and ready wit. Many of us owe to her our first prose and poetry. How we enjoyed the Kinver picnics, studying water plants in the Hyde meadows and heath plants on the Edge, glimpsing for the first time that work and pleasure can be identical. We did not realise then what treasures we were laying up for ourselves when we learnt by heart so much poetry and so many passages from the Bible.
>
> Miss Emms' vivid personality impressed itself on all with whom she came in contact. Whenever Old Girls meet stories are exchanged both of her wit and of outwitting her. Needless to say there are not many of the latter kind and no one appreciated them more than Miss Emms herself.

Two other 'old stagers' left in 1947 – Miss Leigh and Miss Tilley – who both retired after twenty-six years' service to the school. Their colleagues were left with the feeling that 'two of the pillars of the edifice had been removed, and with a sense of their own inadequacy to fill the gap thus created in their ranks.'

As the 1948 magazine describes, Miss Leigh had given the 'Geography Room' an atmosphere all of its own. Many girls past and present could picture vividly the awe-struck file of sober second formers, slightly less silent ranks of the Middle School poring over notebooks for a coming Geography test, stately clusters of sixth formers with scholarly piles of books waiting outside the door. Once admitted, they were expected to behave perfectly and to strive unremittingly to reach the extremely high standard which was set them.

In the staffroom Miss Leigh's mature judgment and quiet humour would be much missed. Her interests had ranged from cookery to cobbling – possibly quite unsuspected outside its walls! Miss Leigh continued to take an interest in the school after retirement and made frequent visits. She had also struck up a lifelong friendship with Miss Sneyd and, as one 'old girl' Cynthia Scott (née Weaver 1936–41) later wrote (1976 *Pear Tree*, p. 19):

> …it is hard to imagine saying Miss Leigh without attaching Miss Sneyd: they always went together like fish and chips! Miss Leigh sat at her desk on a podium rather like a reigning queen, a stately figure, rotund and with grey/brown clothes and a skirt almost to her ankles; one quailed before her beady eye and one look was enough to stifle any uncalled-for remark. Heaven help anyone whose work was not up to the standard expected.

And what of Miss Tilley? As the 1948 magazine (p. 8) reports, her influence upon her pupils was equally marked. She had given to the individual personality of each girl in her charge untiring care and consideration, and each could be sure of sympathetic help in any difficulty. English lessons were a series of happy dramatic efforts, poetry readings, speeches,

SGHS school photograph, 1948.
(2nd row, 13th from left is Pat Wilkes; 15th from left is my sister Pat Davies.)

SGHS school photograph, 1948. Miss Dale is flanked by Miss Voyce and Miss Sneyd.

and discussions, sometimes violent, on any and every topic. Yet, apparently, when examinations came, her pupils realised how much they had learnt without apparent teaching.

The fiction and English reference libraries had been her special care and were used to foster a widespread love of books and reading, and sound literary taste. The school had also often been complimented on the ease and grace with which its senior girls expressed themselves in public (a far cry from those dark early days of the HMI inspections in the old building!) and this was owed almost entirely to the training in oral work given to them by Miss Tilley. She would be sadly missed as editor of the school magazine and there was a worry of maintaining her standards and of making future ones worthy of their predecessors.

The staff remembered with gratitude her hospitality, her gifts of flowers and plants and other work over many years in organising charitable gifts of food, clothes and money to the needy and distressed in many parts of Europe. Everyone regretted the ill health which had made her an invalid since her retirement, and hoped that she would soon be able to enjoy the leisure which she so richly deserved. (In fact Miss Tilley was good for many more years to come, but this does seem to be a time of 'off with the old and on with the new' in the story of SGHS.)

Mrs Adams (known to many later pupils as a teacher of English) joined the staff at this time, as did Miss Margot Clarke (Nonnington Physical Training College); Miss P. Costain (BSc Manchester); and Miss Murray (Domestic Science Diploma).

Unfortunately 'goodbyes' were said to Miss Dromgoole, another real 'old timer', having taught at the school for twenty-nine years. Before she retired, however, after a long period of 'no photographs', the whole school assembled for the first group one since the beginning of the war. My oldest sister Patricia had now joined the ranks of pupils who had passed the entry exam post-1944 Education Act providing 'free education for all'. Perhaps many of us will recognise some staff and pupils in the photograph! (I can certainly recognise some of my sister's peers who came to her eleventh and twelfth birthday parties and who appeared to be grown-up 'ladies' by the time I went to the school. I particularly remember Pat Wilkes ballet-dancing around our sitting room and whose memories, in diary form, of SGHS 1947–55 are recounted so interestingly and amusingly at the end of this chapter!)

Autumn Term 1949 saw the arrival of several more new members of staff – Miss Vincent (National Froebel Certificate and who in a few years to come was to be my own very first form mistress) from Dudley High School; Miss Cooper from Bilston Girls' High School as senior Mathematics mistress; Miss Ball to teach Mathematics; Miss Smith (later Mrs Lloyd) to teach English and Scripture and Miss Wall to teach English and French.

Thus, SGHS was becoming staffed, on the whole, by younger, academically well-qualified teachers. It was growing in terms of societies and activities – there were historical; geographical and scientific; housecraft, art; senior and junior dramatic societies; junior and senior French circles. There was a thriving Dr Barnardo Helpers' League. Trips were made to see plays and concerts and places of interest; House and school sports were played throughout the year (the latter with enthusiasm against other schools). A fairly small nucleus of girls were staying on into the Sixth Form and going on to university and teacher-training colleges after taking Higher School Certificate, when we consider that the total number of pupils in the school was well over 400.

There were to be more changes in the academic/examination field. The School Certificate examinations were to be phased out and replaced by General Certificate of Education (Ordinary and Advanced levels) the 'GCE' which came to be known and perhaps feared by so many of us but probably not so fearsome as was the matriculation system of Higher and

School Certificate to earlier pupils! There would be a wider range of subjects to take at A level, albeit no real combination of three Science and Arts subjects together for many years to come.

Before this happened, however, the school had another momentous point in its history. The *Pear Tree* magazine editorial, reporting on the year 1950, announced:

> It was with a sense of great personal loss impending that we heard of Miss Dale's intention of resigning at the end of the Spring Term after eighteen years as headmistress.
>
> Though some of us had never worked under any other headmistress we all knew only too well how fortunate we were in Miss Dale. In an age when bureaucratic demands for statistics harass the staffs of grammar schools, forcing them to divert energy which they could so much better use in the interests of scholarly work in themselves and in their pupils, we were fortunate in having a headmistress who discriminated with courage and resolution between the useful and the futile of these demands, firmly putting before them the interests of creative work in the school.
>
> In her conception of education Miss Dale showed the same wise judgment. She set a higher value on training every pupil to become a responsible citizen than on achieving for the few brilliant scholastic success. Every girl who comes to a grammar school has not the gifts required for high academic achievement but every girl is capable of learning good manners, self-discipline, and a just attitude of mind towards her responsibilities and rights as a member of a community. In stressing the value of these things Miss Dale catered for the needs of every pupil, recognising the importance to the community of all its members and the value of a grammar school education to the less academic as well as to those whose natural gifts and industry make them especially able to profit by it.
>
> ...girls and Staff alike had reason to respect her and to be grateful to her...but one thing certainly we shall most delight to recall, her shrewd and characteristic sense of humour, a constant source of joy, enlivening many a working day as well as innumerable prize-giving reports. It is not a meaningless tribute to say of Miss Dale that we lost in her a friend to whom we could always look for encouragement and help as well as a headmistress of outstanding personal integrity and courage to whom the school, whatever its future achievement, must owe a lasting debt. We wish her most sincerely all happiness in the Cotswold home and well-loved garden to which she has retired.

There seems little doubt on reading this tribute that Miss Dale was highly valued by the staff as SGHS headmistress, but, reading between the lines one can perhaps perceive just a hint of Miss Dale concentrating *less* on the academic achievements of the pupils and *more* on their whole development? This may have not gone down that well with HMIs and there is the question of the purpose of grammar/high schools – surely some educationists would think that they were intended *for* the more academically able and that SGHS girls should be really encouraged to aim for higher education?

It seems that this was the 'right' time for Miss Dale to retire. She had nurtured the school and guided it through difficult times, such as the Second World War, had survived the 1944 Education Act and its accompanying changes. Many of the 'old' members of staff had also retired (Miss Eastwood, after thirty years of teaching Music in both schools, left in the Summer Term of 1950) and perhaps it was time for a 'new broom'. Before that, the school assembled once again in 1950 for a photograph (by which time my middle sister Ann had joined the ranks of SGHS pupils and, again, readers will no doubt recognise certain faces!)

For a really authentic impression of the 'Dale' years we can do no better than to read

School photograph SCHS, March 1950.

Staff l to r: –; Miss Costain; –; –; Miss Wall; Miss Vincent; Miss Cooper; Mrs Adams; –; Mrs Payton; Miss Voyce; Miss Dale; Miss Sneyd; Miss Wells.

School photograph SGHS, March 1950.

Staff l to r: Mrs Payton; Miss Voyce; Miss Dale; Miss Sneyd; Miss Wells; –; Miss Makin; –; Mrs Hodson; Miss Smith; Miss Woodall; Miss Clark; – (sitting in front of and between Miss Woodall and Miss Smith is a very young Anne Spencer who later taught at SGHS and became deputy head of Redhill School).

My sister Ann is front row 10th from right. (The 'big' girls, i.e. sixth form and prefects, look incredibly grown-up.)

the memoirs of those who actually experienced them, including Miss Dale herself!

From 1976 Summer Term *Pear Tree* magazine (p. 6):

> It is now 26 years since I retired, 43 since I went to Stourbridge, and I have forgotten most of what I should like to remember. I arrived two days before a fog so thick that I had difficulty in finding my way back to the lodgings where I and my 'machine' (i.e. car) were quartered. After that comes a gap.
>
> At my first Governors' meeting one lady was unable to attend through illness, but sent me a pressing invitation to go and see her. I went. Ignorant of the proper entrance I went in through the garden, where I was greeted by two goats. Then a call came from the house bidding me enter. I found my hostess sitting near an open fire with a kind of tripod over it bearing a kettle, while a pot of stew stood on the hearth. In one corner of the room was a bed covered with newspaper on which were two (or was it three?) cats. The window seat and every level space was piled with folded newspapers and magazines. My hostess explained that the hall was covered with potatoes, so that the front door could not be used!
>
> The next thing I remember was seeking out my second Mistress who was putting out stationery. I found her in the stationery cupboard, chewing a carrot! Another mistress kept a hat in her permanent dwelling place. The reason for this I don't remember, but on arrival one morning she found the hat adorning somebody's head. The young lady in question was made to walk, hatted, round the quadrangle.
>
> Then there was Miss Emms. She had lived in an astronomical number of furnished rooms, about which she had many a tale to tell, but the story with the greatest appeal was of the set where a street lamp lighted her bedroom, and she gave the authorities no mercy until they had removed the offending lamp elsewhere. On another occasion three of her Form, knowing it was Miss Emms' free afternoon, decided that they would cut afternoon school and go to the pictures, where, unfortunately, in the foyer they met Miss Emms!
>
> Next came the Great Gale! At 11 o'clock a child came to me saying that the Junior entrance door had broken. I told her to get a dustpan and sweep up the glass. Ten minutes later the Caretaker came in rather a flap, asking if I had seen the flagpole come down; had it happened ten minutes earlier it would have caught some of the children playing. Then half an hour afterwards a message was sent from the Gym to say that the door had blown off its hinges. Lastly, after dinner, one of the Staff came to tell me that a large piece of the roof of my house had been carried away!
>
> The potato peeler was always going wrong. On one occasion the failure was due to a mouse and her husband who had decided it would make a good residence! They were not among the potatoes!
>
> Of prize-givings not much has survived. Dr Sarah Burstall of Manchester H.S. in full doctor's robes, I remember going arm-in-arm up the Hall with the vice-Chairman, a little man. Another occasion which threatened shipwreck was when an artist from Birmingham was invited. He took a long time to answer and then I couldn't discover whether he was bringing his wife; that mattered for the lunch. The proposer of the vote of thanks was a Stourbridge artist. He accepted – for the wrong date!
>
> Three V.L. girls were once sent to me. They had been attending a local café for lunch – not allowed. When asked the reason, the ringleader explained that it was in answer to a prayer that began: 'Help us all to be adventurers, setting out without fear'. Miss Dale was stymied that time!
>
> The war took a slice out of life. The School grew, but not greatly. Some of the railings were removed and we were invaded one night by myrmidons who mixed up all the keys they could find and ate the emergency rations. Then

we slept in various places and listened to hedgehogs making love to each other, but no bombs fell on us. The shelters which sprang up were chiefly used by the juniors, who stood on their heads against them immediately after dinner, which was eaten, the first course in the dining-room, the second in the cloak-rooms, for we suited ourselves to the alert which went usually at about ten minutes to one. The war tools, stirrup pump and bomb shovel, lasted many years into my retirement...'

B. M. Dale (1933–50)

From Olive Barritt (née Clare) (1930–7) (pp. 16-17):

Happy years passed all too quickly, with the high-lights like the annual play, the hockey match against the staff (the New Head proving such a formidable goal-keeper) and not the least the summer outing of the Historical Society to a local place of interest, the simple pleasures of an unsophisticated youth. Almost before we had become used to the status of being Seniors, we were sobered by the realisation that we must 'swot' for School Cert. Soon after came the vital decision whether to go out into the World of Work or remain at school for two more years of even more serious study. I think those of us who stayed for the Sixth Form years gained a sense of satisfaction in the knowledge that we belonged to an elite group. Sixth Forms were much smaller forty years ago. And in retrospect even those of us who did not go further into the academic life must realise what we gained from a period of specialised study. We may all say that we enjoyed these years the most, though we had to spend hours on long essays while other youngsters were at the skating rink or cinema. We enjoyed a certain authority in school and were no longer treated as mere pupils by the Staff. One wonders whether the new system of Sixth Form colleges will do as much for the scholars' ego as I feel the old atmosphere did for ours.

Looking back, I realise I took the devotion and enthusiasm of the teachers for granted, and can only hope that they had their rewards in watching our development, and have received some belated thanks from their former pupils, who as adults begin to appreciate the advantages of a good education.

From Dorothy Myatt (1929–36):

Speech days were formal affairs held in the school hall in the afternoon. Dr Sarah Burstall, one of the pioneers among head-mistresses and at that time at Manchester High School for Girls came one year, resplendent in her scarlet gown. Was it that year that the pupil awarded the Barbara Price medal for the girl 'who was most unselfish at games' dropped – and caught – the medal as she left the platform? With unselfishness as the criterion, how did one decide for whom to vote? Speech days brought to the platform the elegant figure of the ever gracious Alderman Palfrey and the corpulent chairman of the governors, M. J. E. Boyt, who was Head Master of the Boys' School. I appreciate better now the difficulties of the situation, which led to the veiled comments in the Head Mistress's reports. However, these comments achieved some success; for example, the corridors were enclosed and we were no longer exposed to all the rigours of open quadrangles.

Soon I was in the first year Sixth Form: we were six or seven in number. The range of subjects seems very limited when judged by today's standards. Six or seven subjects were available for study for Higher School Certificate. There was no chance of Mathematics and, if I remember correctly, no Geography. French was the only modern language taught in the school.

Miss Tilley, the Senior English mistress, had periods of absence through illness and we struggled to study Wordsworth's poetry with a supply teacher. Goaded by her inadequacy we staged what might be considered the first 'sit-in'. The Sixth Form English group gazed intently at the floor throughout the lesson and refused to participate! It was Miss Tilley who lent us Vera Brittain's *Testament of Youth* and sought to widen our horizons. One of the Sixth form spent a holiday in Germany and, on her return, gave us an enthusiastic account of the work of Adolf Hitler.

In September, 1935, I became Head Girl of the School. The Head Mistress had no secretary: if the telephone rang three times, one assumed that Miss Dale was not in her room and ran from one's lesson to answer it. Other duties seem to have faded from my mind but one last memory remains. Towards the end of that year, I was in the vestibule when I learned of the outbreak of the Spanish Civil War. It was 1936. The life of the School, as I knew it, was to last for a few more years but, although we did not realise it at the time, this event heralded the upheaval which, in turn, was to put an end to the small fee-paying grammar schools, which were characteristic of the first part of the twentieth century. It is impossible to estimate the influence the School had upon me: I do know that much of what I have done and still do is because I was a pupil at the High School for those seven years.

From Elizabeth Coghlan (née Fletcher) (1933–41):

It was Summer, 1975. I was sitting in the Geography Room, formerly the domain of Miss Leigh: now I was a member of staff and I was invigilating. There was a hoax bomb alert, and we all went out to the playing fields while the school was searched. My mind went back to other bomb alerts at the beginning of the war when I was a pupil at the school. I looked round at the girls, in their green blouses and navy skirts. I was a new girl when the green blouses were introduced, more practical than the old cream shantung, but less elegant. Our gym tunics had to be three inches above the knee and black stockings were the order of the day, except for the VIth who were allowed the luxury of beige lisle.

We had inspections to make sure that we were not wearing garters which were said to 'restrict the circulation'. A daring innovation in my time was the introduction of the beret as an alternative to the navy blue velour hat. This privilege was almost withdrawn when fifth-formers started wearing them at an angle instead of straight on the head with the badge in the middle. The girls in front of me did not look very different; their hair would have been tied back with ribbons, or plaited, and their shoes would have been more 'sensible', but their blazers were the same. The doodles on their exercise books were different, as we had no pop idols and television had not arrived in our homes. They had been told to be economical in the use of paper, just as we were, but for different reasons; I can remember, as if it were yesterday, being told that I might have drowned a sailor by wasting half a page in an exercise book.

As I looked through the window, I could see staff cars; in my day the only member of staff who had a car, as far as I can remember, was the Headmistress, Miss Dale. My memory of her is as she was sitting in her study stamping red stars on good work. One could only cross the vestibule in house shoes and then in absolute silence. Order marks were the usual form of punishment, and it was always rumoured that if you had three A order marks you would be expelled. Girls were well behaved, though one of my friends, now a headmistress, was once reprimanded for falling into the pond.

The early years of the war made little impact on us. A few girls arrived from Birmingham schools, and we had our air-raid drills, carrying our gas-masks everywhere. We knitted mittens and socks for the sailors of HMS *Hood* and many squares to be made up into blankets for evacuees. School meals in the dining-room, now the library, seemed to be adequate, and we enjoyed our bottles of milk and slices of cake, or biscuits at break.

The corridors were open, but we did not feel the cold unduly, as we wore more clothes in those days, and they were made of wool. Miss Tilley always wore a red Father Christmas cloak in winter and Miss Leigh had a splendid maroon velour hat which she used to demonstrate mountains and valleys in Geography lessons – those lessons in which, as new girls, we had to wear our names in large letters hung around our necks until Miss Leigh had learnt each one.

The staff were dedicated and spent many hours on out-of-school activities. Miss Voyce took the Historical Society to many interesting places; the Dramatic Society flourished; and Miss Eastwood's choir was popular, as was the little band in which we played our bamboo pipes, made and lovingly painted in Music lessons. Games were popular, and competition for places in teams for Saturday mornings was keen: we had no Saturday jobs and school absorbed our whole lives. When I first went to the High School, cricket was played, but during my time there this was dropped as it was thought to be dangerous and unladylike. The gym was what is now the dining-room, and we were proud on one occasion to put on a display in the Town Hall. Imagine our dismay when we found that the floor was sprung so that it bounced when we jumped! The grammar school boys came to jeer and stayed to laugh. We went to the baths for swimming, which was cold and uncomfortable. How we hated it when the water had not been changed!

The curriculum was much the same, I think, though differently presented. My favourite subject was French. We had no tape recorders or record players, but Miss Edwards had a few pictures and Miss Wells taught us French songs. How the Domestic Science has changed! We made pink and blue bedsocks and laboriously blocked out patterns for school blouses which were too small when we had finished them. We heated irons on gas stoves and spat on them to see if they hissed and were therefore hot enough. We washed in tin-tubs with glorious Lux soap-flakes and left the clothes to dry on horses ready for ironing a fortnight later. We once spent a double period scrubbing and baking potatoes. Latin is still Latin, but Maths is not still Maths but something quite beyond my comprehension. I was not a scientist, but things must have changed there. Men in the school! The only man in our lives was the caretaker.

Not many of us went to University, and many clever girls left after School Certificate. There were not so many openings for girls then. I was impressed, on my return, to see the wonderful opportunities offered to the girls by S.G.H.S., and the high academic standards attained. I hope they will continue to flourish under the new system, but I am glad I grew up under the old one.

Cynthia Scott (née Weaver), 1936–41, wrote:

The High School In The 1940s

For some unexpected reason, I had to collect our elder daughter from school one day during her first term at the High School. As she was not expecting me, I arrived promptly and waited in the car in Junction Road. The girls started to stream out of school after the bell rang, and I watched keenly for Jane. After ten minutes or so I wondered if I had missed her; she might have gone out of the back entrance to catch a bus. Eventually I decided I should have to go into school and ask. Memories started to flood in as I walked through what used to be the Senior girls' entrance and I stopped at the junction of the corridors to ask which was her form-room. I went down the steps and into a room. As I stepped over the threshold I might have been hit by a tranquilising dart. Suddenly I was back at school myself: the smell, a mixture of polish and disinfectant was hard to place – was it chalk as well? In imagination, I was standing in the Geography room waiting to hand a book to Miss Leigh…Miss Leigh sat at her desk on a podium rather like a reigning queen, a stately figure, rotund and with grey/brown clothes and a skirt almost to her ankles; one quailed before her beady eye and one look was enough to stifle any uncalled for remark. Heaven help anyone whose work was not up to the standard expected!

I saw myself on my 'fairy' cycle. I was one of the youngest at the school at the age of eight and usually found no difficulty in locating my cycle in the shed: it was the smallest. My mind darted on in its rush through the decades. Miss Emms who used to teach science – or was it biology? – was another terrifying presence; Miss Tilley, on tiptoes, used to trip along the corridors like a pixie in between teaching English to willing or unwilling pupils. I saw her in a butcher's shop recently, and assured the butcher that she would not remember me; he called her back; she said, 'Hello' and when I mentioned my name she asked me how was my sister. After thirty years, what a memory!

Miss Eastwood! Never can I recall that name without thinking of 'Country dances', the tune she used to play so often when we walked out of prayers in the morning. Was it not she who used to teach music and who helped us to make pipes? We had no recorders in those days. We made our pipes and if the holes were too big or too small our notes were too flat or too sharp. In music classes one dashed to play the triangle or the cymbals, and one's day was made if one was lucky!

Miss Voyce, Miss Wells and Miss Dromgoole; the memories flashed past….the walks to school in the snow and on those occasions we used to stay at school for lunch upstairs in the cookery room. Who was it who taught cookery? The face came to mind, but the name escaped me. My mind rushed on to the time when I waited at school for my sister. The juniors were not allowed to wait in school for their elder sisters who left half an hour later, so I waited in the loos with someone else and we ate some cough sweets, the large square sugary kind. Because we were talking and giggling, mine stuck in my throat. I could not swallow the beastly thing and soon my friend became anxious and went to find help; older girls began to appear and I was taken to the wash basins to have a drink of water. Still the wretched sweet jammed in my throat until a member of staff came and slapped me on the back. By this time of course all and sundry knew I had broken the rules, but no one said anything as far as I can remember.

With a jerk, I was awake again, attracting strange looks from hurrying girls, when suddenly, by my side Jane appeared. I came back to the present with an effort, but the pull was there and the cells of the brain had had a shock which left me lingering in the days at the High School. Immediate memories do not mention Miss Dale, but her presence was omnipotent. At the time, one was very much aware that Miss Dale was at the centre of everything, but unless there was a special occasion, there was very little direct contact with her, (apart from prayers).

On the way out of school, we passed the caretaker's house. Mr and Mrs Evans! Back it all came again! The family became rather frustrated that evening as I alternated between present and past. Inevitably the present won, but there are always memories!

Finally:

Extracts From A Schoolgirl's Diary

Small Fry
1947–48: SGHS at last – no more peering through the railings – rows and rows of girls in assembly, watching the staff climb on the stage, wondering

who will slip – a voice from the back, 'Inwards turn, forward march' – out go the choir – the front row follows, anxious to keep time – only the 'Teddy Bears' Picnic', a rare treat, brings a spring in the step – first French lessons from Miss Morris – School Singing on Tuesday afternoons with Miss Eastwood conducting and Miss Dromgoole playing – complete silence demanded and achieved between each song – first gym lessons – swimming lessons at the Public Baths, one mad rush there and back, the first width ever-elusive – queuing for Miss Dale to stamp those hard-earned stars for three pieces of good work – house meetings to praise the godly and chide the sinners.

1948–49: *Procedite* and *Pax Romana* introduce a world of conjugations and declensions – desperate efforts to create form gardens, trampled on by painters and window cleaners – prize-giving marred by exchanging beloved grey socks for borrowed lisle stockings – an extra holiday, great excitement when the boilers burst – hot dinners, steamed pudding, settle for cold lunch out of a green sandwich tin – spend dinner time rushing through the shelters, hopping round the pond and jumping up the stone steps in the quadrangle – swarm over the games field while Mr Evans holds up the traffic – yell ourselves hoarse at house matches.

Feeling our feet

1949–50: The delights of the fourth form – no longer juniors – as yet unburdened with the cares of GCE and thoughts of a career – play up new staff in a good-natured way – gobble up Symbol biscuits sold by the Lower Sixth – grin fixedly for the school photograph – charge round the hockey pitch brandishing Mother's old stick – make the sudden and momentous choice between Latin and Science – Latin wins in spite of the pleasures of sniffing strange mixtures in Chemistry and playing with pins and prisms in Physics.

Pat Wilson (née Wilkes) (1947–55) (to be continued in Chapter Four)

Notes

1. Newsletter 1980 Stourbridge High School, p. 42 (OGA Archives)
2. *Pear Tree* Autumn Term 1937, pp. 15-16 (OGA Archives)
3. *Pear Tree* Autumn Term 1943, p. 16 (OGA Archives)
4. Worcestershire Education Committee, signed minutes 1941–5 (Ref. BA 1312/4 Worcs. County Record Office)

Chapter Four
Stourbridge Girls' High School and Miss Butler (1950–72)

Miss Doris Audrey Butler was appointed as headmistress of SGHS in January 1950 and actually took office at the beginning of the summer term of that year. She hailed from the Girls' Grammar School, Batley, Yorkshire where she had been headmistress from 1945 to 1950. Previous to this she been deputy head in Cheltenham and before that had taught in Winchester. She held a BA degree from the University of London.

(I wonder how many of us 'Butler era' pupils were aware of Miss Butler's Christian names? Those who later joined the Old Girls' Association may have become accustomed to calling her 'Audrey' but I somehow doubt that many of us knew she had such a 'homely, good, solid' name as Doris. I can't help feeling that if we had known that while we were at the school this might have had some effect on how we viewed or perceived our headmistress. For some reason I certainly always thought of her as a 'Diana' or 'Dorothea' which seemed to me, at least, to suit her rather quiet, dignified but often remote persona, but perhaps I was in a minority!)

Miss Butler's brief was to expand the sixth form and expand the sixth form she most certainly did. Within three years the numbers of the sixth form had doubled and the numbers in the main school were also growing. When Miss Butler arrived, numbers on roll were 432 and by 1953 (when I entered as a slightly nervous but growing ever-confident eleven-year-old because I had an older sister Ann, and our friend Irene Lear in VUX was able to look out for me – it helped) there were nearly 600 girls.

The main school numbers' growth was probably due in part to more places being taken up because of the 'free education' policy. Also (and perhaps a tribute to the high esteem with which SGHS was held) the school was chosen as one to admit a whole additional form of 'late-transfer' girls. These were the girls who had *not* gained admission at 11, but whose secondary school record seemed to warrant a second chance. The catchment area for this second chance to be an SGHS pupil stretched from Bewdley to Oldbury and, as might be expected, competition was very keen. (Miss Butler commented after her retirement that, with very few exceptions, the girls who came did well, and certainly while I was at the school it seemed to me that she appeared to treat the 'T' forms with almost an air of respect and affection. Perhaps they appeared more grateful for their place in school than we 11-plussers!) As Miss Butler put it, '…It was a challenging privilege to be entrusted with these special-entry forms, but a privilege which brought acute accommodation problems…'[1]

SGHS buildings had been designed to house 400-450 girls maximum and with the extra 'T' forms it meant that approximately 120 girls (four streams: II1; II2; II3 and IIIT)

Section of school photo SGHS, 1956.

Staff l to r: Mrs Craddock (secretary); Mrs Hodson; Miss Haig; Miss Mumford; Miss Collett; Miss Riley; Mrs Lowe; Mrs Hewis; Mrs Prescott-Clarke; Miss Goodwin; Miss Sheppard; Miss Wells; Miss Woodall; Mrs Payton; Miss Voyce; Miss Butler.

Section of school photo SGHS, 1956.

Staff l to r: Miss Voyce; Miss Butler (headmistress); Miss Sneyd; Miss Makin; Miss Cooper; Mrs Morris; Miss Nilsson; Miss Polkinghorne; Miss Hill; –; Miss Pritchard; Miss Allott; Miss Gunn; Mrs Adams; Miss Presley.

being admitted each year. Miss Butler was immediately faced with the old problem that Miss Firth had had to contend with many years previously in the public library building – acute lack of space. Some rooms had to be partitioned; a book store, that inner sanctum the vestibule, which surrounded the headmistress's study, and even the hall were also used for lessons. At times, two groups were taught simultaneously at opposite ends of the hall.

At about the time of the Dale/Butler changeover an HMI government inspection took place at SGHS. Their findings were embodied in a lengthy report[2] which would have given Miss Butler much food for thought to say the least. The premises were considered attractive, well-planned and recently decorated but it was noteworthy that there were no shower baths. The lighting in the labs needed improvement; the library was considered inadequate in size – there was a lack of stimulating literature and it needed restocking.

The staff were considered 'moderate' with no 'outstanding' qualifications – in fact a preponderance of Third Class degrees so that work lacked academic distinction. There was practically no Physics in the School; Chemistry started late and there was an urgent need for another teacher. Religious Instruction was good; English was good in upper forms but dictated too much by exams; History – good solid work but lacked liveliness in the upper reaches; Modern Languages were sound and conscientious, lively and a sound appreciation of literature. Geography was varied and interesting; Biology – good; Physics and Chemistry satisfactory within staffing limitations. Latin – the best work was in the first two years but the standard 'falls off' higher in the school. Maths – much sound but uninspired work; Handicrafts was satisfactory; Physical Education was average and posture was very poor! (The latter was also attributed to the fact that the corridor floor surfaces were slippy!)

It was regretted that, as yet, there was no parents' association and that it would be a good idea to establish one so that the headmistress could tell parents to encourage their girls to stay on into the sixth form.

At a meeting following the inspection the two Chief Inspectors, Dr Foster and Miss Dancer, spoke to the governors (headed by Mrs Lunt), Miss Butler and Mr Auty (Education Officer), summing up their findings and thus pointing out various issues which needed attention. They had praise for Miss Butler: 'She is a sincere person who has rapidly assessed the strengths and weaknesses of the School…is thinking deeply about the future and is keenly interested in the needs of the girls.'

They felt that the quality of the staff on the whole showed itself most strongly on the personal side, i.e. good relationships with the pupils, BUT a noticeable lack of scholarship in the upper reaches although they conceded that there were no 'weak' teachers!

There was a large proportion of 'early' leavers amongst the pupils which could be due to the lack of inspired teaching in the Sixth Form, causing the girls to lose interest in their studies. This should be borne in mind when recruiting new members of staff.

The forthcoming GCE Examinations were mentioned as replacing the old School Certificate and Higher Certificate.

On the plus side both inspectors mentioned the 'good manners' that existed in the school. Miss Dancer 'had never found better manners at any school' and Dr Foster felt that 'manners were caught not taught and they had certainly been caught at this school' (Miss Butler had no worries on that score!). School commenced each day with a reverent assembly in the very fine school hall, as was expected. The Catholic girls had their separate assembly in the library with the Catholic members of staff but came into the main hall to hear the headmistress give out important notices.

Clearly, in spite of some praise, Miss Butler's 'lot' was not going to be an easy one and she had got to come up with some results pretty quickly to satisfy inspectors and governors alike. Girls had to be encouraged to stay on into the Sixth Form, take A level GCE and strive for places at universities and other higher education establishments rather than, in the words of the Inspectorate, leave at sixteen years of age and settle for 'clerical occupation'. Was she the woman for the job? It seems that she most certainly was.

In addition to coping with and attempting to solve these problems Miss Butler had to maintain the pastoral/cultural aspects of school life. Certainly during the fifties and early sixties when I was at the school and afterwards, according to the *Pear Tree* magazines, activities, societies, visits, etc. grew enormously in number, variety and appeal for the pupils.

There were regular career talks by outside speakers, visits to theatres, concerts and films. Regular visitors such as Peggy Stack and Betty Mulcahay came to entertain the whole school with their poems, readings and songs. Mr Benoy (County Music organiser, whom we children from Hill Street Junior School, Stourbridge had already met on several occasions) brought quintets from the CBSO and other orchestras to try to instil an appreciation of classical music into us. Girls attended conferences at outside venues; plays and concerts were performed by all forms and there were numerous inter-house competitions and society meetings. My oldest sister was one of a group of 150 girls who attended the Festival of Britain Exhibition in 1951.

There were exchange visits to France (parties accompanied by Miss Wells and Miss Sheppard) with return visits from French penfriends – dressed in a far more attractive and unusual mode to SGHS pupils!

All this and, of course, netball, hockey, tennis and rounders matches against other schools as well as skiing holidays with PE staff to Austria.

It was into a busy, growing SGHS with a fairly new headmistress that I entered in September 1953 along with peers from the same junior school (Hill Street) and many others within the catchment area: Quarry Bank, Brierley Hill, Kinver, Kingswinford to name but a few State junior schools, and there were quite a few new girls from private schools, such was the status of gaining a place at Stourbridge High School at that time.

Summer uniform in the early Fifties.

Miss Voyce supporting her House hockey team.

Linda Adams (née Lemon), who became an SGHS girl at the same time as me, has actually kept her official offer of a place and the list of required uniform. In a short time Miss Butler had taken the school uniform issue in hand and it was she who really established the 'school tie' in school colours of navy, green and gold. (Later on a prefects' tie was added in similar colours but thinner stripes!) The navy box-pleated tunic had been replaced by a slightly more flattering pinafore dress style and the senior girls could wear navy skirts. We all wore quite a nice apple-green tailored shirt. Some mothers no doubt complained that Miss Butler changed the summer uniform too frequently. It began in Miss Butler's reign as blue-and-white-striped dresses with collar in revers – the more daring wore white plastic belts with them but it should have been self-made. This changed within quite a short while to blue-and-white-striped dresses with a 'roll' collar and similar belts. The mothers who were brave enough to make these themselves with material from the approved shop in Stourbridge, Gwyneth Postlethwaite's, had a good deal of trouble with the roll collars, and there was quite a variety in the way these were cut and lay!

Round about 1959 Miss Butler changed them again to a top and skirt in the same blue-and-white-striped material but pupils who were leaving in the near future were allowed to wear out their 'roll' collar dresses! Navy blue berets with school badge were usually the order of the day until the first Commemoration Service when suddenly light grey felt hats with brims with school ribbon (navy, green and gold) were phased in. I think we still wore navy berets in wet weather.

There were always those brave pupils who tried to deviate – black skirts instead of navy blue; pencil slim instead of flare or pleats; a hint of make-up and jewellery! Having a ponytail at this time I had great trouble with a beret and had to fold it and arrange it somehow with a hat pin!

What did the girls wear for PE/Gym and the various sports? There was not much deviation there – new young juniors (Forms II and III) *had* to wear the ubiquitous navy blue knickers with a short-sleeved blue tee-shirt (regardless of whether they were well-developed or not). As a concession, they were allowed to keep their tunics on top if they were menstruating but had to ask the Games staff's permission first. No privacy there! Entry into Form IV brought with it a welcome change. For hockey, girls wore navy blue shorts or divided skirts with a green Aertex short-sleeved shirt and for many years there was a short 'Grecian-style' tunic made of pale green/turquoise rayon material to wear for netball, tennis and rounders. There was a tendency for girls to tuck parts of this dress into their knicker legs so that they lost the 'Grecian' look! They were gradually phased out and shorts and Aertex shirts became more the order of the day. Girls who were good at tennis (and later cricket when it was reintroduced) wore white dresses or short skirts and tops for House and other matches and very attractive they looked in them. The following photographs are a good representation of the 1950s SGHS era; also, for nostalgic interest, a copy of the official school uniform requirements for SGHS pupils (kindly lent by Linda Adams (née Lemon)) is included.

It seems appropriate, at this point, to mention Miss Butler's comments on the 11-plus

Carol Weston (l) and Jean Rowley (r) circa 1950 in the quad.

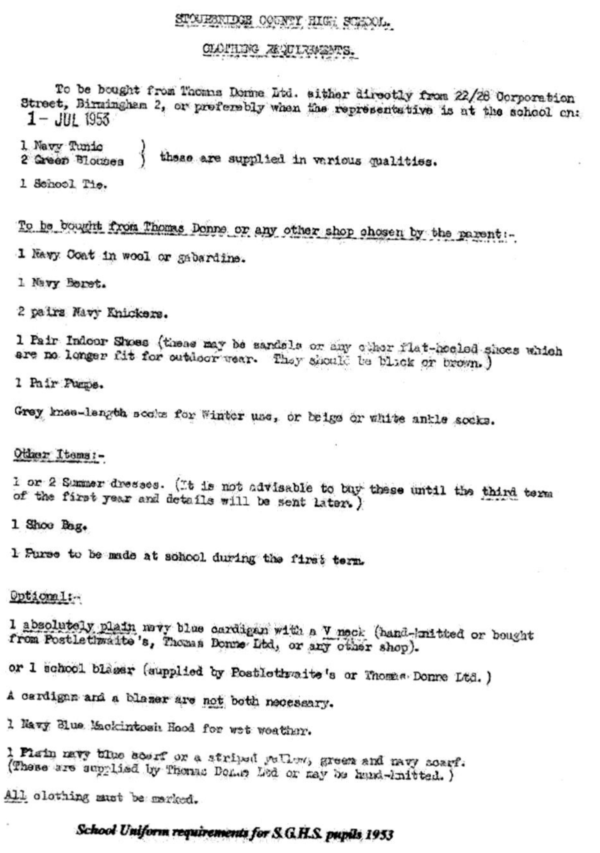

School Uniform requirements for S.G.H.S. pupils 1953

School uniform requirements for SGHS pupils, 1953.

A group of SGHS tennis enthusiasts in the Fifties.

*First netball team SGHS, 1953–4.
Standing l to r: Gill Bullock; Hilary Johnson; Irene Lear; Pat Newnam.
Sitting l to r: –; Katy Pattinson; Jennifer Turner.*

*First netball team SGHS, 1954–5.
Standing l to r: Gill Bullock; Miss M. Clark (Games mistress); Jennifer Turner. Kneeling/sitting l to r: Brenda Spittle; Margaret Priest; Irene Lear; Darrylyn Lawton; Jane Cameron.*

*First eleven hockey team SGHS, 1954–5.
Standing l to r: Ann Vaughan; Vivienne Rushton;
Susan Green; Norma Bird; –;
Sitting l to r: Pat Wilkes; Pauline Poole; Gill
Cheshire; Helen Guttery; Molly Butler.
Sitting on ground: Miss A. Collett
(Games mistress).*

*Irene Lear VUX in pensive mood by SGHS
pond, summer 1954.*

An SGHS group in the mid Fifties.

Form VUX SGHS, July 1954.

Miss Smith and her form pose in the SGHS quad.

Joyce Brown VUX practising her tennis serve SGHS, summer 1954.

About to board the coach home from Evesham circa 1955.

*First rounders team SGHS, summer 1955.
Standing l to r: Rita Priest; Marjorie Norman; Brenda Spittle.
Kneeling and sitting l to r: Vivienne Rushton; Irene Lear; Helen Guttery; Pauline Poole; Jane Cameron; Diana Walters.*

The rounders team wearing those awful gym dresses which were eventually phased out to everyone's delight.

*First netball team SGHS, Dec. 1955.
Standing l to r: Jane Cameron; Margaret Priest; Irene Lear; Darrylyn Lawton; Gill Newton.
Kneeling l to r: Brenda Spittle; Jennifer Turner; Miss Margot Clark (Games mistress).
(As mentioned earlier, we liked tucking those games dresses into our knickers!)*

Saturday morning SGHS home netball match (half-time) – opposition on RH side, circa 1955.

Tennis team SGHS, summer 1955.
Standing l to r: Jennifer Turner; Gill Bullock; Susan Green.
Middle row sitting l to r: Gill Cheshire; Helen Darby; Pat Wilkes.
Sitting on ground: Ann Horridge; Miss Margot Clark; Janet Forrest.

School prefects, 1955–6.

First netball team SGHS, 1956/7.
Standing l to r: Sylvia Taylor; Marjorie Norman; Jennifer Doley; Pat Newnam.
Sitting l to r: Miss Claire Turner (Games mistress); Jane Cameron; Brenda Spittle.

Rounders team SGHS, 1957.
Standing l to r: Jennifer Hinchley; Pat Curry; Marjorie Norman; Darrylyn Lawton; –; Josephine Hinchley.
Sitting l to r: Sylvia Taylor; Jane Cameron; Mary Witherford.

*First eleven hockey team SGHS, 1957/8.
Standing l to r: Ann Vaughan; Jennifer Turner; Susan Green; Gill Balderstone; –; Jennifer Hinchley.
Sitting l to r: Pat Curry; Vivienne Rushton; Miss A. Collett (Games mistress); Pauline Poole; Barbara Bishop.*

Ena Mobberley (l) and Maureen Lowe (r), circa 1957/8, share a moment of friendship in the school garden!

*First tennis team SGHS, 1957.
Standing l to r: Vivienne Rushton; Pat Newnam; Gill Balderstone.
Sitting l to r: Joan Price; Pauline Poole; Jennifer Turner.*

Some members of VLC, circa 1957.

examination in one of her headmistress's reports (1957) given at prize-giving.[3] Her remarks were revealing in that they seemed to attempt to dispel the rumours surrounding the exam – that all depended on a child's performance on one particular day. What is also clear is that Miss Butler was *not* in favour of the 'comprehensive school' system.

THE HEADMISTRESS'S REPORT

Miss Butler began her report by speaking about the new buildings in use from the beginning of the autumn term. During the last few years we had struggled to meet the rapidly increasing demands of the VIth forms and to give the girls the opportunity of studying all the subjects asked for, but shortage of teaching space for the various groups had made this very difficult. This problem would now be solved but even so our buildings are still far from adequate for the present size of the School.

After next reviewing the year's work and achievement in all the various activities of school life, Miss Butler referred to the vexed problem of the eleven-plus examination. She felt that parents should be told what happens in the selection of children for our own School, a typical maintained school in Worcestershire.

'There never has been any desire to conceal procedure, but I think many people may be totally unaware of what takes place.

'In the Spring, I receive a list from the County Office showing the combined score for the Intelligence, English, and Arithmetic tests, plus an assessment by the primary school Headmaster or Mistress. In addition there is a detailed confidential report form showing the child's score in English and Arithmetic at 9 and 10, and details as to character and perseverance. The children with the highest score are automatically offered a place. Then comes a big group whose scores at 9 and 10, and report forms, are carefully checked. After this, when further evidence is needed, the Heads of the primary schools are asked to meet one of the County administrative staff, and the Grammar School Head. Further discussion takes place, and offers of vacancies are then made. I do want parents to know that hours of time are given to this question of selection, and that it is neither soulless nor arbitrary, and I have heard it called both.'

Miss Butler then referred to the British Psychological Society's recent report on secondary school selection which stated that such a method of selection as this reaches a very high degree of validity and is about as accurate as it can be in view of the natural alteration in interests and abilities as children grow older.

Many people believe that the comprehensive school solves the difficulties of the 11 plus selection test, but it may be that the comprehensive schools will not adequately cater for the intellectually gifted children. They have not yet existed long enough to prove their worth, but if it should happen that they failed to attract staff of the intellectual calibre needed to teach the VIth form, or if the VIth form groups were too small to offer a wide range of subjects, or the stimulus of adequate competition, then the universal adoption of these schools would be a national disaster.

Miss Butler concluded: 'In England we have not the teeming millions of the USA or of Soviet Russia, and in the interests of survival we cannot afford to waste the talents of the intellectual minority. Whatever may be the future fate of the grammar schools, I hope that here, and in other grammar schools, we shall go on striving to see that the fullest and richest opportunities on both the academic, and the moral side, are given to every child entrusted to our care.'

Extract from Miss Butler's Headmistress's Report 1957

How did Miss Butler attempt to meet her brief of expanding the sixth form?

The 1953 official offer of a place actually advised that girls should stay on until 18 to gain full benefit from their High School education.

The changeover from School and Higher Certificate/matriculation to GCE occurred from 1951 and this would perhaps have attracted more girls into the sixth form anyway. There was a far wider choice of subjects (Physics, Chemistry and Biology included) on offer with specialist teachers and life in the sixth form would thus have presented a more attractive proposition to girls considering A levels than previously. There were regular careers talks; the guest speakers at the annual prize-givings never missed an opportunity to encourage the girls to stay on until 18 and then go into higher education to make full use of the opportunities on offer.

Slowly there was a growing realisation that more careers were, in fact, open to women in the science field, hitherto mainly a male domain.

Miss Butler encouraged parents to come and talk to her about their daughters' prospects and she would certainly have 'pushed' for them to stay on after O levels. School was probably becoming a more interesting and even enjoyable place to be so that many girls were not tempted to 'escape' straight after O level GCE into what could be a dead-end, boring job.

Social and educational changes may have made girls feel that there was actually more to life than just getting married and having children. This was quite radical thinking, of course, and obviously it didn't suit every girl to stay on into the sixth form, but slowly the news of 'Girls Who Had Left School' in the *Pear Tree* magazines expanded in numbers and scope. We read of girls who had won exhibitions, scholarships, county awards to universities and more and more were going on to teacher training colleges. Some girls were following scientific careers such as laboratory work and medical technology. Without doubt 'the times they were a-changin'!'

Meanwhile staff members came and went. Sadly, the *Pear Tree* Spring Term 1954 magazine (p. 1) reported on the death of Miss E. Dromgoole (4 June 1953) who had, as we have seen from earlier chapters, taught at SGSS and SGHS during the years 1920–48. Miss Tilley wrote the tribute:

> Not only by the skill and clarity of her teaching, but by the manner and conduct of her life, Miss Dromgoole unconsciously made a great impress on the character of many of the hundreds who passed through her hands. She went about her work, quiet and unassuming; but one could not fail to be struck by her strict integrity, her sense of justice, her tolerance, her endeavour to attain a high standard in life and in work, in her own work as much as in that of others.
>
> So well realised was her sincerity, her impartial appraisement of the work and manners of those who taught, that her opinion in council was always listened to with the greatest attention. Never was she swayed in her judgment by emotion, sometimes felt in estimating children. She had courage too, quiet and strong, in combating any misjudgment.
>
> During the war it was quietly accepted by all of us that she should be responsible for comforts for the Services. She arranged for bales of wool to be sent; she distributed it and all, even the bad knitters, felt they must turn it into garments. A few weeks later she would be seen packing up great parcels of pull-overs, helmets, socks, scarves – there was no noise, no fuss; one just saw this happening.
>
> Many of her pupils have expressed to me their appreciation and admiration. They realised how much they owed to her clear teaching, how much it helped them in their struggle to learn. Some, now almost middle-aged, tell me how much they valued her, how they trusted

her, what an inspiration she was to them.

She never in any way sought popularity among them, this, perhaps, unusual in girls' schools; but for her help, her kindness, and her generosity could be always relied on, but it was so quiet that it was sometimes unnoticeable.

My mother's tribute to her (she was taught by Miss Dromgoole from 1926 to 1930) is simpler but no less sincere: 'Miss Dromgoole was really nice.' These words from a maths-hater speak volumes!

Another article in this same magazine illustrates how much the girls (particularly the sixth formers) were broadening their horizons, both educationally and geographically. Madeleine Johnson (VIU2) describes a visit to London with six other girls to attend a series of lectures and discussions held by the Council for Education in World Citizenship. Their mornings and most of the afternoons were taken up by the conference, which was found to be stimulating, enjoyable and of great educational value. They also had time to explore London and attended a lecture by Dame Sybil Thorndyke, saw three films and did some shopping!

A school outing.

Miss Z. Wall left the school in 1954 to teach in her own county of Northumberland. Miss Shand and Miss McKnight also left, Miss Shand to take up a post at the Hittorf Gymnasium, Münster, Westphalia and Miss McKnight one at Wharfe Lane School, Shelton, Stoke-on-Trent in order to be near her home. Goodbyes were also said to Miss E. Ingoldsby, whose teaching of Music had given many girls a lifelong enjoyment of the subject they might never otherwise have had. Mrs Drane, who had been teaching English part-time, left and Miss Irons (always a popular teacher) left to take up a commission in the WRAF.

It seems that there was a much higher turnover of staff in the 1950s than had hitherto been the case in the earlier days of SGSS and SGHS. Women had perhaps become accustomed to travelling away from home to teach; there were more grammar and secondary schools in *which* to teach and a wider scope of subjects *to* teach. Ever so slowly the permanent 'fixtures' on the staff who had devoted practically the whole of their adult life to the school were gradually disappearing and in their places were coming younger, more ambitious teachers who, seeing an opportunity to broaden their horizons, were keen to take it – not always through marriage either! And yet there was always a small nucleus of graduates who were very eager to return to SGHS as members of the teaching staff. Swings and roundabouts!

Miss Allott arrived from the Mount School, York to teach Latin; Miss Haig, from Stanford High School, to teach general subjects; Miss Polkinghorne from Westminster College to teach Scripture and Miss Riley from a school in Bremen, where she had spent a year as an English assistant, to teach German. Mlle Duvignère came from the Université de Bordeaux to take French conversation. Miss Nilsson was welcomed back to teach domestic subjects – she had been absent for one year teaching in her native Sweden. Miss Nilsson was a very jolly person and reigned over the little needlework room where girls struggled to use sewing machines, some manual, some electric, some treadle, to make various garments such as skirts and blouses which she praised fulsomely but which perhaps, at times, did not deserve her praise. Girls enjoyed 'trying on' these clothes in this room at various stages of completion and it was always quite a relaxed atmosphere. Miss Nilsson also made a formidable, well-padded-up goalkeeper in the Staff versus Girls hockey matches – carrying on the former headmistress's (Miss Dale) tradition!

SGHS also lost its secretary at this time – Mrs Morgan, who had become very much part of school life and had been untiring in her response to incessant demands made on her by pupils and mistresses, never impatient when her more important work had constantly to be put aside to deal with trivialities. She was replaced by Mrs Craddock who stayed for many years and who will be remembered by pupils as bringing a sense of long-term stability to the office, and no doubt to Miss Butler's peace of mind. She was also a comfort to girls who were forced to spend any time in the sick bay – over and above her secretarial duties.

A 'first' for the school occurred on 10 July 1954. A service of commemoration and dedication was held at Oldswinford Parish Church. This service was conducted by Canon A. V. Hurley, Archdeacon of Dudley, and attended by governors, staff and pupils, parents, friends and old girls. The first lesson was read by the head girl Anne Millward and the second by Miss Butler. The collection was taken by four school prefects, representing each school house. The school choir sang the anthem 'Worship'. The service became an annual tradition with a crocodile of pupils accompanied by their form mistresses making their way to the church. Canon Hurley became a familiar figure, especially to girls in the Senior Choir who had to attend a rehearsal at the church a few days before the actual service. Having daughters of his own, he was not embarrassed to mention to choir members that they should take care not to let any 'slips' show beneath school dresses when they processed in from the vestry which, of course, caused a bit of giggling at the time. He was an impressive figure (at well over six feet tall) bringing up the rear of this procession and wore full regalia of military medals, etc. on his surplice for these auspicious occasions. There seemed to be something akin to tetchiness between himself and a Mr Lamb who was the church organist in the 1950s!

And so the 1950s moved on – Miss Butler became very established as headmistress (Miss Voyce always referred to her reverently as 'The Head'). Plans were afoot for the first extension to the school which included a new Physics lab, large sixth-form room and an extra cloakroom. Meanwhile it is doubtful whether the lack of space truly bothered the pupils. One became very used to members of the sixth form setting up folding desks and chairs all over the building and particularly in the hall and vestibule. Many of us were assigned to 'travelling form rooms' such as the domestic science and

Canon A. V. Hurley of Oldswinford Church.

art rooms where one had to pack up books in satchels for most of the day's lessons quite early in the morning, with a quick return at breaktime. In my own experience this had disastrous results one day. Mrs Lowe (French teacher for a while) had kindly promoted Pauline Griffiths and me to the 'A' Division for this subject (I had been quite content to cruise along in the 'B' division with many of my other friends but Mrs Lowe must have seen some kind of hope for me). On the day of the O level French Dictée examination Pauline and I had to set off from the upper regions of the domestic science room (our form room at that time with Mrs Payton as Form Mistress – two years running) to sit the exam in one of the downstairs rooms. We were not late – the examination wasn't scheduled to start until 9.00 a.m. but when we arrived nervously clutching pencil cases and rulers we found to our horror that the rest of the 'A' division (whose form rooms were downstairs) had actually started the Dictée (by Miss Wells). Pandemonium was let loose – we thought Miss Wells was going to collapse and eventually those who had already done half of the Dictée were put on their honour not to change anything they had already written and Pauline and I were read the Dictée to do on our own.

Miss Wells was *most* apologetic and asked us whether we felt this had affected our performances –'No, we didn't think so' – and told us that she would enclose a letter with our papers to tell the examiners what had happened! We both passed, not actually with flying colours, but the Dictée was only a small part of the French O level examination and we forgot about the incident very quickly. I don't think Miss Wells did and always called a register after that!

Sadly, Mrs Lowe died, quite unexpectedly, on 13 March 1957. She had taught for fourteen years at Bilston Girls' High School before joining the Staff of SGHS in September 1955 and so quickly did she become part of the school that it was strange to realise what a short time

Miss Makin (front right), crouching down, looking very jolly. Is she going to throw a snowball? School Easter holiday trip 1955, Pic de la Corne glacier.

she had actually been there. Staff and girls alike (myself included) were quick to appreciate her scholarship and sound teaching so that French became enjoyable. Perhaps many of us didn't realise that Mrs Lowe was also a great lover of music and an able pianist and helped in the choir and French Circles. Miss Wells wrote 'In Memoriam' that Mrs Lowe's 'happy personality and lively sense of humour were a constant source of pleasure in the staff-room. Her death has left the School the poorer, for by it we have lost not only a highly skilled teacher, but a valued friend and colleague.'[4]

Her death came as a great shock to me personally, and I always wished afterwards that I had sought her out to thank her for elevating me to the 'A' division and now it was too late. One more step on the ladder towards maturity perhaps.

At this time there were several staff changes – Miss Gunn returned to teach English at her own old school Bilston High; Miss Riley gave up her post as German mistress to train at Mount Hermon Missionary Training College. Mrs Drane returned in a full-time capacity to teach English again (how I had enjoyed her lessons in II3 when we devoured *Treasure Island, Prester John, David Copperfield* and *Cranford,* and I envied those children who were going to be taught by her). Miss Eldridge (University of Hull) arrived from Brockmoor School to teach French and Mrs Gorringe (Royal Holloway College, London) came from the Nonsuch School, Cheam to teach Maths, and Miss Wylde (Westfield College, London) to teach German and French. Little did we know at this time that Miss Wylde was to become very much part of the future of SGHS.

During the Fifties the joint play-readings with the Boys' Grammar School really became an enjoyable part of school life, particularly in the Senior School. Mr Chambers (headmaster), Mr D. Waters (his head of English) and our own Miss Voyce were all enthusiastic organisers of these evenings held at their various homes with very welcome refreshments. Such was the success and popularity of these play-readings that they led to joint public play performances with the two schools which made a great deal of sense (remembering how Miss Voyce had to don male attire for Professor Higgins in the 1930s).

The first of these plays was *The Teahouse of the August Moon* (performed in the November of 1957 at the grammar school) and our own Joan Price took the female lead which she performed fantastically well. Those of us who were not old enough to be in the cast were no doubt very envious of this opportunity to 'mix' with the boys from the grammar school at such a worthwhile and enjoyable venture – a sure 'carrot' to tempt many of us into the sixth form! *Teahouse* was to be the first of many, many plays to be performed in future years by both schools as a joint venture.

It was always of some interest to SGHS pupils when a member of staff married and this was the case when Miss Selwood (Biology) became Mrs Hadley in 1956, marrying the brother of one of the SGHS girls. Disappearing, slowly, were the days when the majority of the teaching staff remained confirmed spinsters and we were equally interested when we got to hear that Miss Z. Wall, Miss Gunn and

Scene from **The Teahouse of the August Moon,** *Nov. 1957, SGHS/KEGS.*

Miss Mumford had also married, even though they had left SGHS. Members of SGHS staff were doing exciting things in this decade. Miss Irons had become a Flight Officer in the Education Branch of the WRAF. Miss Hill (Music) left to go off to Jamaica, not only to teach in a full-time government post there but also to be an associate missionary. She had shared a house with Miss Polkinghorne (RE) previously (who left SGHS a couple of years later when she married Revd Michael Edwards, a Methodist minister) and went out to Kenya to do church work there. Many SGHS girls (myself included) were privileged to know Miss Hill and Miss Polkinghorne as fellow members of New Road Methodist Church, Stourbridge congregation where it was good to see them, not as teachers at school but as 'friends'. Both were excellent local preachers – Miss Hill sang in the church choir and Miss Polkinghorne bravely guided some of us around the local Methodist church circuit where we were allowed to take part of the services. (We were known as the Mission Band and my heart always sank when it was my turn to do part of the sermon!) We were pleased to hear that Miss Hill became Mrs Ruddle a year or so after going out to Jamaica.

Miss Collett poses in the school garden with the tennis team.

At this time, also, the *Pear Tree* reported, as usual, on the achievements and successes of old girls, especially the more 'recent' old girls. It was clear that a much higher number of girls were graduating from universities and teacher training and other colleges and that more were going on to take postgraduate courses as well as entering the professions when compared with the 1940s and earlier. Also, old girls were taking advantage of posts abroad and making names for themselves in their particular fields.

In short, SGHS was moving onwards and upwards. This was due to a certain extent, of course, to the fact that the actual number of colleges and universities were slowly increasing so that there were more places for which to apply. But surely some of the credit should go to Miss Butler who was pushing for girls to stay on into the sixth form and realise their full potential: this in spite of the ever-present problem of lack of space in the school.

Old pupils of SGHS looking back on their headmistress's persona may not perhaps always think of her as an inspiring ruler/presence in the school. She was a rather thin, wiry person usually dressed in slightly baggy tweed suits and occasionally an old mackintosh when she cycled to school from her nearby home. She was certainly not a 'laugh a minute' person but how many heads of high/grammar schools were in the days of the 1950s? She almost gave the impression of an 'old' school girl at times when her face crinkled and went red with amusement whilst at the same time giving a slight illusion of shyness and awkwardness of manner. But there was no doubt about it, Miss Butler commanded respect, fear, deference...call it what you will. New intakes were 'introduced' to her (during my seven years at SGHS) on the second day of the September term in no uncertain terms. After the school had marched into the hall for assembly (II1, II2 and II3 were usually squashed down the side aisles) there was meant to be utter silence as the staff filed in and up onto the platform. A bell rang out in the vestibule (by a special monitor); we girls heard the click of the headmistress's study door open and shut which was the signal for everybody to rise to their feet. In swept a gowned figure in the form of Miss Butler, down the centre aisle and onto the platform to her table and dais: 'Good Morning', 'Good Morning, Miss Butler', and assembly had begun! Our first glimpse, usually, of 'The Head'.

One was never much in doubt that SGHS was Miss Butler's life.

Maybe it was because she gave the impression of not being 'quite of this world' or detached from ordinary, everyday life outside school. Until the sixth form, many of us probably found Miss Butler quite a remote figure unless we were sent to her for breaking rules, etc.! She taught RE to the new forms and in this way she must have become familiar with girls' names early on and observed them as they progressed up the school. Certainly the staff seemed to treat her with great courtesy and respect (again I feel I want to use the word 'fear' at times), but one feels that there was little camaraderie between her and the staff when she visited the staffroom or at staff meetings. She changed her image very slightly towards the end of the 1950s by having a new hairstyle and slightly smarter clothes.

When it came to deciding to do A levels Miss Butler came into her own and I personally found her very kind, sympathetic and

School prefects: SGHS 1957.

encouraging when I wanted to go into the sixth form slightly against my parents' wishes (my older sisters hadn't wanted to), and by the time I left I felt I had a reasonably good 'working relationship' with her.

She appeared to like and rely upon the prefect and house system, and during the 1950s the four Houses York, Stuart, Tudor and Windsor were expanded into six houses – the two extra ones being called Kent and Lancaster. This was to give more girls a chance to play sport, etc. for their House and to allow a few more prefects to become House Captain and Deputy. Sensible thinking – but this caused consternation in the school. The Autumn Term of 1959 saw the whole school split up into the six Houses regardless of which had been their previous House and to which they had owed former allegiance. A person such as myself who had been loyal to York now found themselves a member of Windsor House, a former 'enemy'! A change of coloured badge was also expected of course, but it wasn't too long before everyone had shaken down into their new Houses and wore their badge with pride: red for Windsor, green for Tudor, yellow for York, blue for Stuart. The two new Houses were pale blue and orange.

Pauline Poole (l) and Gill Balderstone (r), Sixth Form prefects, support their House netball team, 1958–9.

SGHS cricket team, 1959.

Whilst on the subject of badges, Miss Butler, no doubt after discussion with her staff, introduced striped deportment badges in the 50s decade which were awarded each term after staff had noted in the staff room those girls who held themselves up straight around the school! (Perhaps Miss Firth and Miss Dale should have introduced these in those dark days of HMI criticism of the girls' poor posture.)

Sport was taken very seriously at SGHS and colours and girdles were awarded to those who deserved them for playing well. The girdles were a blended weave of navy, green and gold worn around the waist over the skirt – not like those lovely silk ones of Miss Firth's day that hung somewhere around the hips!

Great was the rejoicing of the school when

A quiet 'girly' gossip.

Miss Butler announced in assembly that the SGHS hockey and netball teams formed all or part of the Worcestershire County Team.

Cricket also reappeared on the sports agenda during the late 1950s after a break from this particular sport since Miss Firth's days.

Sadly, Priscilla Chambers (sitting on the right of a Hinchley twin wicket-keeper, front row), who was without doubt to have been Head Girl for 1959 to 1960, died early in the summer holidays of that year. Priscilla was the oldest daughter of Mr Chambers (headmaster of KEGS) and his wife and, although she had been very ill from time to time during most of her SGHS life, always seemed to bounce back and was very able, both academically and sports-wise. Miss Butler somehow got a message to Priscilla's sixth-form peers (remember this was before email and not everyone had telephones then) and quite a group of us attended the funeral held at 'our' church St Mary's, Oldswinford, where Priscilla had attended with the rest of the school for the annual SGHS commemoration services.

It was, to say the least, a sobering experience – for many of us it was the first funeral we had ever attended and certainly for one so young and familiar to us. Our hearts went out to Mr and Mrs Chambers and her sisters, Felicity and Victoria – the latter did not attend the funeral. Also, we felt great sympathy for Miss Voyce, a close friend and neighbour of the family, who was openly weeping.

At Miss Butler's request we wore our school uniform and she waited outside after the service to thank us for coming. I think quite a few of us grew up a lot that day.

Perhaps it was the first experience of belonging to the SGHS 'family' and losing one of our peers sadly and prematurely.

Happier events during the school year 1959 to 1960 were the annual school play *Mr Pompous and the Pussycat* and the school carol service. Several of us had hoped to be sent to KEGS for an audition for the joint play, but Miss Woodall managed to convince us that we were much

Mr Pompous and the Pussy Cat *SGHS school play, Christmas 1959.*

needed for what we privately considered to be a children's play for younger pupils to perform. She felt it needed senior girls to 'bring out the humour' (the play had been performed many years previously) and, much to our surprise, we all thoroughly enjoyed ourselves and rose to the occasion. Miss Woodall worked like a Trojan producing the play and we played to packed houses on one afternoon and two evenings. The members of the cast more or less had to manhandle her onto the stage after the last performance to take a bow and receive

SGHS senior choir following the carol service, December 1959.
(I hadn't realised my skirt was that much shorter than the other choir members – I think I grew a lot that year!)

a bouquet of flowers, so modest was she. I do hope we also thanked Hilary Jones and Sheila Russell who I can remember playing away at the piano to the side of the stage accompanying the lovely songs, 'Mr Pompous is giving a party' and 'There's many a slip twixt the cup and the lip' (Janet Bett née Homer and I met up recently after a gap of thirty years and easily got back into the parts of Artaxerxes Bunn and Mother Crosspatch, remembering the words! Sadly, Richenda Brown, who played Melissa who 'turned into a cat', died several years ago. We're sure that Barbara Bishop who played Mr Pompous and the rest of the cast will still remember the words wherever they are!)

In spite of pending A levels those seemed to be halcyon days in the sixth form – accompanied perhaps with the feeling that 'something' was coming to an end fairly soon – possibly childhood and close friendship.

Mrs Davies, the Music mistress who had arrived a few years earlier, teamed up with Mr Thomas (Music master at the Grammar School) and formed a joint Sixth Form Choir which met weekly. We sang a wonderful selection of music made possible by the wide range of voices, culminating in a lovely evening concert in SGHS school hall for staff, governors, parents and pupils. There were refreshments, and we could wear our own dresses! We sang 'Vienna Woods' and many other pieces but the one which sticks in my mind, on the more serious side, an unaccompanied full-harmony 'Ave Verum' (I can still remember the alto part in this!).

The joint choir also went on an outing to Cambridge where we punted on the river (with the gallant efforts of the boys of KEGS) and then took part in Evensong in King's College Chapel.

Trips also took place to Le Mans during the Easter holidays of 1959 (accompanied of course by the Misses Wells and Sheppard) and Miss Collett and Miss Turner took 23 girls skiing in the Austrian Tyrol for two weeks.

In the Spring Term 1959 *Pear Tree* (p. 5)

SGHS school trip to Le Mans, 1959.

Miss Butler, in her report at senior Speech Day, mentioned the academic successes of the year in which the school had a record number of university entrants. For the first time the number of people taking science at university almost equalled the number of arts candidates. State and open scholarships and exhibitions had been won, and over the last five years the school had sent an average of 20 students a year to teacher training colleges. She added these poignant words: 'If the Grammar Schools should be destroyed, would it really be in the interests of education, or the country, or would it not rather be an act of blind, doctrinaire folly?'

For the first time the school motto *Non Sibi Sed Omnibus* appeared on the front cover of the 1960 Spring Term *Pear Tree* magazine. Girls had always been made aware of the motto and its meaning (Not for one but one for all) but it's doubtful whether this was actually 'thrust down their throats', so this was quite a subtle way of reminding them of the ethos of the school. (Interestingly it appears that many other schools, including that of the boy Gordon Brown who was to become prime minister in the twenty-first century, shared this same motto.) From this date on, the motto appeared either on the cover of the magazine or on the first inside page for many years.

This seems particularly significant when Miss Butler wrote in a subsequent magazine (Spring 1960) about public-spiritedness and that some of the senior girls were visiting elderly people in Swinford Old Hall (carrying on the tradition of previous years). Some of the Lower Sixth had spent part of their holidays working in residential nurseries or children's homes. Miss Butler felt moved to mention the previous year's head girl, house captains and prefects who had been particularly public-spirited, who

> ...gave themselves unsparingly to their tasks. It is the tradition here that the House Captains take much of the responsibility taken in some schools by the House Mistresses, and they rose splendidly to the task. For the rank and file of the school I think that literally hundreds on Open Day worked without any thought of themselves, not only to prepare the exhibits and to serve the refreshments, but to overcome the difficulties created by the weather. As, at the time of many big functions, I appreciated their cheerfulness and their willingness to give, I hope that they will take some of that spirit with them when they leave...

It seems fitting then to include a photograph of those referred to by Miss Butler and it was a good time to be alongside them!

During 1959 new members of staff arrived: Miss Round from Manchester University to teach Geography; Miss Petersen from Lady Mabel College to teach PE. Miss Collett, who had taught this subject at SGHS for six years,

SGHS prefects including House Captains, 1958–9.
Centre sitting head girl Joan Price, flanked by Viv Rushton on her right and Angela Kay on her left (an example to us all in public-spiritedness!)

had also hailed from Lady Mabel and she was now returning there as a lecturer. Mr Love (violin teacher), the *one* male figure (apart from Mr Evans the caretaker who had also left by this time and vacated the caretaker's house just inside the front gates of the school) to be seen in the SGHS corridors, also left to do some teaching in some of the newly opened schools in the county.

In July 1960, one member of staff retired who had had a very long connection with SGSS and SGHS both as pupil and teacher – Miss Sneyd. She had not changed in appearance much at all during the years she taught and had in fact taught many of our sisters *and* mothers. Miss Sneyd was my Upper Sixth form mistress during my last year at school. On the last day of term, after returning to our form room for the very last time, following Miss Butler's 'Goodbye, girls. Good luck!' and, after the last notes of the stirring 'Jerusalem' had faded away some of us were overcome with tears and emotion and clung somewhat hysterically to each other vowing friendship for life. Miss Sneyd, rather to my surprise, did not appear emotional at all. She told us rather briskly not to be silly and that the friends we had made at school were going to be our friends for life – she was retiring to Sussex to be near to her old school friend (Miss Leigh)! It never dawned on me until years later that Miss Sneyd was only human after all and justifiably had probably been waiting to be free of us and of the school for a long time. At any rate she certainly had a very long, happy and healthy retirement and did, in fact, return occasionally to SGHS as we shall read later in this chapter and in the one about the Old Girls' Association.

Miss Butler wrote a short tribute to Miss Sneyd in the Spring Term 1961 *Pear Tree* magazine (p. 8):

MISS D. N. SNEYD 1928–60

It came to me as a great surprise when at the beginning of the spring term in 1960 Miss Sneyd told me she would be retiring in the summer. Miss Sneyd was firmly established as Upper VIth form mistress when I arrived, and it was hard to imagine what school life would be like without her. Her connection with the School had begun when she came as a pupil. After the years she spent at the University, and two terms in a school in Cambridgeshire, she returned here in 1928, and has given a life-time's service to the school, acting as second mistress for several years, and as Upper VIth form mistress since 1948. We thank her for her cheerfulness, for her friendliness to the girls, and to members of the staff both young and old, and for her unruffled dealings with situations, and people. She was an unfailing source of information about school ways, and school people, both past and present. All this – and much more – we miss. Miss Sneyd will always be welcome when she comes back to Stourbridge, and we hope that her present well-being and very evident enjoyment of her retirement in Sussex will continue for many years.

I think many of us fell foul of Miss Sneyd's occasional rather violent outbursts of temper when we had committed some misdemeanour. She rose to her full (less than five feet?) height, going bright red in the face, and really ranted and raved and then, almost before commencing, finished with 'don't do it again, will you, dear' and all was forgiven and forgotten. Miss Sneyd harboured no grudges. Her long, foolscap notebooks from which she taught us History were a source of amusement at times, and I do remember that she dealt very efficiently with my bleeding nose which threatened to flood the senior cloakroom on one occasion before the dress rehearsal of *Mr Pompous and the Pussycat*. Her old Girl Guide skills must have come to the fore!

Before moving on further into Miss Butler's second decade – the 'swinging Sixties' – it's interesting to read the memoirs of two pupils who experienced the 'Butler' Fifties decade first-hand. Firstly Pat Wilson (née Wilkes) again, who made a great contribution to SGHS as Head Girl and House Captain – Miss Voyce

Miss Sneyd's and Upper Sixth Form's last day at SGHS, July 1960.
Standing l to r: Brenda Beale; Gloria Kirton; French penfriend of Margaret Jones; Kathleen Rowberry; Katherine Brown; Janet Homer; Elizabeth Faulkner; Gaynor Webster; Shirley Smith (wearing a suit for an interview); Marion Davies; Louise Lloyd; Barbara Bishop.
Sitting on seat l to r: Pauline Griffiths; Margaret Jones; Miss Sneyd; Margaret Lea; Janet Powell.
Sitting/crouching on ground l to r: Brenda Green; Mary Witherford; Josephine Hinchley; Jennifer Hinchley; Ann Platt; Sheila Russell.

often used to refer to Pat and ask us why we, as sixth formers, couldn't be more like her!

Feeling our feet

1950–51: Societies, societies, Historical, French, Geographical and Scientific – the delights of afternoon expeditions, Webbs seeds at Droitwich, the sweet, sickly smell of chocolate at Cadbury's, the damp, steamy atmosphere of the dyeing sheds at a Kidderminster carpet factory – French films barely understood and soon forgotten except for the haunting *Les Enfants du Paradis* – the summer expeditions – Windsor Castle closed for cleaning – exploring the ruins of Hailes Abbey and visiting Miss Dale and Miss Eastwood at Guiting Power – the Festival of Britain, symbol of hope for the future.

Reaching the Heights

1951–52: Frustrations, frustrations – O level year except for those under sixteen – work hard at the syllabus with no results to show – play hockey endlessly and see Hockey Internationals – to stay on or not to stay – some inspired RI lessons from Miss D. B. Clarke – Uniform, uniform – Put on your hats! hats! – wear an over-large felt, WRNS surplus or a very small beret, invisible from the front – school dinners improving fast.

1952–55: In the Sixth – exchange tunics for skirts, long grey socks for nylon stockings – grow very responsible with the cares of state – officers of societies, house captains, games captains – the endless round of prefects' duties – taking preparation, counting dinner numbers, reading in assembly, turning out of the cloakrooms – school splitting at the seams with no space for private work – camp out in the vestibule, the book cupboard, the corridors, corners of the hall or the dining room – enjoy reading the personal columns of the School copy of *The Times* and even try the crossword – sell Symbol savoury biscuits

– no fraternisation with King Edward's Sixth Form – official that is – except for the Christmas party and annual debate – propose 'that the power of the United States of America has increased, is increasing and ought to be diminished' – must concentrate on work – History, Latin, French – drive Miss Voyce, Miss Sneyd, Miss Shand to distraction at times – life governed by revision, examinations, prospectuses, forms, examinations, results, interviews, acceptances, examinations, results – suddenly it is all over – call 'Inwards turn, forward march' for the last time, wish Miss Butler and the staff goodbye and rush down town to celebrate the end of one life and the start of another.

Pat Wilson (née Wilkes), 1947–55

(From *Pear Tree* magazine, Summer Term 1976, p. 20)

Also in the same edition of the magazine (pp. 20-1) another pupil, Kathryn Morfey (née Waterton), with whom I grew up at the same junior school, reminisces about SGHS in the 1950s. (I had drama/speech training with Mrs Waterton, Kathryn's mother, who I remember with great affection from the New Road Methodist Church days.) Kathryn must go down in the history of SGHS as one of its greatest academic achievers, taking and passing O and A levels long before her peers and winning a state 'Oxbridge' scholarship, whilst at the same time remaining incredibly modest and likeable.

THE HIGH SCHOOL IN THE 1950s

In looking back to the High School as it was to me as a pupil in the 1950s, I have tried to draw out of my memories some things which were probably special to that period and some things which I remember with particular warmth.

When I arrived at the High School as an eleven-year-old in 1953, ration-books were not far in the past. In school we were still rationed in many ways. Miss Sneyd watched over the school's use of stationery and woe betide the pupil who could not show that every inch of her exercise books had been used before she was issued with another. In 1953, the Sixth could be found in all kinds of odd places, working at collapsible desks, not just for free periods but even for their small-group classes.

I was never in one of those unfortunate classes whose 'classroom' was a laboratory and who were therefore compelled to move from room to room, carrying all their books, each period. My first encounter with these space problems was when I started French conversation classes in what was then the dining-room to the clatter and smell of dinner preparations.

During the 50s, things were just beginning to improve, though the new gym and dining arrangements were not even thought of; at least by the time I reached the Sixth, we had the new block down by the old music room (shades of *Peter and the Wolf* on how many 78 rpm records!), so that only our free periods were spent in holes and corners.

Not only did the physical amenities slowly improve, but the social climate was changing too. In 1953, further education was the hard-won privilege of the few, and who, from our school, dared try to enter Oxbridge! By the time I left at the end of 1959, the gates of further education, including universities and even Oxbridge, were opening wider and wider, bringing, I think, a new confidence to both staff and girls that they were indeed capable of many things they had not dared to think of before. To me, as one of the first of a long line to march into Oxbridge with colours flying, such events were an assertion that ordinary schools could mobilise the talents of staff and pupils as effectively as any of those prestigious Birmingham schools to which we had tended to kow-tow. I have remained an iconoclast with respect to supposedly prestigious

educational establishments ever since.
The winds of change were blowing in other ways too; much credit must go to all the staff, particularly Miss Butler, who sensed what was happening and urged it in a good direction. There was dancing in the lunch-hour for the Sixth; ball-room dancing for girls over sixteen may not cause much stir now, but it merited mention in the *County Express* twenty years ago. There was the advent of Sixth Form democracy over the perennially vexed problem of school uniform. We saw the start of Sixth formers (just a few) having time off to take motor-scooter tests or the ordinary driving tests, in the affluent 50s.

The winds of change were not just for the Sixth. In my third year a beauty consultant came for the first time to talk to all the school on cosmetic problems; this was not just a recognition of what interested us outside school-hours, for the talk included mention of the cosmetic problems of mastectomy – very avant-garde for those days. Another talk by a careers consultant around that time contained words of wisdom twenty years before the Equal Opportunities Commission arrived: we teenagers should look well ahead, recognise we should be likely to get married and have children but not throw up any career ambitions we might have, rather face squarely the prospect of interweaving a career and family life. One may now wish the implications had been spelt out in more detail, but at least the thought had been implanted.

Opportunities for women, physical provision – so much has changed in the last two decades. But two impressions of enduring value remain with me from my school days. I remember the real enjoyment so many of the staff took both in their subject and in us: a combination that made learning really pleasurable. Too often either pupil or subject (if not both) is a bit of a bore for the teacher. We were lucky that it was not so for us, and that our standards for the future were set so high.

I also developed an appreciation of nature at school. I do not mean I enjoyed Biology; what I enjoyed was being at a school that had water-lilies and lilac trees, lawns and playing-fields. I learned not to ruin next spring's greenness by playing thoughtlessly on the grass on muddy winter days, and was rewarded by lawns to rest the eye at hot examination time. A walk over the playing fields; idly making daisy-chains; the smell of lilac and mown grass – these memories make me thankful it was not a school of tarmac and concrete, treeless, grassless.

I take it for granted that schools ought to be concerned with creating liking and respect for knowledge, and also for people – 'Manners maketh man, and woman too,' said the posters in the corridors in those days. However, I view it as a pleasurable bonus of my school days that they gave meaning to the words of Blake's 'England's green and pleasant land'. Long may all school children remember their school, as I am lucky to remember mine, as a green and pleasant place.

Kathryn Morfey (née Waterton), 1953–59

Jane Staples (née Green), a pupil at SGHS from 1954 to 1961, wrote very poignantly her tribute to the school.

When I think back to my school days a host of jumbled memories come flooding back. I picture the classrooms, and the pictures awarded for tidiness, the corridors with the white lines down the middle (we were supposed to 'drive' on the left) and the posters done by the art mistress saying, 'In the Street we do not Eat' and 'Two abreast, pity the rest'. I think of coach outings, the annual trip to the International Hockey Match at Wembley, and the joint expedition of the Geographical and Scientific Society with the Historical Society every Summer. Sport played an important part in my own school career, with many Saturday mornings spent in school for matches. The Inter-house sports and Music Festival also enriched the school year. During my time as well as Stuart, Tudor, Windsor and York, two new houses, Kent and Lancaster, were created so that more people could have the chance to represent their house. Music played its part in the school, and I still have a record of the school choir singing carols – on a 78 rpm record! The school taught us to consider those worse off than ourselves, and a weekly collection was made for the Save the Children Fund throughout the school. I remember school plays, in particular *Twelfth Night* in which I played the Fool, and some of the highly successful joint productions with the Grammar School, such as *The Teahouse of the August Moon*. During the 50s the new block was opened – the new Physics Lab and classroom above it. Since then there has of course been further new buildings.

All these recollections are trivial though; what sort of education did the school give me? Academically the standard was high, and I personally owe much to the staff who taught me and helped me to gain a university place, but education is much more than examination marks, important as they are. Education should develop the character and equip one for life. I am grateful that the standards of honesty, integrity, self-discipline, responsibility, kindness and love were so high. These were enforced not only by staff but also by prefects, enforced not only by punishments but by example. As I look back I realise what a high standard of teaching we received, and the hours the staff must have spent preparing lessons, marking our work and taking trouble with individual girls. I am thankful for the stability of the school. Many of the teachers were there for all my school career and longer, and I was fortunate to receive all my secondary education at the same school. Today I see families moving frequently from one town to another, and children having to adapt to a succession of different schools, teachers and courses and also friends. Teachers too tend to change school much more frequently, so children today are not so often taught by the same person throughout their course, making further changes inevitable, sometimes at crucial times like their O level year.

I have recently become a teacher myself. I did not set out to be a teacher, but as the years have passed by I have appreciated more and more how much we owe to the good influence of our school. As I see children clearly in need of this kind of guidance I have felt I must try to play my part in giving them what I have received in such full measure. This is my greatest tribute to the High School. I can wish for nothing better for the new school than that it will continue to give this kind of education.

Jane Staples (née Green), 1954–61

During the 1960s SGHS was endowed with some extra much-needed accommodation – the first extension included a Physics laboratory, a large sixth form room and an extra cloakroom. The former gymnasium became the dining-room and the old dining-room and kitchen were eventually transformed into the library, needlework room and a small pottery. A new gym was built across the road on the playing field. These additions solved some of the immediate problem of space which allowed Miss Butler to concentrate on an 'extra' which had long been very close to her heart, i.e. a swimming pool.

In the spring of 1962 an appeal was launched for £6,000 and a Swimming Pool Appeal Committee of parents was eventually formed. Generations of SGHS girls had had to use the public swimming baths in Bath Road and this had proved to be better than nothing but enormously inconvenient and disruptive to the school time-table – memories of running back up the hill in Church Street, still damp, or borrowing someone's bicycle to try to get back to school in time for another lesson! However, it was to take a few more years before Miss Butler's dream of an SGHS pool was realised.

To this end on 19 July 1962 a bring-and-buy sale was organised. Fine weather brought many purchasers to buy the home-made goods, flowers, vegetables, fruit, sweets, drapery, groceries, toilet requisites, records, books, ornaments, etc. all most generously supplied by parents and friends. Mrs Lunt (chairman of the Governors) declared the sale open. There were sideshows, displays of art, Stourbridge Industries (arranged by the sixth form), French dolls, records of the Exhibition – 'Fifty Years at Stourbridge Girls' High School' (Oh, to be transported back in time to see that!). There were ices and light refreshments for the weary.

There was also a display of Movement, something of a new venture for SGHS, by the first years and members of the sixth form. The highlight of this performance was an interpretation of the life of a river; the streams flow to a river, the hunt enters, a wedding dance takes place on the banks until night falls, the moon appears and water nymphs dance by moonlight. (The 'Vltava' from *Má Vlast* by Smetana.) This programme, somewhat surprisingly perhaps, was produced by Miss Haig (she seemed to 'wear many hats' for, including the teaching of her own subjects, she also had some responsibility for remedial work for pupils who were in need of help on occasions in some areas.)

Performance of 'Vltava' SGHS, Bring-and-Buy Sale, summer 1962.

The programme was repeated on Monday 23 July when it was preceded by an orchestral concert arranged by Mrs J. Bird, this being the first public performance of the orchestra and very well received. The collection was added to the proceeds of the bring-and-buy sale to go towards the swimming pool.

During 1960 a visit was arranged to Oberammergau and the Rhineland, the highlight being a visit to the Passion Play. This must have had a lasting effect on the SGHS party with the performance conforming to its strict principles of no make-up, no artificial lighting on the stage (no married women actresses) and lasting for seven hours. The school party was lucky enough to occupy some of the front seats.

There was a good deal of going and coming amongst the staff in the early Sixties. Mrs Andrews went off to Melbourne, Australia and Miss Eldridge to teach in West Nigeria at Abeskuta Girls' Grammar School. She continued to keep in touch with SGHS by sending regular newsletters telling of her rich and varied experiences out there!

Mrs West went to teach at the Princess Mary School, Halifax; Mrs Davis, Mrs Johnstone and Mrs Atkins retired from teaching.

First Form Movement SGHS, Bring-and-Buy Sale, summer 1962.

To take their places came Mrs Allman (BA Reading) to teach Classics; Mrs Best (BA Birmingham) and Miss Smith (BA Manchester) to teach Music. Miss Parsons (also BA Manchester) came to teach French. Miss Bryan (formerly Gloria Bryan, an old girl) returned to teach History. News came through that Miss Mumford (who had taught Geography) had married and had become Mrs Morris. The *Pear Tree* magazines can be appreciated not only for their school year information and team and play photographs, but also for the ever increasing number of marriages of old girls, teachers, the births of their children, and, sadly on occasions, their deaths. One such announcement was the death on 4 October 1962 of Miss W. M. McDonald who had been Physical Education mistress at SGHS from 1930 to 1936 and who had thus served under both Miss Firth and Miss Dale. Miss Voyce at least would have remembered her.

The joint KEGS and SGHS play for 1962 was G. B. Shaw's *Pygmalion* and was very successful, Miss Turner again acting as prompter and Miss Voyce the giver of encouragement and support throughout. This must have brought back many memories for her of the staff's performances in the early war years. Such a nice change to have the genuine article for the masculine characters!

The official school photograph taken in March 1962 shows a significant increase in numbers in the staff line-up and there were over 600 girls on roll. No great changes in school uniform, but were the hairstyles gradually becoming a little more sophisticated and bouffant?

Christmas 1963 brought with it a new experience for the school in that the Dramatic Society, Recorder Group, Orchestra, Chorus and audience joined in a single act of worship in place of either a school play or a carol service. The Nativity story was simply presented with the minimum of properties, relying for effect on sincerity, contrasts in characterisation, e.g. the homely shepherds, richly apparelled kings, boisterous townsfolk at the inn, the Holy Family and the angels. Musical items were selected to fit in with the story at appropriate places – *La Follie*, music from Handel's *Messiah* and Bach's *Christmas Oratorio* with new and traditional carols. An ambitious undertaking, but 'Light Is Come' was a memorable and moving departure from the usual form of school service at Christmas.

The Student Christian Movement (SCM) which had played a regular part in school society life for many years had weekly meetings during 1963/4 based on the filmstrip of Reverend Storr's book *Your Confirmation*. These meetings were very well attended. They concerned themselves with Christianity in the twentieth century and led to much discussion

Scenes from Pygmalion joint performance KEGS/SGHS, 1962.

about the relationship between spiritual and material things, often with convincing scientific facts to substantiate the theme 'Facts of Faith'. The spring term open meeting placed St Paul in an unusual 'trial' position of defending himself against charges of heresy.

Another new venture in the Spring and Summer Terms of 1964 was a series of lunch-hour career films. Careers advice for SGHS girls up until this time had usually consisted of a rather small noticeboard at the bottom of the stairs by the Geography room with one or two advertisements for the Civil Service and similar organisations pinned to it.

A 'Careers Convention' evening for parents and girls, which was largely manned by local employers such as the *County Express* newspaper, police force, etc., was organised once a year and also chats with representatives from the Youth Employment Service/Agency (based down the road in Church Street). Girls could always make an appointment to see Miss Butler to discuss university courses/career options – some of her favourites obviously being teaching or nursing! There were on occasions talks by visiting speakers pertaining to certain jobs/careers such as the armed forces.

Thus the career films in the lunch hours aroused much interest especially among older girls. Among the subjects covered by these films were work and training in retail pharmacy; the work of nurses and others in the naval medical services, work in public libraries, the production of *The Guardian* for girls interested in journalism; training and work in dentistry; social work with children; the work of a childcare officer, of an opthalmic optician and of a WRAF officer. (The public library film must have been of special interest, because many SGHS girls have worked at Stourbridge Library – myself included – and together we have almost formed a small OGA of our own over the years with many reminiscences of school during our coffee breaks!)

There was also a forum in May 1964 in which the speakers dealt with the wide range of careers following on Institutional Management qualifications, the opportunities for physiotherapists and work with handicapped children. For those girls who were not sure what they wanted to do with their futures these talks/films must have helped a little. SGHS also hosted that year's SCM Conference where a number of fairly local secondary schools came together to listen to and discuss ideas pertaining to the day's theme, opening with a controversial talk by Reverend Ronald Milner – 'What Has God To do With Me?'

There was certainly a lot of meat for SGHS girls to get their teeth into at this time.

The school orchestra was coming into prominence during the early Sixties. It started to play in assembly and at the school Christmas performance (previously described) when it provided much of the incidental music along with the choirs and recorder group. Mrs Bird was the guiding power behind this with Mrs Best at the piano. All sections of the school were represented from the first years up to the sixth forms and the orchestra was slowly increasing in size and variety of instruments played.

Every year the orchestra attended the festival which took place at the Grange Secondary School, Stourbridge with old friend Mr Benoy in charge, playing such contrasting numbers as the lively 'Tartan Polka', the precise 'March from an Occasional Overture' and the solemn 'Cast thy Burden'.

Scarborough SGHS school trip, 1964.

School photograph SGHS, March 1962.

School photograph SGHS, March 1962.
Miss Butler is flanked by Miss Voyce on her right and Miss Wells on her left.

There were many interesting expeditions made by the Geographical and Scientific and Historical Societies, and there is a very nice photographic record of one to Scarborough in April 1964.

During the 1962/3 school year there were some significant staff changes. Mrs Gunn, Miss Nilsson and Mrs Prescott-Clarke all left to take up other posts – Mrs Gunn accompanying her husband to Copenhagen; Miss Nilsson to join the staff of South Wilts. High School, Salisbury, and Mrs P.C. went back to her own old school, the Ladies' College, Cheltenham. Miss Haig went to live in Weston-Super-Mare.

In September 1963 'replacements' were Miss J. Butter (Froebel-trained) from the Friary School, Lichfield to teach mainly in the first year forms, Miss Elliott from Halesowen College of Further Education and Churchfield Comprehensive School to teach Needlework and Pottery. Finally, and at long last, a male teacher joined the permanent SGHS staff in the form of Mr Rudd (BSc London) from the Dudley and Staffordshire Technical College to teach Physics!

During that year news had come through of the death of Mr Palfrey who had been one of the school governors for 42 years and also of Mr Evans who had, as many of us remember, been the school caretaker for many years, wrestling with the grounds and the coke for the boiler and countless other jobs. (When he and his wife retired they had gone to live in Norton, Stourbridge.)

In the early sixties Miss Butler renamed the forms in the school. Previously the first years had been the Second Forms II1, II2 and II3, moving onwards and upwards to IIIA, IIIB, IIIC plus IIIT (late transfer) and so on until the GCE year which became VU X, VUY and VUP. The Lower Sixth had been divided into VI lower A and VI lower alpha and then Upper Sixth. (Maths had been streamed into A and B; Languages had been streamed into A, B, C and D.)

Whether the change of 'names' was purely a psychological act (were pupils traumatised by being in a C form?) is not clear, but certainly there was no A, B, C from now on, but L, M and G forms came into being and sensibly the first years became the First Forms.

And so the Sixties moved on. A sign that time was marching on was the announcement in the 1965 *Pear Tree* magazine of the death of Miss Firth – first headmistress. She died in Southport and, very aptly, a tribute was written by Miss Sneyd, now retired, but who had known Miss Firth personally both as a pupil and member of staff. Miss Firth had retired early (due to ill health) in 1933 and it is somewhat surprising to read that she did, in fact, live on until 1965. Retirement must have come as a welcome change to the rigours of running SGSS and SGHS.

Appropriately, in the July of the following year, a stained glass window in memory of Miss Firth was unveiled (by Miss Sneyd, who returned for this special event) in the school hall. On this occasion, a committee of her former pupils, with Mrs Hale as chairman, met to present the window, a gift to the school bought by subscriptions from the Old Girls, to Mr Brooke, Chief Education Officer for Worcestershire. (The window had, as we know, on either side similar memorial windows to Miss Harris and Miss Turner, Miss Firth's deputies who had died many years previously.) When she unveiled the window Miss Sneyd paid tribute to Miss Firth's foresight and zeal in planning for the future. Miss Firth had looked forward to a time when girls would enjoy the privileges of a full education and unrestricted opportunities, too long accepted as male prerogatives! Ivy Freemantle, who attended the ceremony as a former pupil in Miss Firth's time, has kept her copy of the 'Order of Service'.

Further indications of *tempus fugit* amongst the staff were two major internal staff changes. At the end of the Spring Term 1964 Miss Voyce decided to resign her post as deputy head, seemingly worn out by all the many changes,

THE UNVEILING OF A
WINDOW
IN MEMORY OF
MISS ETHEL M. FIRTH

FIRST HEADMISTRESS
OF
THE COUNTY HIGH SCHOOL
FOR GIRLS
STOURBRIDGE

IN THE SCHOOL HALL
ON FRIDAY JULY 22nd, 1966
AT 7.30 p.m.

Service for unveiling of memorial window to Miss Firth, July 1966.

increases in numbers of pupils; expansion of buildings and a much more complex organisation within the school which had put an increasing strain on the deputy head. She had been deputy head for 18 years and had, of course, been teaching at SGHS since 1932. It was hoped that a slightly lighter load of work might postpone her retirement. Miss J. Sheppard, who had arrived in 1953 to teach French, was appointed as deputy head in Miss Voyce's place, a well-deserved promotion which one feels would have been seized upon with relish and enthusiasm.

At the same time, Mrs Payton, who had for many years been responsible for dinner-time organisation, resigned from this responsibility and her place was taken over by Mrs Morris and Miss Croft who were going to share the work – an indication of the volume of work involved for one person. Mrs Payton had, of course, seen vast changes in her years connected with the dining-room (which had now been transformed into the library). Until fairly recently, before such changes, no more than 90 girls were provided with a hot meal and staff and girls dined together, with sixth-formers acting as heads of table, and junior monitors (wearing the ubiquitous green-and-white-checked aprons made in Needlework lessons) fetched food from the kitchen and carted away dirty plates.

Gradually, increasing numbers had necessitated two sittings, senior and junior, and the staff ate in the Domestic Science room. The new (former gymnasium) dining-hall had come into being and there were now 200 girls at each sitting, bringing with this many complicated changes of organisation – little wonder then that Mrs Payton thought it was time to stand down!

The new library which grew out of the old dining-room had its first movement of books into their new home in the summer of 1964 and a very welcome move this was. It retained the dining-room partition to begin with as this allowed sixth forms to have a section divided conveniently into alcoves, where they could work with reference books close at hand. With its restful, subdued colour on the walls, white paintwork, light beech-wood furniture and attractively designed curtains the room had a pleasant and airy aspect. Little wonder that many girls wanted to be 'librarians', and they put into operation the ticket and card system of borrowing for the lower and middle school sections and kept a watchful eye on overdue books. Their efficiency resulted in a sum of almost £2 10s being collected in library fines in the Autumn Term and this money purchased the first librarians' badges which were presented just before Christmas to junior and senior librarians. Professional librarians in the making!

Because the library was no longer being used for teaching purposes this meant that the sixth formers had a place where silence was observed and where study could go on undisturbed. Many girls took advantage of this facility but a number still seemed to prefer the odd corners where lighting, ventilation and noise must have hindered concentration. Miss Butler hoped that the tradition of silent study would continue and increase, to provide training for college and university students to be! (On reading this in a *Pear Tree* magazine I have to confess that some of my peers and I used to escape to the little Book Room (in the old days of 1960) with the best of intentions to study but, inevitably, we collapsed into chatting, and chat that was not always connected with work! How our boyfriends' ears must have burned.)

Goodbyes were said to two staff members – Mrs Allman and Miss Allen – and in their places came yet another male teacher, Mr Cameron (MA Oxon) to teach Classical Languages and Philosophy (the curriculum was indeed growing) and also Miss Jane Cameron (an old girl known to many of us) from Dartford College of Physical Education to teach PE.

It seems appropriate at this point to include a photograph of the school prefects during 1965–6: easy to see how they were growing in number and looking rather more 1960s. Hairstyles were definitely changing and many were wearing their hair longer – we earlier pupils will wonder what Miss Presley had to say about that. Anyone pre-Sixties who had 'untidy' loose hair was thrown a rubber band or piece of string to deal with it straightaway!

The 1966 Summer Term *Pear Tree* magazine contained the small but *very* significant announcement of the marriage of a long-standing member of staff. Mr Jack Haden (chief reporter for the *County Express* newspaper and an absolute authority on Stourbridge and its history) married Miss Joan Makin (head of Geography). This marriage was not without some accompanying amusement for all those who knew Jack Haden. He apparently got up from his desk at the *County Express* office one day and told colleagues that he would be 'a bit late back' as he was going off to marry 'Joan' in his lunch hour! This would not come as a surprise to those familiar with his slightly eccentric figure in a mac and bicycle clips over his suit, cycling busily all over Stourbridge reporting and collecting copy wherever he went for the newspaper.

The couple must have known each other for years, as Miss Makin associated herself with 'Stourbridge Playreaders' and the Historical Society and had numerous other local interests.

Mrs Haden, as Miss Makin now became, continued teaching for a few years and by all accounts became slightly less severe in the classroom, and often regaled girls with stories of her husband and his eccentricities!

Other changes amongst the staff during the year 1965–6 meant that Miss Banner, Miss Parsons, Mrs Cox and Miss Cameron all left. Miss A. Spencer (another old SGHS girl) came to teach French; Miss M. Guest to teach French and Spanish; Miss S. Grant to teach PE; Mrs Bowen from Homerton College, Cambridge to teach Mathematics and Mr Handley (to swell the ranks of the growing male teacher contingent) (BA Wales) to teach History. (Miss Ruth Besso, who had taught Chemistry at the school during the war years (1938–41), had sadly died that year.)

Without doubt, the highlight of 1967 must have been the official opening of the much-longed-for school swimming pool (at a cost of £7,500). This was made possible by individual and collective enthusiasm (the scheme being inspired by Miss Butler), Mrs Hodson and a devoted band of parents undertaking to carry it through.

In the light of this great achievement, the Foreword of the Summer Term *Pear Tree* considered the growth of the school since 1905. It paid tribute to Miss Firth's pioneering years: she not only established a tradition of hard work, academic achievement and sound discipline,

SGHS prefects and netball team, 1965–6. Some girls had long, loose hair – what would Miss Presley have to say?

pride in the school and loyalty to it, but also the physical, social and moral training aspects of school life.

It was also important to realise, when comparing the school in 1905, what had been accomplished by Miss Firth's successors – how the school had kept pace with modern developments in education and the need to prepare for more varied opportunities for girls leaving school. Under Miss Butler there had been rapid development in the sixth form and that year there were 127 girls in the four sixth forms. In VI Upper alone, 15 subjects were being offered at A level GCE. This article also emphasised the large and increasing numbers of girls who were going on to university, colleges of education and other centres of professional training and to exciting, challenging work in the adult world at home and abroad.

However, towards the end of this review of the school and its development appeared the first 'warning bells' of comprehensive education and perhaps the death-knell of the High School (p. 4):

But while we review its history with gratitude and pride we now have to look forward only with misgiving.

We hoped that under the adoption by Worcestershire Education Committee of the comprehensive system our school would continue as the nucleus of a single comprehensive school. Modification and extension we have had in the past and these on an even greater scale we knew we must accept in the future but we hoped that the school would live on adapted to the needs of a new generation.

We who love the school, who have worked in it for many years and have seen our girls go out into the world equipped to make a full contribution to the larger life of the community deplore the decision to alter it so radically that it will lose its character and traditions.

If the School had outlived its usefulness it would be another matter, but the value of the contribution our former pupils are making in their various spheres is undeniable and we have no reason to suppose that future leavers will not follow in their path. It seems inevitable that a completely new system, however worthy in its ultimate purpose, must lead to a lowering of academic standards and a waste (which the nation cannot afford) of first-class ability. Moreover the modern world, insecure, sceptical, needs to preserve the values the grammar schools have cherished, to build on the past, if it is not in a technological age to lose sight of any end in life beyond material prosperity.

Stirring and meaningful words indeed, although it was to be several years before the 'threat' of such radical changes came about.

In the summer of 1967 Miss E. M. Scarratt came (Honours Graduate of Manchester University) from Trowbridge Girls' High School to teach French and German; Mrs Barton to help with sixth form Mathematics and Mrs Lester to help with the Science teaching. One gets a sense of how much the school was growing with extra teachers being drafted in to 'help'.

The time had come for Mrs Payton to retire and Mrs Hodson to move on to a new venture. As the magazine pointed out so poignantly, others would take on their work but nobody could replace them in the school's affection or more deserve its gratitude for the contribution they had made to the life of the school. Mrs Hodson had, of course, been instrumental in the raising of funds and support for the building of the swimming pool and it was very pleasing that she would see the fruits of her 'labour' before actually leaving. (Mrs Hodson was to take over the running of a hotel and restaurant with her husband – The Mill at Alverley – to which establishment many girls, parents, members of staff and old girls would make their way in the future years to sample the delicious food, wine and ambience. Mrs Hodson was also going to help temporarily with some Art classes.)

Who better than Miss Voyce, a colleague of many years, and also Ann Hindle, a former pupil and teacher herself, to pay tribute to Mrs Payton? (Tributes to Mrs Payton, *Pear Tree* magazine, summer 1967.)

MRS PAYTON

When Mrs Payton leaves SGHS at the end of the present term, she will have given almost the whole of her professional working life in unstinted service to the school in every sphere of activity.

We salute her without doubt as an excellent teacher of Domestic Science, and as an efficient and tactful manager, for many years, of dining room organisation and staff, domestic and otherwise. She has been a Sixth Form Mistress, a House Mistress, and has given invaluable help for many years to the Deputy Head. Yet the older members of the school community have also the memory of a centre forward streaking up the field for the staff Hockey Team, of a graceful member of the staff Tennis and Netball Teams, and of a most competent actress, whether as heroine in *Arms and the Man* or as Professor Higgins' mother in *Pygmalion*. The recent and younger members of the community know that they have never appealed in vain for help with play costumes or society teas, or indeed in any emergency, serious or trivial.

Finally, members of the staff are aware of their great debt to a wise counsellor, a sympathetic colleague, and a staunch friend. We wish her the happiness in retirement which she so fully deserves.

C. J. V.

I was very sad to hear that Mrs Payton was leaving the High School and I'm sure it must be even worse for the staff and pupils to part with her. Mrs Payton or Miss Lewis, as she was known to many former pupils older than myself, has been part of the High School scene for so long that it is hard to imagine the building without her calm and smiling presence.

I, personally, have known her since I first entered the school as a very new pupil in 1943, and over the years have come to value her friendship and advice firstly as a teacher, then as a form mistress and in latter years as a member of the same profession.

Looking back over my very happy nine years at SGHS Mrs Payton figures fairly prominently in my memories. I had the good fortune to have her twice for a form mistress and in this role she was always so very fair in her dealing with girls. She never pre-judged and always listened, with patience, to both sides of any argument between members of the form. But, perhaps, it is in her domain upstairs that most of us think of Mrs Payton. She has, throughout her time as a teacher of Housecraft, seen many changes in that field. Throughout the war and post-war years her task of planning interesting lessons, when all she could provide for pupils was 2 oz. flour and 1 oz. fat for pastry-making was immense and required great ingenuity on her part. Today, as she plans lessons on budgeting and the wise use of Convenience Foods she must, on occasions, reflect on the problems of those days. Even so, with all these difficulties she gave her pupils sound training in the basics of Housecraft, and there must be many housewives in the Stourbridge area and far beyond who feel indebted to her for this. She was as sympathetic to girls with little practical aptitude as to those who had a flair for her subject. There is though, I know, one former pupil who will never forgive her for making us whilst members of 2 Lower, knit school uniform gloves on four needles!!

Mrs Payton's interest in school life was not confined to the Domestic Science room. She was the instigator behind the founding of the school Housecraft Society, whose members enjoyed a wide variety of activities under her guiding hand, and house matches and the many practices leading up to them nearly always found her on the sideline, cheering her team on and giving every encouragement to them. She has always, too, taken an active interest in meetings of the Old Girls' Association and when she has been able to be present, obviously enjoyed being among her former pupils and hearing about their careers and families. The Old Girls' Association are also extremely grateful to her for her co-operation in allowing them to use her room for the preparation of refreshments for their meetings.

After so many years of loyal service to the school Mrs Payton will, I'm sure, be leaving with mixed feeling, but many present and former pupils will, I feel, echo my sentiments in wishing her a long, healthy and happy retirement with time to pursue gardening and the many other interests she has and the hope that we shall continue to see her on occasions at School and Old Girls' functions.

ANN HINDLE

Also in summer 1967 a tribute to Mrs Hodson:

MRS HODSON

For twenty years Mrs Hodson has given the High School a lesson in the art of humorous living. Completely competent yet utterly relaxed she has handled the complexities of her work with easy grace. To a great store of commonsense has been added the leaven of cheerfulness and charm. No-one turns to her with a request – from painting scenery in a free period to chauffeuring home the sick and needy – without being sure of immediate co-operation. Content to take people as they are, in many cases she has brought out a hitherto unsuspected best in them.

She has been an enthusiastic house mistress for many years; she has won the affection of the many children whose form-mistress she has been; VIth form girls have discovered new skills in her craft lessons. To all she has taught the art of gracious living.

It is largely due to Mrs Hodson's unflagging efforts that we now possess our own swimming pool. It will remain as a fitting signature of her unselfish work here. Yet material things are not *always* as valuable as spiritual ones. What those of us who have had the privilege of working with Mrs Hodson, will most cherish will be the recollection of her imperturbable good humour.

P. M. D.

Sadly, there was news of the death of a former teacher, Miss Vincent, who had retired to Malvern a few years earlier. Although she only taught at SGHS from 1949 to 1955 Miss Vincent had soon established herself as a 'granny-like' figure for those in their first year at the school, and many of us will have fond memories of nature walks over the playing fields with Miss Vincent gamely climbing over stiles and carrying bunches of 'nature' for Biology lessons. Miss Butler seemed very shocked to hear of Miss Vincent's death on 11 September 1966 and wrote a short tribute in the *Pear Tree* magazine, 1967 (p. 10):

> Until she retired we had enjoyed, and been stimulated by, her zest for life, her ready wit and her forthright manner…She shared fully in the life of the school and because of her alert, independent mind, she was always ready with constructive suggestions. When I visited her in retirement at Malvern I was always amazed by her vigour of mind and body, and it is that impression of vitality which we shall treasure of her.

It appeared that Miss Vincent's Christian names were Flora May which seemed to fit in beautifully with her persona which always seemed to have about it something of yester-year.

It was a busy and varied year for the school. The joint play with the Grammar School was Sheridan's *The Rivals* (performed on 8, 9 and 10 December) which was an ambitious but very well-received production. Mrs Malaprop – a demanding character – was finely played by Margaret Brookes. Bridget Waters was Lucy, the scheming maid, and the lovesick maiden Lydia Languish was played by Philippa Kelly. Susan Whitehouse was Julia and Alison Collins the other maid. By all accounts, the handling of the play and the acting were remarkable and striking effects were created by the scenery.

It is interesting to note that the Senior Dramatic Society was replaced now by the Theatre Group to promote interest in the theatre. Members of the sixth form went to see a variety of plays and lectures on them where possible, ranging from Shakespeare to Arthur Miller. Many of the plays were those selected for A level GCE and it had been possible to make joint outings with KEGS.

The school continued to contribute to the pleasure of the lives of local 'old folk'.

For example, at Christmas forty food parcels were made up and despatched by girls of SGHS and thanks were due to Miss Morris and

A scene from The Rivals joint SGHS/KEGS production, Dec. 1966.

Miss Wyld who offered to deliver them with the help of the SCM committee. At this time also, and very appropriately for the 1960s, the SCM and the Music Society joined together to form the Folk Group which provided entertainment for the old folk of the area. The Group sang at Beulah Court, Halesowen and at Swinford Hall.

The SCM had, as its aim for that year, the enlivening of its activities by being useful to society and certainly seemed to achieve this. They had cake stalls, knitted baby clothes to help the Leprosy Mission, launched an appeal for old spectacles, scrapbooks and knitted squares and made a patchwork quilt. They cleaned cars and were able to send money from all of these ventures to Oxfam and Christian Aid – practical Christianity to say the least and very commendable.

A group of girls went off to London's Albert Hall and one of their number, Susan Newey, had been chosen to present a golden purse containing a cheque for Dr Barnardo's to Princess Margaret. There was a procession of purse-bearers from many different countries and all the counties of Great Britain, each carrying a banner, and Susan must have been extremely proud to represent the school and Worcestershire.

SGHS Folk Group, 1966–7.

(Miss Woodall, with her very strong interest in Dr Barnardo's, had organised the trip in connection with the Barnardo Centenary celebrations, but was unable to attend herself.)

On the visits side, a party went to Le Mans at Easter led by Miss Sheppard and Miss Spencer – it must have felt quite strange for the latter to be going on this trip as a teacher rather than a pupil.

A girl from Germany (Irmela Filz) wrote in the magazine of her impressions of SGHS during her term's stay at the school: 'I soon became familiar to all the strange school customs, so much different from the German ones which (but do not tell anyone) I prefer, because they are not by far as strict!' – a sentiment with which many SGHS girls would have agreed!

On the academic side, Miss Butler in her annual report at prize-giving remarked that although 51 girls gained certificates for A levels (ten with distinctions), on the whole the quality of results was not quite so high as usual. However, 16 girls had been offered places at university, three were taking degree courses at colleges of technology and over 30 were going on to teacher training colleges. Significantly, for the first time girls who were not expected to pass Mathematics at GCE O level were entered for the new CSE examination. Ninety per cent passed with two girls obtaining Grade I. Two girls were also entered for CSE French, successfully.

On the games side there was a particularly good spirit amongst the players of various sports and for the first time, the school entered three teams in the district athletics held in May at Brierley Hill. The intermediate team achieved the honour of winning the Richard Payne Cup.

A chess club had joined the list of SGHS societies and met once a week during the winter months and it was hoped to expand this club the following year with a greater supply of chess sets and the acquisition of a cup for the best individual player. The Housecraft Society had held a design competition where a variety of curtain materials, dinner plates and evening dress designs was judged. A cake-decorating competition was also held before Christmas. They were shown two films – *Everything, but Everything in Bri-Nylon* (this was definitely becoming the era of man-made fibres!) and *1,000 Years of Cotton*.

The choirs and orchestra provided entertainment at Speech Day/Prize-giving instead

SGHS visit to France, Easter 1967.

SGHS Intermediate athletics team with the Richard Payne Cup, 1967.

of having a speaker (probably a very popular decision for many members of the audience!). At the end of the Summer Term 1967 the joint choirs of SGHS and the Boys' Grammar School performed Gilbert and Sullivan's *Trial By Jury* – another very enjoyable venture for all concerned.

Could the late 1960s be seen as SGHS's 'finest hour'? Certainly there seemed to be plenty going on both academically and culturally and with a strong sense of social responsibility and Christian service thrown in for good measure.

The year 1968 saw a departure from the traditional format of the *Pear Tree* school magazine with its dark, somewhat austere olive-green jacket it had sported since its inception. It had a spanking new cover (still showing the Worcestershire pear tree) psychedelic orange for 1968, lime green for 1969, probably more in keeping with the 1960s! The cover was designed by a B. Wadsworth who was also responsible for the lino cuts in some of the contributions.

The magazines were beautifully and clearly set out, but sadly from then on contained very few photographs.

There was a magazine committee consisting of some ten girls although the editors were still Miss Woodall and Miss Pritchard.

The 1968 edition was something of a 'bumper bundle' of news – not all good. There were three deaths, and the people concerned had all been prominent figures in the history of SGHS.

Mrs M. Lunt, chairman of the Governors since 1948 had resigned in the autumn of 1966 due to ill health. She died in November 1967. Many of us will remember Mrs Lunt leading into the hall with the party of school governors on Speech Day, usually wearing a fur coat, after a glass of sherry with Miss Butler in her study. She was something of a magnificent figure on the platform with a very distinctive voice, and those of us who won prizes have her signature on the book or certificate with which we were presented. No rubber stamp for Mrs Lunt and it must have taken her hours to sign everything. She was an all-important part of the SGHS scene, although we didn't actually get to speak to her much except at large functions. On retirement she had been replaced as chairman by Mr Leather, another longstanding and loyal governor of the school. Mrs Lunt's interest in and loyalty to the school was expressed by Miss Butler in the 1968 Summer Term magazine (p. 7):

Mrs M. H. Lunt

After being Chairman of the Governors since 1948, owing to failing strength, Mrs Lunt resigned in the autumn of 1966 though she still remained

1968 new-style Pear Tree school magazine, but still showing Worcestershire pears.

on the Governing Body. She died in November, 1967.

We all owe her a great deal of gratitude for her absolute loyalty and interest in the school. Until almost the last year of her life she never missed a meeting or a function. She was an excellent Chairman, and all the Governors will remember how she watched the clock and insisted that every meeting and function began punctually.

She was a shrewd judge of character and had a ready wit. I personally could always turn to her for advice and depend on her fund of commonsense and her unfailing support. For this, and her friendliness to me, I shall always be grateful.

In the same month, another governor died, Mrs Charles, who maintained her interest in the school to within a few days of her death when she expressed a wish that the prizes she gave every year should not be forgotten because she was ill.

The third was Miss A. E. Tilley, whose photograph appeared regularly in the early chapters of this book and who in 1968 would probably only have been remembered by SGHS pupils' mothers and aunts, but was, nevertheless, part of the fabric of the school's history.

Ruth Killon (1926–35) writes about Miss Tilley (*Pear Tree* magazine, Summer Term 1968, pp. 8-9):

Miss Tilley as I knew her

My earliest memories of Miss Tilley go back to the times when, as an eight- or nine-year-old member of Lower 2B, I descended to her dark form room on the ground floor near the Church Street entrance of the old 'Tec.' Building, to be spell-bound by a session of her story-telling.

> And still the little mill, hidden
> behind the door, went on
> Grinding our porridge

At this, one looked round, half fearfully, expecting to see the sticky flood steadily oozing between the desks.

Then I knew her as the organiser of frequent Saturday trips to Stratford, dealing so tactfully with a young and naïve theatre-goer who intended to eat an orange in the middle of the second act of *Macbeth*. School journeys were not the two-a-penny occasions they are today, and Miss Tilley's money as well as her time was spent ungrudgingly, so that we should think of the plays of Shakespeare as warm, living words and action, not just so much cold print.

The junior and senior dramatic societies offered staff and girls together weekly play-reading opportunities, and what a range we covered under Miss Tilley's guidance! Other schools might produce their annual performance (and we did do *The Weather-friends*, Galsworthy's *Little Man* and Lady Gregory's *The Dragon*) but we had a schoolgirl equivalent of a do-it-yourself repertory company. With the book of words in one hand and using the minimum of props. With the maximum of imagination, we got used to hearing our own voices clothing with life the thoughts of other people.

I don't remember very much about time-tabled English periods with Miss Tilley, except that she interested me in poetry sufficiently to take her advice and compile my own anthology – to which I still add occasionally. But her influence on the methods of teaching the subject in the school spread beyond her own classroom and, when in the lower forms, we enjoyed 'lecturettes', drawing our imaginary 'islands' and writing about matters of enormous personal importance as well as trying our hand at versifying. Years afterwards, she explained how, as a young teacher, she had sat in Caldwell Cook's classroom at the Perse School and saw the methods at work which he was to write about in *The Play Way*.

Miss Tilley was one of the team built up by Miss Firth, the team who put into practice ideas about methods of teaching far ahead of their time. Latin as a living, conversational language in which one could act plays about naughty boys in school – *Marcus dextram tollit*, history as finding out how real people lived and worked in houses, monasteries and on the land; geography as going for a walk with a map in one's hand and experimenting damply with the flow of the stream in the field in Old Junction Road; even the nightly line of 'Graily Hewett' handwriting – these were just some of those ideas. As a result, I had little to unlearn when the time came at college to study the art, craft and science of my profession, and teaching in the way I had been taught was not the disaster it usually is. Miss Tilley and I talked about such matters during the very occasional visits I was able to make to her since moving from the Midlands eighteen years ago. But as recently as 1966 we had a lively discussion on present-day developments in mathematics teaching in primary schools, and she took an informed interest in the educational articles I wrote for publication.

My feelings for Miss Tilley have extended from awe at nine years old, through amusement in adolescence, to a sincere professional appreciation and real affection for her as a person – critical, enquiring, sympathetic in mind, triumphing over ill-health and eccentric in many ways. She who took the part of Miss Prism in the staff performance of *The Importance of Being Earnest* in 1932 or thereabouts, caricatured herself delightfully. It is said that unmarried women teachers are becoming extinct: how sad to think that future generations will not know people like Miss Tilley. I'm glad I did.

Anice Smith (née Dewey), a former pupil (1936–41), and Miss Woodall added their tributes:

> She never walked, she tripped lightly along the stone corridors of the school, bringing the gay philosophy of her life and teaching to the prosaic minds of her pupils.
>
> Hers was a wisdom tempered with wit; a deep love and knowledge of English verse and prose balanced with a tolerance toward the young and untutored; a versatile vocabulary that transformed even a mundane conversation into something of beauty; yet she had such a quiet, patient ear that the hesitant, stumbling participator found confidence and assurance and blossomed in the presence of this small, vital, ageless personality.
>
> To me, personally, she exhibited an interest that extended far beyond the bounds of the form room, embracing the peculiar problems of my youth, helping me bear the aching loneliness that those problems brought. She imparted to me a lasting joy in the beauty of the written and spoken word and my life will for ever be the richer for its contact with Alice Tilley.

MISS A. E. TILLEY

Among girls now at school there are many whose mothers and aunts will remember Miss Tilley, for no-one who had the experience of being taught by her has ever forgotten her. She loved children and she loved her work, but behind all her enthusiastic enjoyment of a lesson there was sound scholarship. Her interest communicated itself to her pupils and she made English one of the best loved subjects in the curriculum.

It was, for me, a privilege to succeed her as head of the English department and editor of the magazine she began.

Of her it was so true that her life was her work that for years after her retirement she had no interest except in news of the girls and the school. Happily, after years of physical incapacity, she recovered sufficiently to enjoy active life again, several times going with her sister by air to Spain, but never revisiting her beloved Norfolk.

Her death at the beginning of this year was followed very soon afterwards by that of her sister who came to live with her after her retirement.

L. W.

Another longstanding member of staff retired during that school year – Miss Voyce. It was almost impossible for pupils, staff and old girls to visualise SGHS without her. Many pupils (and probably some members of staff) 'crossed swords' with Miss Voyce during their time at SGHS. She attempted to wither the 'wayward' with a certain 'look', but there was no doubt that she made History interesting for us and had invaluable tips up her sleeve to help us remember dates and battles for exam time. (I have sometimes wondered why Miss Voyce (as far as we knew) never applied for a headship at another school. After all, she had years of experience of teaching and of being deputy head. I think the answer must be that she actually truly loved her job at SGHS, although some of us doubted it at times, and particularly her interests in Stourbridge, such as being involved with the joint plays performed by KEGS/SGHS. She always dressed extremely smartly and expensively.)

Mrs Payton, who would have many memories of their very early days together at SGHS, wrote a tribute (*Pear Tree* magazine 1968, p. 11):

Miss C. J. Voyce, 1931–68

The school suffers an immeasurable loss in the retirement of Miss Voyce who, for 37 years, has contributed to its life – academic, administrative and social. When I knew her first she was 'the leader of the younger set' on the staff. Hers was the driving force behind school plays and several staff dramatic productions. As Henry Higgins she was superb!

In the staffroom our lunch hours were enlivened by working with her on *The Times* crossword puzzles or in the enjoyment of amusing conversations, which always thrived when she was present, and noticeably wilted a little in her absence.

She was a tower of strength in more ways than one, in the Staff netball team and in tennis when her skill was responsible for some of our victories. I think her enthusiasm for games was outstanding and many House Captains will remember with gratitude the advice, encouragement and coaching which she so generously gave.

In one sphere Miss Voyce and I had little in common. As a historian I know she is exceptional, but my own neglect of the subject, when I had the opportunity to study, made me wish I could have crept in unobserved to benefit from Miss Voyce's lessons. The opportunity never came my way and I am the poorer as a result.

When Miss Voyce was Deputy Head Mistress her skilled administration ensured the smooth running of our day-to-day life. Her judgment was such that many members of the Staff and senior girls consulted her over their problems, always finding her ready to consider them and give kindly and sound advice. As a form mistress she must have been invaluable.

I know many will be glad that Miss Voyce will still be living in Stourbridge where she will enjoy a less active, but no less interested connection with the school. In her retirement I hope she will find greater pleasure in her garden and home than she has had time for in the past. Her great capacity for friendship will not be wasted, as I am sure she will have many visitors.

I speak as though I am still a member of the school community when I say – 'we' wish her much happiness in the future.

Also, from Elizabeth Crawford, a former pupil:

As one of Miss Voyce's former pupils I can readily appreciate how much her present pupils will lose by her retirement. Those who have been taught by her will not easily forget her many gifts as a teacher. The most important of these is undoubtedly her lively approach and sense of humour which has made history so enjoyable, even to those with no special talent for it. Through her teaching she has communicated her own great enthusiasm for history and her conviction of its importance. In relating past events to those of modern times, she has also aroused in many of her pupils a keen interest in the affairs of today which has persisted beyond their life at school and into their future careers.

She has always encouraged her pupils to think for themselves and to express their opinions coherently, guiding them to read widely and form their own judgments. Her skill in this has been invaluable especially to those who have gone on to further study from school.

A good teacher must have not only a love of learning and the ability to pass this on to pupils, but also a real interest in the pupils themselves. This is what Miss Voyce has always shown. Her sympathy towards those in difficulties, her willingness to give advice and her genuine affection for those she has taught have been very obvious.

It is understandable that many people should regret Miss Voyce's departure from school and regard this as a loss, but this is also the time to remember the great gain which her work has been to school and pupils. All of us fortunate enough to have benefited from it are grateful and wish her every happiness in her retirement.

Sponsored walks to raise money for charity started to take place for SGHS girls and the Duke of Edinburgh Award scheme was popular. The photograph of school prefects and VI Upper 1967–8 shows a different 'look' compared with earlier ones, especially regarding hair styles and uniform.

The year 1969 saw a new long photograph of the entire school and this is the last official glimpse of some long-standing members of staff. Miss Woodall, Miss Wells, Mrs Haden and Miss Presley were on their way 'out'. Never had the school lost, in one term, so many heads of department.

There were many other staff changes at this time. Miss D. Cooper resigned her position as head of Mathematics but would continue on a part-time basis for a while. Miss R. Croft was going to Taumarunui High School, New Zealand; Mrs Frayne and Mr Handley were leaving for other posts in the UK. New members of staff included Mrs Skidmore for Domestic Science and Miss Wadsworth for Art (this must have been the B. Wadsworth who designed the new magazine cover). Yet another old girl, Dorothy Blakeway, joined the staff to help with Domestic Science, part-time. Not only were old girls returning to teach at SGHS but often on a part-time basis so that they could juggle home, family and work. Also, members of staff were spreading their wings to teach in the far corners of the globe. What a difference from the very early days of SGHS!

Part of SGHS school photograph, 1969.

SGHS school photograph, 1969. Hair is being worn long and loose and even the juniors are in skirts rather than gym slips/tunics.

School prefects SGHS and VI Upper, 1967–8. A change of uniform is becoming evident.

Because the swimming pool had now been completed and in use, largely owing to the tremendous zeal and hard work of the Parents' Committee, it was decided to try to continue this link of parents with the school by forming a Parents' Association, with Miss Butler presiding. (The HMI report in 1950 had recommended that such an organisation be set up.) The parents' response was enthusiastic and a committee was chosen and a constitution duly set up. Staff and old girls were also represented on the committee in addition to parent representatives from each year in the school. A programme of theatre visits, talks and films was planned. Its purpose was to benefit the school and all its members with a social and educational function rather than fund-raising although money did have to be raised annually for the maintenance of the swimming pool.

Miss Woodall said 'goodbye' to SGHS in the *Pear Tree* magazine (Summer Term 1969, pp. 1-2):

> It is not easy to write one's own obituary, but this is what I feel I am doing in attempting an introduction to my very last *Pear Tree*. When Miss A. E. Tilley retired in 1947 she bequeathed to me, then a very inexperienced sub-editor, responsibility for the annual production of the magazine. It has not only survived my early struggles and the pressures of rising costs, but has grown apace following the almost incredible expansion of the school, over the last twenty years especially, of which it is the magazine's main purpose to preserve a record.

Over the years many changes have been recorded, including inevitable staff changes, but in no year has the school lost at once so many senior members of staff as are retiring this year: Miss Wells, Mrs Haden and Miss Presley. All these Heads of Department have given to the school far more than their individual teaching, excellent as this has been. The debt felt is reflected in the tributes to them from colleagues and pupils which follow this Editorial.

Miss Wells came to the school in 1929 and became Head of the French Department when Miss Edwards retired in 1943. Her love of France, her people and her literature, has inspired all her teaching, communicating itself to generations of pupils. Mrs Haden, who joined the Staff in 1941 and became Head of the Geography Department when Miss Leigh retired in 1947, Miss

Presley, who came to us in 1943 as Head of the Science Department and Miss Wells have made vital individual contributions to the vigorous life of the School community, but for one thing especially the school will always be indebted to them, the fact that they have maintained an inflexibly high standard of work and conduct, of reliability and good manners, the *sine qua non* of a grammar school education, our school's proudest tradition in face of the many tendencies which threaten it in the modern world.

When such people leave, the school cannot but be the poorer.

We wish them all much deserved happiness in their retirement.

Also leaving this year is Miss Cook, who is to be married and will then live in Loughborough. During her nine years here, teaching both Physics and Mathematics, Head of the Physics Department since 1966, Miss Cook has won the goodwill of girls and staff alike by her good sense and good humour and readiness to participate in all ways in school life, as form mistress, house mistress, coaching girls in swimming, helping with their games, arousing their interest in photography, looking after national savings, and sharing in many other activities.

Miss Grant also leaves us, after four years of enthusiastic and selfless work, to take a senior post in a Birmingham school, and Mrs Lofthouse, who, in the two years she has been here, has done excellent work in Art, introducing new approaches, stimulating new interest, is leaving to go to London. At the end of the Spring Term we most regretfully said goodbye to Mrs Skidmore, who has been Head of the Domestic Department for not quite two years. We thank all leaving staff for their work with us and give them our best wishes for a happy future, assuring them of a warm welcome whenever they can visit us.

Finally, may I add my personal best wishes for the future of the magazine and of the school. To my successor I cannot wish greater happiness than I have had myself in every relationship with members of the school, past and present, and in all aspects of my thirty-two years' work here. I am pleased that with Miss Wells and Mrs Haden I shall be returning next year to continue some VIth form work.

Miss Woodall, ever modest and unassuming, fully deserved the tributes paid to her by Miss Pritchard (a member of the English Department) and an anonymous pupil in this same magazine.

Miss Woodall

After thirty-two years of devoted service to the life of the school, Miss Woodall is resigning from her position as Head of the English Department, though she will continue her work with us as part-time teacher of the VIth form. This then is not a melancholy occasion for saying 'Goodbye' but an opportunity for us to express something of our affectionate gratitude to her while she is still with us.

Her scholarship and the infectious zest of her teaching have opened to many a schoolgirl a life-long pleasure in English literature. This has been further nourished by the innumerable theatre outings she has organised to Stratford, Ludlow and Birmingham, and by a host of dramatic productions, ranging from Society readings to school plays, through which she has excitingly communicated her own love of the theatre. So much of her most valuable work has been behind the scenes; in ungrudged dinner-hours and after-school coachings she has given patient and unstinting help to many who would not have succeeded without it, and though she herself has perhaps found most enjoyment in her work with the Upper school, her sympathetic encouragement has gone out to any child, however stumbling, who needed it.

As Editor of the school magazine; as organiser of the Barnardo Helpers' League, on behalf of which she has worked indefatigably for years; as organiser and supervisor of refreshments on Open Day – a very necessary and much appreciated service! – as well as in countless other ways, Miss Woodall has poured out her energy and enriched our lives. As form-mistress and as colleague, she has won the love and admiration of girls and staff. Warm-hearted, generous and self-forgetful, to those of us who have had the privilege of working with her, and to the many girls who have gained by her teaching, she has made vivid the educational ideal of Michael Sadler: 'Childlike faith, intellectual reverence, and, not the least, gaiety and cheerfulness of mind'.

J. M. P.

When I hear or read speeches of appreciation, I always feel they have been written according to a rigid formula in which the requisite number of exuberant epithets have to be used. Doubtless, these are meant sincerely, but the over-florid style seems to give the impression of forced sentiment. I say this, only so that if what I have to say seems mundane, or even trivial compared to your expectations, you will understand that it is meant to reflect the sincerity of what I have to say. Besides, I am sure Miss Woodall's fine ear for the rhythms of English prose will be offended at an excessive use of superlatives – and if I can pay her no other compliment, I can at least prove that I have learned something from her!

Looking back over my school career, I find that the outline is landmarked by the influence of only a few teachers out of the many. By far the greatest influence has been Miss Woodall's. Throughout my turbulent academic career at Stourbridge High School she invariably took a firm grip upon the situation, guiding me through success and disappointment, always ready to encourage, but sensibly, never flattering. It is a great pity that many more teachers do not realise that honestly telling their pupils the true value of their work is often more use than instilling in them false hopes of soaring to academic heights.

In teaching her subject, Miss Woodall was always scrupulously thorough, at times, I fear, putting a great deal more effort and enthusiasm into the lesson than the whole class put together. On the other hand, I think it is quite true that much of the enthusiasm for her subject rubbed off onto her pupils.

The profit we gained was more than a good grade in an exam; it was much wider and more useful than this. By having pieces of literature criticised with such evident pleasure and in such a scholarly way before us, we were drawn, without even realising it, into worthwhile discussions which made us think about the principles of English literature and language. Once this power to assess the value of a book is learned, reading becomes a much more enjoyable and satisfying occupation. I would imagine that few, if any, of Miss Woodall's pupils have not profited in this respect from her teaching.

However, by no stretch of the imagination could you term Miss Woodall a dry academic. The same interest which she showed in her subject also spread to other areas of school life. What would have happened to our poor attempts at acting if Miss Woodall hadn't always been there to make sure rehearsals were going ahead and to tactfully suggest improvements in our amateurish acting? But as always, the person behind stage who makes everything possible never sought the limelight. So I think it only fair, if we could have just one minute of your valuable time, Miss Woodall, to bring you to the front of the stage and say 'Thank you'.

Miss Spencer and Miss Sheppard paid tribute to Miss Wells:

When Miss Wells retires from full-time teaching at the end of this term, she will have given a lifetime of service to the School.

As a form teacher she has shown patience and understanding towards the girls in her charge and has guided many a new girl in the ways of the school. She has also been a House Mistress, a faithful spectator of inter-House competitions, and she has taken a keen interest in many aspects of school life. Members of the Old Girls' Association owe her special thanks and assure her of a warm welcome at future meetings.

We are, however, most indebted to Miss Wells as a teacher of French. When parents of present First-formers praise 'this new idea of introducing the language orally' I have to admit that it is not an innovation – I was taught in this way by Miss Wells! As a ten-year-old I was immediately caught up in her infectious enthusiasm for France and things French and I still have nothing but admiration for her sound teaching and her ability to make her subject come alive.

The activities of the French Department have not been limited to the classroom or to the French Circle meetings. Inspired by Miss Wells, the school has gained a reputation for its success in the Verse-Speaking and Prose-Reading competitions, organised by the Birmingham Anglo-French Society. Also, together with Miss Sheppard, she established the link with Le Mans and has participated in all the exchange visits arranged subsequently.

Over the years we have all enjoyed Miss Wells' sense of humour, her encouragement and loyal support and her appreciation of the smallest service rendered. To a gifted teacher, a respected colleague and a valued friend, we extend our grateful thanks for the past and our sincere good wishes for the future.

A. S.

Miss Wells

When I came into the IVth Form, I had already done two years' French. I had been well drilled in verbs and vocabulary, but it was not until my first term here that it was borne upon me that French was not just a question of grammar, or of questions and answers, or of reading a text-book: it was the language of France. This discovery – with its far-reaching results! – I owe to Miss Wells.

From France in the classroom (Brittany – the Mont Michel...) to France in reality; at the end of our first year in the 6th, two of us set off to stay with our correspondents at St Servan, an exchange visit arranged by Miss Wells. A normal enough procedure now, but then we were pioneers indeed!

How wide have the ripples spread! Individual visits; Le Mans exchanges. (How many of our laggards would have failed to arrive, or even depart, but for Miss Wells' capable 'whipping in'!) Nor has the traffic been only in one direction: more than one young French girl owes her happiness in an English family to Miss Wells' kindness.

And so for forty years Miss Wells has shared with us all her love for France and the French way of life, along with the discovery of its language and literature. As pupils and colleagues, we owe her an unpayable debt for her inspiration, her patience, her ready sympathy and wise counsel, her tact – and teasing!

Visits to France have invariably led to the finding of 'ideal spots' for retirement. We wish Miss Wells much happiness and a well-earned rest, be it in that cottage in the Berry, a 'cabane' in the Pyrenees, a chalet in the Alps – or simply 'chez nous'!

M. J. S.

Mrs Hadley, who had long been a friend of Mrs Haden as well as a colleague, paid tribute to her, as did Gaynor Hadley (née Beauchamp), an ex-pupil.

Mrs Haden

I first came to know Mrs Haden when I was having difficulty in finding accommodation. She spontaneously offered me a temporary home (which incidentally became a permanency of six years) and this kindness and effort to help someone in need has always to me been one of Mrs Haden's great qualities.

During her years in school, many girls have discovered this and have benefitted from her sympathy and interest.

Mrs Haden has followed the lives and careers of girls and staff even after they have left school and has usually been able to supply information on both when discussions have developed in the Staff room.

When the Government policy on Comprehensive Education threatened the present identity of the school, Mrs Haden acted as a liaison between school and the local press to help Miss Butler's efforts to publicise the work and achievements of the school.

Mrs Haden's 'out of school activities' have brought her into contact with many local societies and personalities, and she has been a valuable source of information when lectures and visits have been planned.

We hope that when her full-time work with us is over at the end of this term she will be able to enjoy all her other activities more fully, and we wish her well in her partial retirement.

F. H.

As a former pupil of Mrs Haden (better known to girls who like myself, left school some time ago, as Miss Joan Makin) I can readily appreciate the great loss to the School on her retirement.

My first and most vivid recollection of Mrs Haden was the ritual of waiting huddled together, in the draughty alcove outside the Geography Room before being allowed to proceed in complete silence into class. This was only part of her adherence to strict discipline, but a discipline which earned her the greatest respect and admiration, rather than the reverse.

In her position as Senior Geography Mistress she had the ability and enthusiasm to make a subject, never the easiest to teach, extremely interesting. She was always ready to give extra attention to those of her pupils who found the subject particularly difficult, and her patience in this respect was unlimited. She encouraged individual thinking and always had time to lend a sympathetic ear to any problem, however trivial. The successes which her pupils achieved prove her ability as a teacher and her great gift for passing on knowledge of a subject so dear to her heart.

We sincerely hope that even though she will no longer be a member of the teaching staff we shall not lose touch with Mrs Haden altogether. I am sure all her pupils past and present will be delighted to see her whenever the opportunity presents itself. Although the school will certainly be the loser by her retirement, the impression she has left on the girls she has taught over the many years will never be lost. Those of us who were fortunate enough to come under her instruction and influence owe her a great debt of gratitude. We do wish her many happy years of retirement, and hope that with more leisure time she will be able to do all those things she has never found time to do before.

GAYNOR HADLEY (née Beauchamp)

Mrs Haden, in turn, paid *her* tribute to Miss Presley:

Miss Presley

Miss G. H. Presley a graduate of Aberystwyth, came to Stourbridge to teach Chemistry in September, 1943, when Miss Grimwood left to go to St Felix School, Southwold (at that time evacuated to Hinton St George, Somerset). She came to a school which was also a Rest Centre, fully equipped with blankets and other essentials to receive those who might be bombed out; a school where lessons might be interrupted at any time by an air-raid alert, where the staff spent many nights on the school premises 'fire-watching' (by no means the comfortable occupation that those words may conjure up in the minds of the present generation of girls!); one in which every form had a garden, where they enthusiastically grew vegetables – later to be eaten with equal enthusiasm at school dinner, for this was a time of strict food rationing. It was also a school of about 450 girls, with forms of less than thirty – what changes Miss Presley has seen in her twenty-six years of service to the school!

In 1946, the late Miss A. E. Tilley wrote in the school magazine, 'a teacher has to occupy the minds of others during the whole day – a day that is completed by an arduous evening of marking and preparation'; this has been no easy task for Miss Presley, battling as she has with patches of indifferent health. Her subject is one which has changed radically in the last twenty years or so, yet she kept up-to-date with current advances, maintaining a standard of sound scholarship. This was not always appreciated by junior forms, as it was combined with a strict discipline, desirable in any aspect of life in a school community but essential in the environment of a Chemistry laboratory with its potentially lethal equipment. Many generations of sixth-formers, however, will remember with gratitude the painstaking way in which she successfully guided their studies, revealing her basic humanity and interest in their future careers. The need to widen her pupils' horizons led her to organise many out-of-school visits – to the local gas-works, to the ICI and BIP factories, to Round Oak and to other works in the same area. It is fitting that her final year in the school should coincide with Kay Partridge's successes in the entrance examinations for the universities of Oxford and Cambridge.

One side of Miss Presley's activities not generally known to her pupils has been her keen interest in and enjoyment of her home and garden, though many staff have benefited from her advice and experience, and latterly she has taken up golf with enthusiasm and no small success. We hope that she will have many years of retirement in which to enjoy these pursuits.

J. M. H.

Janet Vale, an ex-pupil, thanked Miss Presley for stimulating her interest in Chemistry:

> On the occasion of Miss Presley's retirement I am happy to have an opportunity to express my thanks to her.
>
> Although leaving the field of Chemistry some years ago, I am still aware that I owe her a debt for stimulating my interest in the subject, which was largely instrumental in my choice of University, study and career, a choice which I in no way regret.
>
> When I first entered the school, I must admit that I regarded Miss Presley merely as a stern disciplinarian who was on no account to be disobeyed, but as I advanced through the school (and since leaving school), I became better acquainted with her and realised that this is only one aspect of her character. Thus I express my appreciation, not only towards a member of staff, but also towards a friend, whom I wish happiness on her retirement and for the future years.

(I think many of us would agree with this tribute – with the callousness of youth, it was often a source of nervous amusement amongst junior forms when Miss Presley confessed at times to having 'rheumatism in the head' and often sat through a Chemistry lesson wearing a woolly hat!)

A lot of space devoted to tributes, but essential I feel as these people had been such a part of SGHS history and will be remembered by generations of pupils all over the world. Perhaps we *may* visualise them in a slightly different light after reading them now we are 'old girls'!

Several deaths were recorded in the 1969 magazine and, in particular, a really tragic one. Patricia Downing, who had left SGHS in 1963, had been killed at the age of only twenty-three during the Easter holidays when she had been accompanying a party of girls from the school where she taught (Hill and Cakemore Secondary School). This was much more unusual to read of then than perhaps it is nowadays.

We learn of the death of Claire Wright, Miss Sneyd's great friend and also an old girl. Miss Sneyd wrote that she had first met Claire on the steps of the Girls' Secondary School in the old Technical College/Library building when they were both new girls arriving for their first day and from that moment there began a friendship which lasted until Miss Wright's death at the end of 1968.

New members of staff were welcomed – Mrs Ashmore (BSc Manchester) to teach Chemistry; Miss Mills (BA Cantab.) for History; Miss Yates (BSc London and another old girl) came to teach Biology; Mr Taylor (BA London) came as head of History. Mrs Lee (who was actually French herself and graduated from the Sorbonne) came to share in the teaching of French and Mr Bendall, formerly head of English at Bromsgrove County High School, to teach some sixth form English. The school was becoming much 'busier' and Mrs Hynd, who had been giving part-time help with Domestic Science, was now to become full time; Mrs Smith (née Margaret Orford) and another old girl took on a part-time post as assistant librarian, thus relieving Miss Round of some of the work the rapid growth and use of the library had made very demanding. Also, there was some much needed help in the dining-room (now that members of the teaching staff had, at long last, been freed from supervising meals) and Mrs White was appointed to share this work with Mrs Cooper and Mrs Millinchamp.

Miss Butler did quite a lot of reorganising herself during the year 1968/9, particularly with the prefect system. The sixth formers now numbered 140 and it had become impossible for all worthy girls to have recognition as school prefects. She considered that many had felt hurt and unwanted by being omitted from the prefect body so, under the new system, all sixth-form girls were given authority and responsibility with the staff for the smooth running of the school.

The sixth forms were divided into six groups made up of all girls from all four sixth forms and each group had a leader. The groups were responsible in turn for all prefect duties for one week and when A level examinations began, VI Upper were freed from further duties which then became the sole responsibility of VI Lower.

(Some of us may perhaps have vague memories of a 'sub-prefect' system in the 1950s when a few non-prefects were allowed to take 'office' for a while from A level people.)

From then on there is definitely an impression, via the school magazines, that the sixth formers, with members of the teaching staff, had a very strong say in the running of SGHS. There appears to be more consultation between the headmistress and the senior girls, for example on the issue of uniform. The Sixties decade gave way to the Seventies and with it yet another 'new' look to the *Pear Tree* cover and shape, and there is a strong, informative editorial from the two editors, Janet Billingham and Anne Wood, which reflects the inevitability of change within the school.

Perhaps it is appropriate at this point to read what Mary Edwards, an ex-pupil, wrote in the 1976 *Pear Tree* magazine (p. 22) about her time at SGHS in the Sixties.

THE HIGH SCHOOL IN THE 1960s

'As from tomorrow you may wear summer uniform [pause] and so you need not wear your hats!'

I have fond memories of the delight that greeted this announcement each year; Miss Butler always managed a knowing smile as she said the second part. School uniform was an emotive subject, but like House Netball, the Swimming Pool Fund, Deportment Badges, and STCF, it was ever with us. During my time there, there were many changes, including the introduction of grey suits for the Sixth Form, and the abolition of the blue and white summer dresses, which looked like mattress material made up to the requirements of a Reform School.

I was fortunate to be one of a very lively year. We supplied most of the Hockey Team, and some of my happiest memories are of matches against other schools, particularly Kidderminster, with whom we were lucky to draw, and Worcester, whose hospitality and cream cakes made it all worthwhile.

At the end of each term came the Final Assembly. There were Form Conduct and Tidiness Prizes, which always seemed to go to a First Form, Games Reports, Colours and Girdles for the lucky ones and 'Jerusalem' for all. This last sounded particularly good at our final assembly in the Upper Sixth.

Dare I mention Miss Presley? How could I leave her out? The epitome of the phrase 'stern disciplinarian' her iron rule made Chemistry our Most Feared Subject and I had great admiration for anyone who took it to O let alone A level. I had more luck with Maths, thanks largely to my teachers. Mrs Hewis used to come to our Wednesday afternoon lesson straight from her sessions in Court (as a magistrate, I may add!): 'Girls, I must tell you...' she would begin, and Maths would take second place to the maintenance of Law and Order. She gave us jargon for getting the right answer ('Cross the line, you change the sign'), too much homework ('into Neat, Girls'), but most of us passed, and I for one caught an enthusiasm for the subject that I still retain.

Now the schools of the area are to be re-organised, and Stourbridge High School will be no more. Even Postlethwaite's where I bought my Regulation Uniform, hat and all, has long been swept away by the Ring Road. Is nothing sacred? I must be one of the many Old Girls who have gone into Teaching and I work now in a large Mixed Comprehensive with new buildings and such things as a Sports Centre and a Computer Link. But there is still something about a bright, frosty morning in January that jerks my memory back to the brown benches of the Old Physics Lab.

Mary Edwards (1960–7)

The year 1970 brought yet another 'new look' to the *Pear Tree* magazine.

Miss Cooper, who had taught Mathematics to countless SGHS girls, finally retired in 1970. Mrs Morris (staff) and Jane Staples (former pupil) paid tribute to her:

MISS COOPER

When Miss Cooper leaves at the end of this term, we shall miss her steady, reliable influence. Some years ago, she was faced with illness and difficulties which she met with matchless serenity and courage. She has been an inspiration to those of us who have known her well, never too busy to give sympathetic and practical advice on personal or mathematical problems.

Her great contribution to the life of the school has probably not been realised by the majority, as it consisted largely of monotonous 'back-room' jobs carried out unobtrusively and with a smoothness and efficiency we have all taken for granted: for example the practical arrangements connected with external examinations and the counting and tabulating of proceeds of 'Bring and Buy' Sales away from the excitement and 'limelight' of the more colourful activities. One could always depend on her being at the point at which she was most needed.

If one called at her home towards the end of the Summer Term she would probably be found 'playing' cards – a

'New' look to cover of 1970s **Pear Tree:** *dark purple with pale blue lettering.*

game of patience she devised herself. It involved many different colours arranged on an easel affair in special permutations and combinations. Out of this contraption, by some magic known only to herself, emerged the school time-table, a work of balance and precision.

The Maths staff appreciate their good fortune in having such a person as Head of their department. Many past pupils who realise that their satisfying careers are largely due to her have kept in touch and she takes a real interest in them long after they have left school.

We all wish her the very happy retirement she so richly deserves.

K. M.

MISS COOPER

Somehow Maths never seems to have achieved much success in the popularity ratings of school subjects, and I suppose many people would expect little of someone who had spent her life teaching it. Those people would be in for a surprise if they knew Miss Cooper. She hardly fulfils the image of the austere and perhaps inhuman Maths mistress. She is a born teacher, and her own warmth of personality and enthusiasm cheered even her most unmathematical of pupils, and stimulated the more gifted.

My chief memory of Miss Cooper is of our Sixth Form lessons when she taught three of us for no less than fourteen lessons a week. Before anyone lifts their hands in horror or weeps tears of pity for such ill-fated pupils, let me say that we really enjoyed those lessons. We inevitably got to know one another quite well, and were able to share many a laugh. She was always interested in all our activities, not just whether we could determine the answer to some complex equation! Her competence as a mathematician was matched by her ability to teach, and her enthusiasm was infectious. We cannot be alone in thanking her for her part in what little success we had, both in our exams and in our future careers.

I wonder what Miss Cooper felt about those lessons. She always appeared with a smile, and never seemed tired of us, though we were not exactly angels, but I hope and believe she enjoyed them too – perhaps one of the best signs of a good teacher.

Some will remember Miss Cooper better as a form-mistress – capable, calm and kind. Others will recall her interest in House activities, and yet others her magnificent work in working on the time-tables each year.

I count it as a very great honour that I have been asked to write this tribute to her. Perhaps I may sum up by saying that there are few people to whom I personally owe so much. We all wish her a long and happy retirement.

JANE STAPLES (née Green)

Mrs Hewis likewise retired that year, and Miss Cooper paid tribute to her colleague of sixteen years.

MRS HEWIS

Mrs Hewis came to the school in 1955 to teach Mathematics. In the classroom, she displayed energy and enthusiasm and made a subject, which is not always considered easy, interesting to all those whom she taught. Her encouragement and generosity in giving of her time helped many pupils over what might have been a difficult hurdle.

It is not only in the Mathematics Department that Mrs Hewis will be missed when she leaves the school. Her abounding energy, lively good humour and friendly manner have made her popular with Staff and girls alike.

As a form mistress, she quickly gained the affection and respect of those girls in her charge. She was always ready to listen to them with sympathetic understanding and to give help where it was needed.

In the Staff-room, she always gave willing and unselfish service. In fact, she contributed most generously to all aspects of school life.

When Mrs Hewis gives up full-time teaching, she will by no means retire in the full sense of the word, for she has a wide variety of interests which will keep her busy. She will be greatly missed in the school, but we sincerely wish her every happiness in the future.

D. C.

The 1970 magazine was certainly not short of copy and is packed with amusing and interesting articles and poems from the girls. One struck a chord in the hearts of generations of SGHS girls who had ever read the lesson in assembly (p. 19).

THE READING FOR TODAY IS TAKEN FROM…

I filed into the Hall with my form. At this time I was feeling quite calm. The rest of the School was fed into the rows of chairs. The empty seats were gradually filled with dark blue bodies. The faces meant nothing at all. It was only the large number of people that concerned me and not whom the blue bodies belonged to.

My friends were chattering to each other as if they had no cares in the world. The Staff walked into the Hall and took their respective positions on the stage. The bell was rung in the vestibule. It was a shrill, harsh noise that only meant that my nervous system became more active than before.

Miss Butler walked onto the stage and announced the hymn number. The few introductory bars of the hymn were played on the piano. The Hall was filled with music. The hymn was long. It comprised four, eight-lined verses. I could hardly hold my hymn-book. I smiled sickly at my neighbour. The last verse of the hymn was being sung. I was encased in a bubble and shut off from the world…My friend's hand dug into my side. I was back in the School Hall. She gave me a desperate look and glanced up to the stage.

'The reading for today is taken from…'

I heard my own voice thrown back at me from the four walls. The Hall was filled with my voice and my voice alone. Do not look up. Do not look up at the mass of faces staring at you. I was shaking. Could people on the back row hear me? What did I look like, standing up there? I did not know what I was reading. I just read.

I walked down from the stage. People stood up for the prayers. I prayed hard.

HILARY BLOOR, IVM

The editorial of this same magazine draws attention to the 'spirit of change' that seemed to be present in the school, perhaps in line with the 1970s and the forthcoming changes in education.

EDITORIAL

Change is inevitable. People change from generation to generation, thus influencing society with their new ideas and actions. Compare the High School of fifty, even five years ago, with the High School of today...

Looking back nostalgically over our seven years in this school, we can now see how our daily lives were affected by progress and change. During our first year, we were caught up with the enthusiasm at the prospect of at last having our own swimming pool. Surprisingly enough, we have been able to make use of the pool, as it was completed two years ago. Unfortunately, many of the staff who worked to achieve this were unable to see it materialise, owing to retirements, marriages, births, deaths or emigration.

We were impressed by the influx of new ideas and methods of teaching from new Staff, whose arrival made it possible for us to pursue a greater range of subjects. It is perhaps because of this that many more girls have chosen to stay on for a further two years. As a result, the prefect system proved to be outdated: now, by the new scheme, each Sixth Former is given the 'privilege' of compulsory duties!

The changing social environment has influenced all, thus leaving its mark on school life. New ideas have been exchanged with mutual understanding, and a new level of communication has been established between staff and girls. We can now discuss freely all our problems, including that of school uniform, as new modes of fashion have inevitably infiltrated into our secluded community. None greater, perhaps, than the introduction of grey suits for girls in the Sixth. This 'non-uniform' uniform is attractive and practical, and has itself contributed in the narrowing of the gap between the pupil and the young 'girl of the world'.

Change, however, occurs not only in people but in the school itself. Vast sums of money are being spent in improving and extending buildings. You might have noticed that for the past few months, holes have continually been appearing in the new building. Lessons have continually been disrupted by the 'gritty machinations' of the cement mixer, painters whistling, and other slight distractions. Occupants of Room 15 and the new Physics Lab, and people using the stairs have had papers, hair and clothing disarranged by frequent gusts of wind from the 'holes-in-the-wall'! All this is to provide more much-needed Sixth Form amenities, which we hope will be completed before the end of term.

As you proceed through your copy of the magazine, you will doubtless notice how the spirit of change has affected the *Pear Tree* itself. It is hoped that the new layout will appeal to the majority, if not all, of our readers!

A. W., J. B.

The school year 1969–70 began with 637 pupils and a varied year it was too, with numerous visits, performances of plays, etc. The Christmas Carol Service, probably because of the vast numbers of people, was now held at Oldswinford Church. The academic records showed a greater number of O level subjects being obtained – not uncommon now to have nine passes – and the CSE included Needlework in addition to Maths and French. That year also saw the return of Spanish as an optional subject on the Lower Sixth Form curriculum, the aim being to reach O level standard in nine months. All eleven candidates passed.

Miss Butler enjoyed attending SGHS Old Girls' Association meetings as did several of the retired members of staff and by all accounts she very much appreciated any opportunity to 'catch up' on the old girls' news.

There was a 'Knit-In' on 10 April 1970, the last Friday of the Easter holidays, when ten girls arrived at the hall with knitting needles, packed lunches and paper bags. This idea (originally Miss Morris's invention) was to raise money for the Nsambya Babies' Home in Kampala, Uganda. This home had been built by Oxfam for abandoned and orphaned African babies under three years old. The matron, Margaret Hobbs, was an old girl of SGHS. Much of the wool had been collected at school during the Spring Term, the remainder being brought by Firkins, a confectionery firm who had kindly used their Quinton shop as a base to which customers brought wool. Knitters were given a suitable thickness of wool for their knitting needles and left to knit as many squares as possible. Throughout the day about 40 knitters came and went. Coffee was constantly provided by helpers with Miss Wyld and Miss Morris in charge. At 4 p.m. named paper bags filled with squares were handed in to be counted and the amount per square that each person had been sponsored for was recorded. The total amount collected was estimated at being between £70 and £80 – a good day's knitting and for a very worthy cause.

The 1971 magazine brought news of the newly created Sixth Form Common Room – eagerly awaited by the girls. According to Lynda Harris and Angela Marshall (the editors) it had proved to be both successful and popular, helping to provide a less divided atmosphere amongst the Sixth Forms. The size of the room had also made it most suitable for society meetings and the kitchen facilities were an added asset. (Such facilities would have been beyond the dreams of avarice for us earlier pupils!)

Two new societies appeared – chess (with regular weekly meetings attended by both staff and girls) and a debating society which was flourishing. Perhaps this was something to do with the fact that they had joint debates with the Boys' Grammar School!

A sadder part to 1971 was that Miss Woodall was going into permanent retirement after the last two years of part-time teaching. Miss Tolley wrote a short tribute to her and mentioned Miss Woodall's long, devoted service

SGHS Old Girls' Association annual dinner at Old White Horse Inn, Stourbridge, 1970. L to r: Mrs E. J. Cooke (Treasurer); Miss A. Spencer (Vice-Chairman); Mrs G. Hadley (Chairman); Miss Butler (Headmistress and President); Mrs Hale; Miss C. Oakley (Secretary).

and untiring efforts as head of the English Department. Her last two years of part-time teaching had been devoted to a Sixth Form English group and had been fully appreciated.

(From a personal point of view I can add that I feel that anyone who was taught by Miss Woodall was indeed privileged. My own time in the sixth form many years beforehand had been enriched by her A level English Literature lessons and discussions. Somehow one never felt like 'playing Miss Woodall up'; she was so sweet and sincere – usually coming into the form room at a slight run – and told us sadly on one occasion that she wouldn't be able to accompany us to Stratford to see a play because 'Mother wants me to wash the curtains'! At the same time we never doubted her academic prowess and powers of scholarship.)

There were well over 60 girls from fourth, fifth and sixth forms visiting elderly and handicapped people on a regular basis and some girls found time to do odd jobs for them – shopping, dusting, reading, writing letters and even cleaning windows. They also raised funds to give the local old people a Christmas party at the school with food and entertainment provided by the girls, supported by members of staff.

SGHS certainly had a strong presence in the local community.

There were a few new members of staff – Miss Eaton from Homerton College, Cambridge to teach Maths and Junior Geography and Miss Pope from the University of Bristol to teach Maths. Mademoiselle Grémy came (at her own request after an exchange visit) as French Assistante and Fräulein Pankopf as Assistentin from the University of Marburg.

The Parents' Association was going from strength to strength and had suggested as a major project a minibus for the school. However, after much discussion it was decided to defer this and concentrate on assistance with the provision of music practice rooms.

The 1970 and 1971 school magazines did not make much mention of Miss Butler.

Nor was there a great deal of copy referring to the House system. One cannot imagine that Miss Butler was taking less interest in the school; rather, the new, younger and enthusiastic members of staff, with the ever-growing and enterprising girls of the sixth forms, were enjoying a slighter closer involvement (plus the PTA) in the school's development and daily life.

Miss Butler was certainly nearing retirement age and in the 1972 magazine came the inevitable news that, after 22 years as headmistress, she was to retire. The editorial, written by Janice Hill and Nicola Forrest, paid tribute to the fact that the many changes in the last few years at SGHS, both in structure and administration, had been brought about as a result of Miss Butler's influence and concern for the school. Whilst they felt that there might have been a tendency for members of the Lower School not to recognise all her contributions, the Upper School could not fail to appreciate her untiring efforts, her guidance and advice with regard to further education and careers.

Miss Wyld, who had now become a relative 'old-timer' at SGHS and had worked with Miss Butler for many years, wrote a much fuller tribute (*Pear Tree* 1972, pp. 3-4):

MISS BUTLER

It is a well-nigh impossible task to attempt an evaluation of Miss Butler's influence on and contribution to the life and development of the school during her twenty-two years at Stourbridge. Her self-giving in terms of time, energy and interest has been apparent to us all and has invariably covered almost the whole of the school holidays as well as term-time.

When in 1950 Miss Butler took over the headship of the High School, the roll numbered 422 girls, including 31 in the Sixth Form. Our present total stands at 625, which included a Sixth Form of 136. This enormous expansion of the Sixth Form has been matched over the years by a wide increase in the range of subjects offered, particularly at Advanced Level, steadily rising academic standards, and a considerable increase in the number of girls applying to and accepted by Universities for degree course. Here is evidence of healthy growth, inevitably reflecting in its turn the unremitting hard work and unwavering commitment of the Head of the school.

As successive generations of Sixth Formers no doubt appreciate, one of Miss Butler's major contributions has been the considerable help and guidance given to intending applicants for University and College of Education places. The Autumn of each year has seen her almost snowed under with piles of UCCA forms to be completed, and constantly pressing the bell on her desk in answer to the tentative knock of yet another bewildered member of the Upper Sixth seeking advice on choices of University or course. That this time-consuming task has been worthwhile has been borne out over and over again by the appreciative and grateful comments of old girls visiting us in the University vacations.

But there is more to school than the academic side, and Miss Butler's influence has been equally great in other directions. Never afraid to break with tradition when present-day conditions demanded it, she has initiated changes in, for example, the organisation of first Junior, and latterly Senior Prize-giving, the prefect system, Sixth Form uniform, and summer and outdoor uniform for the whole school. The aim of such changes has always been to give greater freedom and flexibility where appropriate, to encourage a sense of responsibility, and quite simply to make life in school as enjoyable as it may be.

Perhaps in a sense one of the school's greatest achievements during Miss Butler's headship was the building of the swimming pool, a project which she initiated, and to further which the Swimming Pool Committee was formed, involving parents in the affairs of the school more closely than had ever been possible before. When the long years of money-raising reached their fulfilment and the Committee's *raison d'être* ceased, another of Miss Butler's far-reaching ideas was born. Appreciative of the 'tremendous fund of goodwill' towards the school among the parents, and anxious that it should be recognised and allowed to flourish, she was largely responsible for the founding of the Parents' Association, to whose interest and generosity we are indebted in so many ways.

The school has gained immeasurably from Miss Butler's years as Head, and it is our earnest hope that when she looks back upon those years it will be with a sense of achievement and fulfilment. We for our part know how much we shall miss her, and our affection and gratitude accompany her into what we very much hope will be a happy and satisfying retirement.

Two more long-serving members of staff were also to go that year – Mrs Adams and Mrs Morris – and they too had well-deserved tributes. On a personal note I was never taught by Mrs Adams but was always aware of her presence about the school, dressed very attractively and very feminine in her looks. We girls were aware of a dark, handsome husband accompanying her about the town of Stourbridge on occasions or at a school function.

Mrs Morris, on the other hand, had the very doubtful privilege of teaching me Maths for many years. She had a very definite way of speaking and almost exploded on the words '*decimal point*', giving them an exclamation mark all of their own! She also delivered her small boy to a nearby private school on her way in to teach, and asked some of us to meet her at the back entrance of SGHS to help carry her heavy bag of books. Somehow, we never minded.

MRS ADAMS

It is with much regret that we have to record the retirement of Mrs P. M. Adams. An Old Girl of the school, she joined the staff in 1950 and since then has taught the two major subjects of English and History with equal facility and success. She has brought to both the same liveliness of approach, enthusiasm and erudition, and her lessons have inspired many girls to continue with their studies. For she has been quick to see the best in those she taught and given them steady encouragement to develop their talents.

Mrs Adams has been a quiet, effective and popular form mistress, at first of junior forms, but latterly of the Sixth Form; her rule has been gentle but firm. With her quick sense of humour, graciousness and lively interest in everyday affairs the girls have found her easy to approach and ready to assist them in every way.

She is an avid yet discriminating reader with a particular interest in drama and music. In school choral activities she has been happy to lend her not inconsiderable talents when the staff have been asked to participate, and she has always supported musical functions with enthusiasm. But indeed her support of all School functions has been beyond praise, and with her husband she has formed an appreciative and cheerful nucleus of the audience.

Perhaps in her knowledge of drama has Mrs Adams been most outstanding. There can hardly have been a performance at Stratford or Birmingham which has escaped her attention; she can discuss all forms of drama with insight and appreciation. For many years, her own productions of form plays were watched with interest for the expertise of direction and the attraction of the costumes. These latter she often provided herself or fashioned from materials given by eager but unhandy supporters.

Never has Mrs Adams sought the limelight, but her quiet, steady work in the background has helped the wheels of the school to turn smoothly. She has been a pleasant, reliable and hospitable member of the Staff, held in affectionate admiration by all who worked with her. She is an example of the best that the High School has produced in the past, and if the present generation can aspire to her devotion to duty, sound scholarship and integrity, we have no need to fear for the future.

P. D.

MRS MORRIS

We are sorry to say goodbye to Mrs Morris. She has given excellent service in the Maths Department for the past twenty years and has been an exceptionally good conscientious teacher, taking a personal interest in the success of her pupils.

Mrs Morris was always willing to assist with any task which presented itself with the running of the department. In other ways Mrs Morris contributed much to the school, one of these being the way she organised the smooth running of the school dining-room arrangements. Also for many years she gave untiring help in dealing with the collections for the Save the Children Fund.

Mrs Morris will be greatly missed by members of Staff and pupils and we wish her much happiness in the future.

D. C., K. H.

A new era was indeed on the horizon for SGHS and Miss Butler was leaving behind her a much changed High School from the one she had taken over from Miss Dale way back in 1950!

The Old Girls' Association (of which we will hear more later in the book) presented Miss Butler with a clock, a handsome cut glass bowl, and perhaps somewhat surprisingly, a set of copper-bottomed stainless steel saucepans!

The chairman, Mrs B. Price, thanked Miss Butler for having been president of the Association and invited her to become the first honorary vice-president.

For Miss Butler was not going to leave the area (she did *not* want to sever ties with SGHS) and remained living, as she had been whilst headmistress, at Garth, Oakleigh Road, Oldswinford for many more years. Stourbridge Girls' High School's loss was to be the Old Girls' Association's gain!

Before leaving Miss Butler's 'era' it's interesting to read the memoirs of SGHS pupils who experienced the 1960s and early 1970s under her 'rule':

> House gymnastic competitions took place, as nervous energy there caused the wobbly leg syndrome, the shaking legs causing the mottles to merge into the solid area of trembling, yet deeply concentrating being.

> That was not the only time our legs trembled during the first school year. Prime numbers provided another stimulus for the same response, for everybody else, it appeared, managed to understand the principles without the struggle of wasting half a maths book and going to sleep full of anxiety about the next day's mathematics. However, when we reached geometry, the battle was not so tense.

> The second, third and fourth years seem to merge together in a welter of insignificant, yet remembered events. The trivia tends to remain, whilst the rest evades mental recapture; for example, the only memory of the eminent Robert Walpole is that he ate Red Norfolk apples in Parliament!

> Rumour has it that the allotments adjacent to the lower courts are to be covered by new buildings. How sad! The topic of apples reminds me of scrambling under the wire to sample the forbidden fruit of the apple trees on the allotment side of the fence, and also of smuggling pounds of fruit in the spacious pockets of our summer dresses back into the classroom. There, desk lids provided ample cover for their consumption when less vigilant staff were teaching.

> The highlight of the school year after O levels (it is peculiar how vague are the memories of that then traumatic experience) was the Geographical and Historical Society outing. Unfortunately, as far as I was concerned, so much time was spent playing tennis that the blisters patterning the soles of my feet prevented me joining the expedition. The others went, of course, and one

Presentation of retirement gift to Miss Butler from OGA, April 1972.
L to r: Mrs E. Cooke (Treasurer); Mrs J. Higgins (Chairman); Miss Butler (President); Mrs P. Johnson (Secretary).

gaggle of three girls strayed too far from the coach before the outing started. Consequently, they were left behind to catch another coach which took them to visit a place where they did not really want to go.

Work in the sixth form was both interesting and stimulating, whilst occupation in free time in school demanded enterprise and ingenuity, particularly when trying to find vacant rooms. Those with Bunsen burners or points were preferred in order to cope with our Heath Robinson appliances to boil milk or water for coffee. We had no such luxury as the sixth form Common Room. Those last two years were hectic in work and play, the balance being well maintained by some, but tipping disastrously one way or the other for others of us. This if nothing else will remain the same during the last year of students in the new school.

Pandy Brodie (1963–70)

Amazingly, it is only 6 years since I left the High School. So much has happened in my life since then that my school days seem very much a feature of my past and outwardly appear to have little relevance to my present way of life here in Leicester. Yet, on reflection, I have realised just how important a part they have played, both in the formation of my character, and in contributing to my present happiness. Most particularly, it was at School that my love for languages was recognised and fostered, especially by Miss Wells. I left eager to pursue these studies at Leicester University, motivated by an enthusiasm that had been generated by experience of life in France via the Le Mans exchanges, resulting holiday friendships, conversation with the various French Assistantes, and not least, by the encouragement of our teachers. It was certainly thanks to these early experiences that I adapted so well to the French life-style when I worked in the perfume manufacturing town of Grasse in the South of France, and it is with increasing pleasure that I return as often as possible to renew friendships gained during the past years.

In this, my first year's teaching, I feel, in my turn, motivated to project some of the same enthusiasm to my own pupils. Spurred on by memories of my own school activities such as dancing 'Sur le Pont d'Avignon' in the quad and the Annual French and German Christmas festivities, I have even the confidence to initiate my own school's exchange visit to Dieppe in France. I have already established a growing network of penfriend links; I might even embark upon 'Sur le Pont…'!!!

All this and more contribute to make my chosen subject a living exciting experience and it is without reserve thanks to my own school memories that I feel confident enough to undertake these activities.

The wheel seems to be turning full circle. As I look forward with eagerness to the future, I feel that I move closer to the High School with the passing years.

Ann P. Wood (1963–70)

In December 1972 Mr Brooke, the County Education Officer, asked Miss Butler to take over the supervision of probationary teachers from Mr Howarth, the County Inspector of Secondary Schools in Worcestershire, in order to free him for the rest of the school year to devote more time to the reorganisation schemes for the new county of Hereford and Worcester. Thus, Miss Butler was retiring in name only – there would be plenty of work to keep her busy…

Meanwhile, a new, certainly more physically robust headmistress for SGHS was waiting in the wings.

Notes

1. *Pear Tree* Summer Term 1976, pp. 6-7 (OGA Archives)
2. Ministry of Education Reports 1950–1 Stourbridge High School (Ref. BA 10838/51(x) 43/3432 Worcs. County Record Office)
3. *Pear Tree* Spring Term 1958, pp. 5-6 (OGA Archives)
4. *Pear Tree* Spring Term 1958, p. 8 (OGA Archives)

Chapter Five
Stourbridge Girls' High School and Dr Beal (1973–6)

Dr Mavis Beal.

Dr Mavis Beal took up her appointment as headmistress of SGHS in 1973. Looking at her dates of headship it is easy to ascertain that she did not stay long, the reasons for this being revealed later. She lived at Worcester, not Stourbridge as had her predecessors.

One might think, therefore, that Dr Beal would have been tempted to coast along during her three years at SGHS. Not a bit of it. During her short era as headmistress Dr Beal instigated many changes and innovations in the school and appears to have taken a very real interest in everyone and everything. A much more robust figure than Miss Butler physically, she certainly made her presence known in her three years at the helm. The school photograph 1975 (probably the very last one for SGHS) gives an indication of the increased number of girls and staff members, particularly of male teachers, compared with earlier photographs.

One change during Dr Beal's first year (which may not be attributable to her) was yet another variation in the school magazine in shape and cover although the pear tree is still discernible. Those for 1973, 1974 and 1975 were in a light tan colour and 1976 a light grey-blue.

The 1973 magazine (p. 3) wished Miss Butler a long and happy retirement, thanked her for her gift to the school of a teak garden seat, whilst at the same time welcoming Dr Beal whose 'efficient administration' enabled the change-over to run smoothly. There seems little doubt that Dr Beal believed in delegation, for during her first year with SGHS a second deputy head was appointed – this being Miss Anne Spencer, who was an old girl of the school and taught French.

The school secretary (Mrs Craddock),

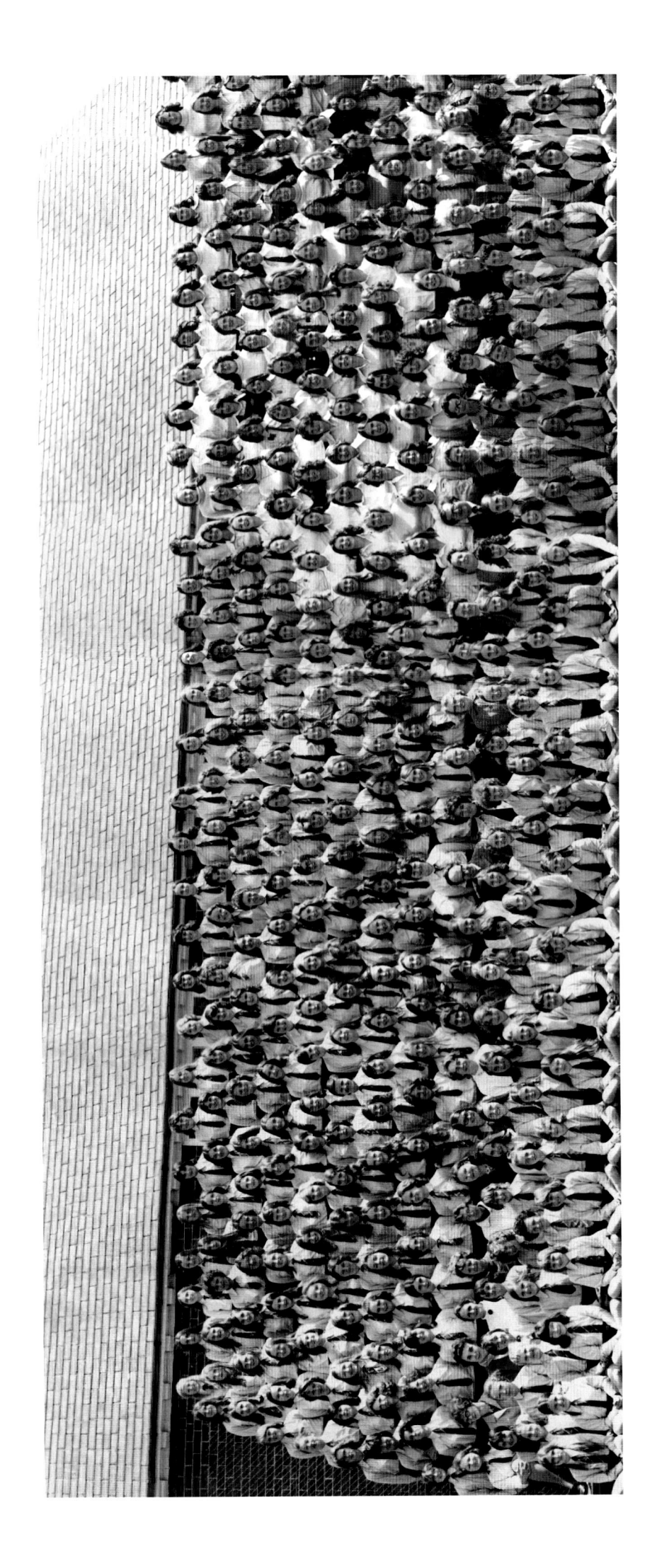

Part of SGHS school photograph 1975.

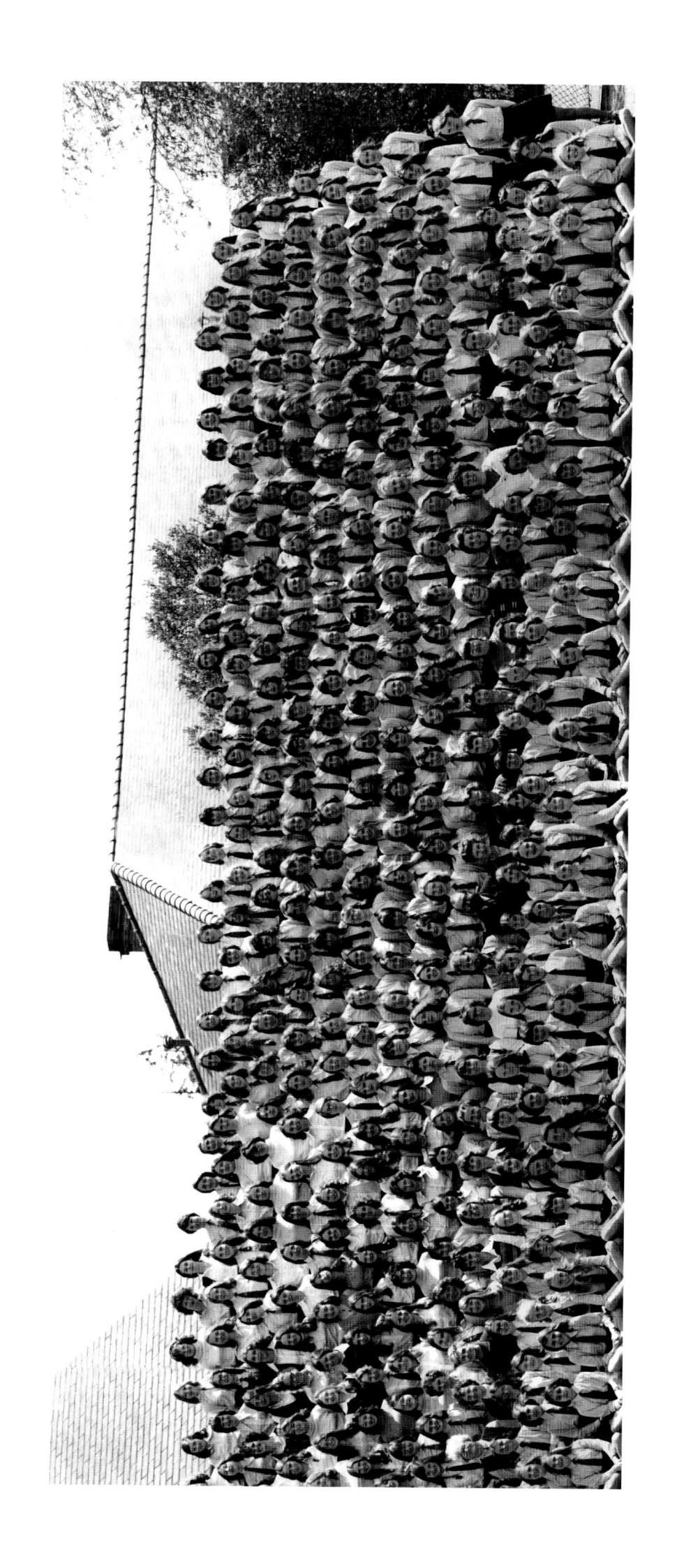

SGHS photograph 1975 (senior girls now not wearing ties!), the staff alone taking up nearly a whole row. Dr Beal on extreme left of row of staff.

New cover for **Pear Tree** *magazine, 1973–6.*

known to many of us from earlier years, had been asked to stay on to aid Dr Beal during her first term. Mrs Craddock could probably have run the administrative side of the school more or less single-handed for she had many years of experience. She postponed her retirement until November 1973 and was then duly presented with some china as a token of the school's gratitude for her extremely hard and much appreciated work.

In addition to saying 'goodbye' to Mrs Craddock the school was also losing Mrs Drane, Mr Cameron, Mr Bendall and Miss Wells, all of whom were retiring, and Mrs Joachim, who was returning to university to take a higher degree. Miss Tolley and Miss Pritchard paid tribute to Mrs Drane (who I remember with great affection in my first year at SGHS in 1953 and who nurtured my love for English Literature and, from time to time, gave us amusing anecdotes about her little boy Timothy).

Mrs Drane

Mrs Drane first joined the Staff on a part-time basis, and after almost twenty years of full-time teaching she will be retiring at the end of the Summer Term. Although she has taught both English and Latin, the greater part of her work has been in the English Department.

Her experience as a teacher and her interest in and concern for all her pupils, whatever their ability in her subject, have benefited generations of girls ranging from First Years to VIth Upper. She combines fastidious scholarship and a lively erudition with the ability to communicate her own love of literature, and her infectious enthusiasm for it.

Mrs Drane has a great interest in drama and oral work, sharing her enjoyment with every form she has taught. She has always been willing to accompany groups on theatre visits to Stratford, Birmingham and Ludlow, and has also been active in helping to provide Speech Day entertainments, which have been appreciated by everyone present.

As a member of the English Department she will be much missed. Her good-humoured, untiring help in the Bookroom has been invaluable, especially in the organisation near the end of the Summer Term, when she has inspired teams of girls to cope with the influx of all the School's English text-books and to check them. In Departmental business her helpful suggestions have always been stimulating.

Mrs Drane has been a form-mistress of girls in every year from First Years to Fifth Years, and in this capacity she has combined meticulous efficiency with a concern for the welfare of the girls at all stages, even when she has been their form-mistress only on a temporary basis. By her interested patience and guidance in her relationships with the girls she has shown the value both of the individual and of the community.

Mrs Drane will be much missed by the Staff as a whole, particularly for her wisdom, humour and penetrating comments. We wish her every happiness in her retirement, and hope that she will often visit us in the future.

M. J. T., J. M. P.

There was also a tribute to Mr Cameron:

Mr Cameron

At the end of this term, Mr Cameron is leaving the school to begin a well-earned retirement. He will be missed both in the staff-room, where his interest in school affairs and his entertaining conversation will not easily be replaced, and in the school where he has made untiring efforts, in both his teaching of Latin and his general Sixth Form work, to impart to his pupils his own appreciation of the need for careful thought and accurate work. Mr Cameron leaves with our gratitude for all that he has done and with our best wishes for a long and happy retirement.

C. H.

Mrs Torode had been appointed head of the Social and Moral Studies Department (an impressive title) at the new Waverley High School to be opened in September 1973.

The school was pleased to welcome some new members of staff – Mrs Bacon, who had taught in Worthing and in Bangkok; Mrs Bartlett from Dudley Girls' High School; Mrs Buck who had taught at St Bernadette's Comprehensive School, Bristol, and Miss Shafee to teach PE, who had trained at the I.M. Marsh college of Physical Education.

There was also news of old members of staff. Mrs Adams had had a serious operation at the time of the hospital workers' dispute and had had to be removed from Stourbridge to Wolverhampton as one hospital was put out of action. However, she was now at home and convalescing.

Miss Banner, now head of the French Department at Folkestone Grammar School for Girls had spent the spring term in Paris in a teaching exchange post. Mrs Hewis, in her capacity as president of the Stourbridge Soroptimist Club, was to be a delegate at the 41st International Conference to be held in August. During her journey she would have travelled round the world in 25 days!

Mrs Johnstone had decided to return to teaching as her youngest child had started school and had a post to teach Classics at Clayton Hall Grammar School, Newcastle-under-Lyme. Miss Sneyd, who until then had been 'going strong', had had an operation for which she had been waiting for some time and because of this had been unable to attend the staff reunion dinner held in July on Miss Butler's retirement.

The magazine was packed again with many poems, articles and artwork and even a crossword puzzle of teachers' names by three members of VI LP, Karen Adey, Catherine Brown and Wendy Slingsby, with the answers provided upside down at the back as one would expect.

The Sixth Form Common Room was continuing to be a very useful place to be for lunch hours and discussion but it seemed that a few users were proving to be untidy and careless and were reprimanded by the committee members!

Three of the ten girls studying Spanish went on a course in Spain for two weeks, spending some time in Madrid. Four girls spent a week in the Corbett Hospital, visiting wards and other departments, playing with children on the Children's Wards and generally getting a clear insight into the hectic and busy life of a hospital.

The school wind quintet had a busy season, playing in a concert in St Mary's Church, Kidderminster which had been organised by the headmistress of Kidderminster High School. The quintet was also to take part in the Cheltenham Music Festival and (with other members of the VI Upper music group) play in a concert in the parish church of Clifton-on-Teme organised by the headmaster of the local

Some of the VI Upper musicians: Hilary Bloor, Deborah Mitchell, Rosemary Wassell, Ruth Hopkins, Amanda Stockley.

school – thus spreading its wings and skills far afield.

On the sports side badminton had become extremely popular and there was a constant queue for use of the court during lunch hours. Badminton was also being played competitively against other schools.

With the publication of the 1974 *Pear Tree* magazine came news and information about some of Dr Beal's initial changes to the school. Apparently she had altered the whole timetable and some extra subjects had been added. School now began earlier and the lunch break shortened. On three days of the week school finished earlier, the extra 'missed' lessons being fitted into the other two days. A cafeteria system had been introduced to try to speed the serving of lunches which had proved quite successful, although queuing had been rather a cold business during the winter.

One of the most outstanding events of the school year had apparently been the production of *HMS Pinafore* performed jointly with the boys of the Grammar School, and Mrs Lefrere and Mrs Best were thanked profusely for their hard work in connection with this production. (SGHS had come a long way from its first joint venture with KEGS, *The Teahouse of the August Moon* in 1957!)

Another enjoyable social occasion was the school dance which took place in the hall, decorated with posters, silver foil stars and coloured disco lights. (No alcohol was allowed or sold but other refreshments were available!) The dance was a huge success by all accounts and many people helped to clear up any mess so that the hall was ready for school assembly the next day. The girls particularly appreciated the co-operation of Dr Beal and other members of staff over this very enjoyable social occasion and the good news was that, as was announced the next day, £50 from the proceeds of the dance had been paid over to the fund for senior citizens' activities organised by the school.

There were some staff changes. In place of Mrs Drane, Mrs Lefrere had come into the English Department and it seems that her lively teaching and enthusiasm for drama were very refreshing. As well as being a major help in *Pinafore* she formed a Junior Dramatic Club and reintroduced the Joint Play-reading Group for the Sixth Form and KEGS Sixth Form which had appeared to have fallen by the wayside.

Miss Sheppard and Miss Wells paid tribute

to Mrs Lee who was leaving the French Department although still staying in Stourbridge with a parent's connection to the school. In her place came Mrs Coghlan, another old girl of SGHS who had settled in very quickly, probably for this reason. Miss Wells had come back to teach French for a while to help out, which she would most certainly have enjoyed, given her long connection as head of French.

Mrs Lee

Mrs Lee joined the staff in July 1968, to give part-time help with the teaching of French. We have indeed been fortunate to have her with us and are equally sorry to lose her.

As a native of France – her parents are still living there, and with her family Mrs Lee returns to them every summer – and with high academic qualifications, she has given inestimable help, not only to the girls who have been lucky enough to be taught by her, but also to all the staff in the French Department. We could always fall back on her first-hand knowledge of French life, language and literature in other words, 'the real thing'.

We have enjoyed her happy, vivid personality. She always brought in with her something indefinably French whenever she appeared in the staffroom. Her keenness to share in the routine work of the department as well as in out-of-classroom activities and her help with oral work, especially preparation for the verse-speaking and prose-reading competitions of the Anglo-French Society, held at Birmingham University, have been invaluable.

Having three children of her own – all of them, (lucky people!) bilingual – Mrs Lee has a sympathetic understanding of young folk and their problems, but she also expects a high standard.

We are glad that she will still be in Stourbridge and we greatly appreciate her offer to help in any way we may need, particularly with tape-recordings. She will still be part of the school as a parent and we hope that she will always feel she belongs to the French department as a former colleague and as a friend, and will come to see us.

We wish her good health and happiness and thank her most heartily for all that she has done for the school in the five and a half years she has been with us.

E. M. W.

Mrs O'Keefe and Mrs Woodend also joined the staff, the former to be in charge of Latin and the latter to teach Biology. There now appeared to be so many more married members of staff, presumably juggling marriage and children with their careers and who, perhaps, 'lightened' the atmosphere in the school bringing in new, fresh ideas and a slightly more relaxed working relationship with the girls. This is not of course to say that their teaching was any the less effective!

The Parents' Association had a busy year, both fund-raising and socially but it was regretted that their numbers were only about 150 – not so high as might have been expected for a school of over 600 pupils. They were hoping to help with the curtaining and redecoration of the hall, the protection of the swimming pool and the provision of a delivery door for the Chemistry lab prep. room. They were also involved with the transport difficulties which some pupils had been experiencing.

The 'Kinver coach' had long been established to bring in girls from outlying areas (before and during my time at SGHS) but it seemed that girls travelling in from Hagley were experiencing inconvenience in the mornings. It was hoped that a private arrangement might be reached with a local coach company to ease this problem.

The Old Girls' Association had a very varied social programme and a photograph at their annual dinner shows Dr Beal and Miss Butler both in attendance with Dr Beal as president and Miss Butler as honorary vice-president.

There was very little mention again of the

OGA Annual Dinner at Old White Horse Inn, Stourbridge, April 1973.
L to r: Mrs P. Cook; Mrs K. Parkes; Dr M. Beal; Miss Butler; Mrs P. Johnson.

school Houses, Stuart, Tudor, Windsor, York, Lancaster and Kent. It therefore came as no surprise that Dr Beal 'seized the bull by the horns' and completely rethought the system. Her changes were generally received with enthusiasm according to the editors of the 1975 *Pear Tree*.

The old system of six houses was reduced to four and girls were redistributed amongst them (similar to the days when we old girls were redistributed amongst six houses) but *this* time to a reduced number of houses. This seems a little strange when the reason to increase the number of houses by adding Kent and Lancaster was to give *more* girls a chance to participate in teams, etc.

The reason given for having four houses was that it would hopefully achieve a more competitive spirit. Perhaps the old system had had its day and girls no longer bothered too much about which was top House. Results were encouraging in that girls seemed willing to support the new Houses – perhaps it was something to do with their warlike names! The four Houses were Viking, Dane, Norman and Saxon, and apparently there had been a competition at the beginning of the year throughout the school to name them. Dane House captains, Christine Forsyth and Karen Johnson, reported that there was a much better 'House spirit' which was the result of regular meetings with form representatives and monthly House prayers which had improved communications. The new system was also thought to give opportunities for those without sporting talent to contribute to House activities, for they were in competition over art and literature, chess, soft toy-making, egg-decorating and gardening to mention but a few such activities.

Many members of staff were leaving at this time, perhaps forewarned by Dudley Education's proposals for the reorganisation of secondary education in Stourbridge. Following local government reorganisation Stourbridge now came under the auspices of Dudley (from 1974) instead of Worcestershire, a change much mourned by many Stourbridge residents.

Miss Butter was leaving to take up a teaching post at the independent Alice Ottley School, Worcester. Mrs Coghlan was going to London; Mrs Farmer would be giving up class teaching in Music at the end of term, but would continue with instrumental teaching. Mrs Hayes would leave in July to join the staff of the Bulmershe School, Reading and Mrs Hayward had been on a course in Birmingham, studying for the Diploma in Art Education. Her place had been taken by Mrs Steveni. Mrs Lefrere would also leave in July to move to Milton Keynes, joining the staff of Ousedale School, Newport Pagnell. Miss Scarratt would leave in July to take charge of French at Chorley Wood College for Girls in Hertfordshire, a residential grammar school for the visually handicapped.

The Parents' Association, too, had a sombre note to its article in the 1975 magazine. Their committee had invited the Director of Education for Dudley to address parents about their plans for reorganisation of secondary education and a well-attended meeting indicated the unease of many parents about their children's future. This initiative taken by the Association bore fruit in two further meetings which resulted in the formation of SPACE, an inter-school action group of parents and other interested people dedicated to fight for a better system than that proposed by the Education Committee.

For their first social event of the year they watched a film *What Did You Learn at School Today?*, a documentary featuring a highly favoured comprehensive school. Although it had a sparse attendance, the film nevertheless provoked a lively discussion of educational aims and methods and the teachers present were both flattered and awed to learn that one parent expected of them nothing less than perfection!

We move on to the school year 1975–6, a dramatic one to say the least. The mood is set by this extract from Miss Butler's article in the 1976 *Pear Tree,* the last and final edition for SGHS.

> When I retired in 1972, we were prepared for coming changes, but we still did not know our fate. In January, 1975, exactly twenty-five years after I had received the mandate to expand the VIth Form, the reorganisation plan was published. The VIth form, in spite of its six-fold increase in size, was to be taken away, and the changes proposed for the rest of the school were so radical that the school in its present form would no longer exist. We are told to believe that the changes are for the benefit of the girls. I wonder how many of their parents would agree? Might they not think that the real reasons for the changes are purely political, and that the present plan happens to be administratively expedient?
>
> However, I do not want the account of the last twenty-five years to end on a carping note. Naturally we deplore the destruction of the High School in its full vigour, as we deplore the similar fate of schools all over the country, including so many old foundation schools; but there are some things which cannot be wiped out. Here, we have reason to be thankful for past successes, whether academic, or in the sphere of music, sport, or social service, and for the sense of achievement they have brought to both staff and girls. We can be thankful too, for the hard work, co-operation, and loyalty of generations of staff and girls, whether they were the most senior members of staff, or the youngest first-form girls. Finally, we can be thankful for something the school has always enjoyed, the easy, friendly relationships of staff and girls. Our hope for the new school community, as it gradually evolves its pattern of life, is that it may be equally fortunate.
>
> D. A. Butler (1950–72)

So the 'worst' in Miss Butler's and no doubt Dr Beal's and some members of SGHS staff's view was to happen. From September 1976 SGHS was to join Lye Secondary School to become a co-educational 11–16 comprehensive school with a new name and identity. There would, of course, be no 11-plus examination for entry into such a school. Boys were to be admitted and the girls who *would* have gone into the sixth forms were to attend a newly formed Sixth Form College which would be housed in the King Edward's Grammar School buildings in Lower High Street, Stourbridge.

Although there had been many rumours about the future of the High School it must have been a shock to all those connected to SGHS to hear officially of its 'fate'. Dr Beal, who had left her post as headmistress of Weston-Super-Mare High School when it became comprehensive and had integrated quickly into the role of headmistress of SGHS was literally 'back to square one'. She lost no time in procuring another post and by January 1976 had left SGHS to become headmistress of Torquay Girls' Grammar School which had no plans to go comprehensive. Miss Wylde wrote a tribute:

Staff News

Dr Beal

At my first meeting with Dr Beal, in the term preceding her transfer to Stourbridge, two things were immediately apparent to me: that the powers that be had selected for us another outstanding Head, and that here was someone with whom it would surely be a joy to work. Both impressions were to be amply fulfilled during the next three and a half years. Although her headship was to prove a relatively short one, much was accomplished in the course of it. She took over a school which was happy, successful, with high standards in academic and other spheres, and under her leadership it has gone from strength to strength. Successes too numerous to record here have come its way, although mention must be made of the ever-increasing academic achievements, impressive by any standard, during her years as Head.

Dr Beal made a distinctive contribution to the development of the school in terms of ideas, vitality, enthusiasm and scholarship. Her capability as an administrator ensured its smooth running, while her emphasis on rationalisation, staff participation and broadening of curricular bases led to a re-thinking of some of our aims and objectives and a re-structuring of some aspects of internal policy. There were contributions of other kinds too!

Her spontaneous and infectious wit enlivened many a staff meeting, and not least among her diverse abilities was her skill in coping with the vagaries of the automatic bell, liable in its early days to sudden and inexplicable fits of pique. On such occasions one would find her, screwdriver in hand, not merely contemplating its mysteries but fearlessly grappling with its interior mechanism – almost always, as those who knew her would expect, with spectacular success!

At a time of change in the school's history Dr Beal showed a genuine care for both staff and pupils, and handed over to her successor a school in good heart despite uncertainties about the future. She carried our warmest good wishes with her on her return to the South-West, and we trust that life at Torquay Girls' Grammar School is proving as congenial and rewarding as we hope she found her years with us.

S. W.

Dr Beal, in her last Speech Day Report for SGHS, wrote as follows:

> I want to make a claim which I feel I am free to do for the simple reason that I have been head-mistress for only three years, and no praise I apportion the school can be interpreted as self-praise...It has been, and is, a very good school. I have been proud and fond of all the schools I have worked in as teacher and head, but I have certainly not worked in better.
>
> Of the future it is difficult to speak. It is a disappointment for the staff not to continue to work as an 11-18 school with the rewarding personal and academic relations it allows them to develop and the inherent benefit to their pupils. In the new situation, especially in this time of financial stringency, it will mean very hard work indeed to build up a school good enough to match the High School in its different way; but there is growing up a determination to do so; there is a tradition on which to build; there are professional expertise, loyalty and courage to use as tools, and so we

have every reason to hope that one day the new comprehensive school on this site will enjoy as high and as deserved a reputation as Stourbridge Girls' High School. I wish it well.

M. Beal, November 1975

This left the rest of the staff to make decisions regarding their own careers. Did they stay with the new comprehensive 11-16 school or did they apply for posts at the new Sixth Form College or elsewhere? This must have been a time of great speculation and worry, but, until September 1976, the school *was* still Stourbridge Girls' High School and with Dr Beal's rather hurried exit it needed a new head to guide it through the troubled times of radical change.

Chapter Six
Stourbridge Girls' High School and Miss Fisher (1976)

Miss B. M. Fisher, SGHS's fifth and final headmistress.

Miss Beryl Fisher was appointed as SGHS's fifth and final headmistress and took up her appointment in January 1976. She had previously been headmistress of Dudley Girls' High School (1971–5) and had in fact been a member of their staff for 20 years and was deputy head there for 12 years. Thus she came to SGHS with an excellent 'pedigree' and was described as 'calm yet energetic, approachable and efficient, and a wonderful organiser, who believed in getting to know all the girls as individuals…'[1]

She would certainly need these qualities in the forthcoming months!

There is a small tribute to her in the summer 1976 (p. 3) school magazine which bears witness to her abilities and personality:

> In January we were pleased to welcome Miss B. M. Fisher…She has so rapidly established herself as one of us that it is sometimes difficult to remember that she has been with us for only six months, and her positive attitude and good humour have already done much to smooth our transition…

(Sadly, it appears that no official school photograph was taken in 1976 with the upheaval and planning for September, so we have no record at the present time of Miss Fisher with SGHS school staff and pupils.)

Structural alterations were taking place already during the months before September 1976 as it had become evident that for a long time there would be difficulties regarding space and accommodation in the future.

Many of the staff were going to transfer to the new Sixth Form College at the end of the Summer Term 1976. Miss Wyld, deputy headmistress since 1967, was one of these. Miss Morris pays tribute to her as a teacher and colleague (*Pear Tree* 1976, p. 3):

Miss S. M. Wyld…will be greatly missed by both staff and pupils. She came to the school ten years earlier to teach German, and her teaching has over the years proved an inspiration to many of her pupils who have themselves gone on to further their studies of German language and literature. She was rapidly promoted to Sixth Form mistress, Head of the German Department and subsequently to the post she has held in recent years.

All have benefited from her good organising ability, which became apparent early in her career, and also from her sympathetic, understanding attitude which has largely contributed to her great asset – an ability to get on with people. The staff have long realised the care and scrupulous fairness with which she has arranged their various duties and have known that any problems would be dealt with promptly and considerately. The fact that the girls have always found her equally approachable and conscientious over her work has meant that the demands on her time and energy have been heavy, but these have always been met generously and without thought of self. The same applies to out-of-school meetings and activities, as members of the Old Girls' Association can testify. Success has not spoilt her unassuming nature and her sense of humour has at all times been lively and spontaneous.

Our thanks and good wishes for the future go with her to King Edward College, coupled with the assurance that she will be as successful there and make as a great a contribution to that community as she has to Stourbridge Girls' High School.

Miss Round, who had come to SGHS in 1959, later becoming head of Geography, was also transferring to the Sixth Form College. She had for some years been in charge of the library and had responsibility for A level examination arrangements and latterly for sixth-form careers advice. She had also organised numerous holiday visits abroad and had supervised the sixth form's social service work for elderly people in the district. (Miss Round became Mrs Flavell in April 1976.)

Mrs Best, who had been with SGHS since 1961, first in a part-time capacity and then from 1964 as head of the Music Department, was also taking her skills to King Edward's, Since her appointment to SGHS orchestral and instrumental music had played an increasingly important part in the life of the school, constantly expanding in scope and variety, and many girls had been encouraged to discover and develop a hitherto unsuspected talent.

Miss Morris, who joined the staff as head of Religious Studies and whose scholarship and dedication to her subject had contributed immeasurably to the growth of the department was transferring. She had been involved in almost all aspects of SGHS's life, and in particular had undertaken for some years the organisation of both O level and CSE examination arrangements. The many who had come to her for help or advice over the years had cause to appreciate her ready sympathy and pastoral concern.

Mrs Hartley, who joined the Biology Department in 1968 and had in recent years been responsible for the smooth running of the library; Mrs Goodman and Mrs Cobourne (old girl), who were appointed as part-time members of staff in 1972 and Miss Cotton, who had been a member of the French Department, would all be on their way to the Sixth Form College in September, too.

This would mean quite a mass exodus for Miss Fisher's staff and many more were retiring including Mrs Barton (Maths Department since 1966), who had never had a day's absence from school until 1976. She had taught a number of the D divisions and had a particular gift for teaching girls who found Maths difficult but at the same time was equally at home with first-class mathematicians in the A division; Miss Page, who had come to SGHS in 1968 and had immediately set about modernising the Maths Department and who had started a Maths

Club, was to retire. She had brought many new aspects of mathematics to light through fascinating puzzles, paper folding and books. It was difficult to imagine Miss Page 'retiring' in the sense of spending her days sitting in a rocking-chair knitting as she had so many interests and hobbies. Finally, Miss Tolley was going to retire at the end of the summer term. She had come as head of English in 1969, very much missed by King Edward VI Grammar School for Girls, Handsworth, where she had taught for 20 years. SGHS had hoped to keep Miss Tolley for many more years, and her decision to retire had been met with utter dismay; 'Is it selfish to be glad that at least we shall not be losing her to another School?' Many hoped that she would not be gone completely from their lives as she would only be living five minutes' walk away! Miss Pritchard, who had taught English at SGHS for well over 20 years, ended her long and heartfelt tribute to Miss Tolley with these poignant words which probably summed up the feelings of the few long-serving staff who were remaining with SGHS:[2]

> So much will have changed when we go back to school in September. While we brace ourselves to meet the many challenges that lie ahead, we shall look forlornly down the corridors for a glimpse of the familiar, reassuring presence of Miss Tolley, and realise again our loss. We shall miss her gaiety, her unconventionality; the sagacity of her judgement; the serenity with which she confronted muddle, and overcame it. We shall remember with grateful affection the kindly advice and help which she was never too busy to give, and the courage with which she rose above personal griefs putting the School first. Seven years have passed all too quickly for those of us who have been privileged to share them with you, Miss Tolley, and we shall sometimes feel very dull without you. Please come back to see us when you can – only a five minutes' walk away – and may your retirement be a very happy one.[2]

Another 'link' with the past for SGHS was gone also as there was an announcement in the school magazine that Miss Eastwood, who had been a member of the school (Music mistress) from 1920 to 1950, had died in January 1976 at Winchcombe. Sadly, there would probably be nobody in the school who remembered her.

And so Miss Fisher, with her 'positive attitude and good humour' to say nothing of her experience as a teacher, former deputy head and now headmistress, guided SGHS towards its final days.

The school magazine as usual was packed full with articles, drawings and poems, accounts of society meetings and visits and details of House awards – the Vikings, Saxons, Normans and Danes showed great competitive spirit. Sports had gone reasonably well but it was regretted that the senior hockey teams suffered greatly from the number of girls with Saturday jobs. Thanks were expressed to Miss Turner (PE), who was staying on with SGHS, for all her help and encouragement throughout the year.

The Parents' Association had presented Dr Beal with a camera when she left the school at Christmas 1975 and gave a very warm welcome to Miss Fisher at its first committee meeting in January 1976. During the last year they had funded the purchase of curtains for the hall windows and stage and in the gymnasium a junior practice beam and a springboard had been provided. New books were also purchased for the Craft and Art Departments and they were endeavouring to raise £1,000 to install stage lighting which the LEA was unable to provide.

Sadly, Mr R. H. Price, a governor of the school for many years, died in April 1976. He had been chairman of the Parents' Association at the time of the swimming pool appeal and for this project he worked indefatigably, never missing a function or a meeting.

The Old Girls' Association too had made a presentation to Dr Beal and then later welcomed Miss Fisher as their new president.

Goodbyes were said to Mrs Nightingale, part-time member of the Maths Department for five years and to Miss Stathers who had given part-time help in the History Department for two years. Mrs Buck, who, after four years in the English Department, was moving with her husband to the North; Mrs Cartwright, who had been assistant secretary for over ten years, was also leaving and Mrs Joachim was giving up her part-time post to do further research at Birmingham University.

At Christmas 1975 Mrs Bacon had left temporarily to become head of Maths at Lye Secondary School (soon to join SGHS in its new identity). Her place had been taken by Mrs Day who had come from the Grange School. Mrs Franklin was also leaving after over four years in the Chemistry Department and was replaced by Mr Zamir from Park Hall School, Solihull.

Mrs Stevens joined the staff from Altrincham Girls' Grammar School to take charge of Latin and teach some Russian (the latter being evidence of the wider range of subjects available). Dr Cotton (PhD Birmingham) came to teach French and Latin; Miss Hepburn from Holly Lodge High School, Sandwell to join the French Department and teach some German. Mrs Lewis came from Hornchurch Grammar School to assist in the English Department; Miss McLeod from St Paul's School, Brighton to teach History; Mr Adams, formerly Music Adviser for Birmingham, to give part-time help in the Music Department. Mrs Steveni came to be in charge of first-year pupils.

A great deal of 'comings and goings' for Miss Fisher to contend with! The wheels were thus in motion for a 'new' school in Junction Road. There would be a new name; motto; uniform; organisation, in keeping with the comprehensive education policy for Redhill School, for that was the name decided upon. Yes, it was to be housed in the same building as SGHS (with many additions); some of the SGHS teaching staff were staying on. There would be a number of SGHS girls continuing their education there who would have to change their allegiance to Redhill School which, of course, in time would create its own traditions and history.

July 1976 came ever nearer and with its approach, in effect, the last days of SGHS. Staff, pupils and ex-pupils looked back (in the Summer Term 1976 *Pear Tree*) at the High School in the 1970s:

Editorial

As this year's School Magazine will be the last produced by Stourbridge Girls' High School, nostalgic thoughts are aroused in us, and these are reflected in the great variety of contributions from former Headmistresses, Staff, and old girls of many generations. These contain recollections and reminiscences of their life here, and show their feeling of affection for the School, and their gratitude.

Many people will already know that the School began in 1905 in the Library buildings. Accounts of those early days show with what energy and enterprise girls and Staff coped with the vertical life imposed on them by the structure. It was in 1928 that the School moved into its present buildings, which had been long-awaited and which, as our contributors declare, were a source of pride, despite the discomforts of the open corridors in Winter.

Although, in common with other secondary schools, we lost our prep. Department in the 1940's, numbers in the School continued to grow. The Sixth Form underwent a more than four-fold increase in its original size, which led to corresponding expansions in the syllabus, and the inclusion of many stimulating new courses. Growth in size also necessitated adaptations and additions to the existing building, culminating in a large Sixth-Form Common Room and a number of Sixth-Form teaching rooms.

Most readers will be aware that from September SGHS will have joined Lye Secondary School to become a co-educational 11–16 Comprehensive with the name of 'Redhill School'. Evidence of this change-over is already apparent, particularly in the structural alterations which have begun. In spite of the obvious difficulties of working on a split-site for a time, and of sharing the building with the builders, we hope that the new School will flourish from its first day, and we wish it well for its future life.

M. J. T. and J. M. P.
[Miss Tolley and Miss Pritchard]

1974–6

The last two years at school have seen some changes and many more are likely to be seen. At the beginning of the Autumn Term, 1974, a new House system was introduced, four Houses replacing the former six. This new House system has been very successful because of greater enthusiasm shown by pupils and staff; House sport events are still popular, but speech competitions, gardening competitions and book collections have also been introduced on a House basis. House prayers too have helped to co-ordinate the various activities.

As we come to the end of the 1976 school year, we see various changes in the building structure, in preparation for the comprehensive system. It is always sad to see an era come to an end, but as we go to our various universities and colleges we shall look back with many happy memories on our seven years spent here. We hope, sincerely, that the school spirit and the school's high standards will be maintained in years to come. We wish the girls, and the little first form boys, success and happiness in their new school, hoping that their years here will be as happy as ours.

Lesley James   Head Girl
Anne Noott   )
Maureen Hanke) Deputy Head Girls

THE HIGH SCHOOL IN THE 1970s

Since I left school almost two years ago my initial feeling of exhilaration and liberation has gradually receded, but has not yet been replaced by the yearning nostalgia one is supposed to feel for school days. The time between leaving school and now I have spent partly in the 'real world' living away from home and friends and now at a college which has a deliberate policy of being liberal and progressive. These experiences have made me realise that possibly the most distinctive feature of my school life was the dominance of rules, regulations, practices to conform to – in fact discipline in its practical expression, which is not necessarily a bad thing. On entering school we were presented with a daunting list of rules varying from the colour of socks for games to prohibition of magazines, paper back books and records.

However, the oppression of discipline is associated with my early days. After what seemed years of being an intimidated and nervous young school girl, I emerged into the later school. By this time, the staff seemed to be on the whole younger and with an increase of male teachers. Teachers then seemed less concerned with wielding authority and commanding obedience and more interested in establishing a productive relationship between themselves and the pupils. This could of course be due to the natural process of growing up when one can at last be treated as a human being with valid opinions to be expressed. There was a change in goal from aiming merely to restrict personal behaviour and encourage conformism to perhaps the more laudable aim of developing inquiring minds and a genuine interest in learning. For these opportunities, I shall always be grateful.

Carmel Elwell (1967–74)

In writing such an article as this, it is difficult to avoid pompously bewailing the passage of time. However, having been 'set free' (or banished!) forever, I sometimes think that the 'bondage' of school is not undesirable! For all they may say, most people have at least some affection for 'The Slave Cave'.

As my major interest was music, I naturally remember first the many opportunities offered to me in that field. The sheer discipline (or is that word taboo nowadays?) of regular rehearsal and public performance is excellent training. The orchestras are the best of their kind for miles around, having proved themselves to be unbeatable at the Worcester Festival. The Junior Choir, too, has a good reputation. Chamber music has for a number of years been fostered at the school with a great success, and the recorder group forms a useful link between junior and senior schools.

The High School benefits from many hours of weekly tuition from peripatetic teachers. For years the Worcester Education Authority has loaned instruments to many girls who would not otherwise have learnt to play. Much of the school's musical strength lies in its enormous number of instrumentalists. Thus, progress is encouraged by means of a little healthy competition. Speaking of competitions, the school has become well known for its annual 'Grand Slam' at the Worcester Festival, followed by a triumphal concert at the end of terms. The Carol Service at St Mary's Church was another regular event.

There are numerous other ways in which one's general musical education was helped. Even the playing of hymns for assembly steeled one's nerves! It was generally through school that one joined the Worcester Youth Orchestra, often leading to those idyllic summer courses at Pershore. Singing and playing in joint opera productions with the Grammar School was great fun and valuable experience. All this was made possible by Mrs Best; with her unbounded enthusiasm, energy and encouragement she has built up the school's music to a tremendous level (with, of course, the help of Mrs Farmer, Miss Butler and Dr Beal). At least the school will disappear in a blaze of musical triumph.

The benefits derived from the High School last a lifetime. I could write volumes on my seven years there, but must conclude, hoping that the future pupils of Redhill School will strive to feel as much pride in their school as we did in ours.

Clare Hingley (1968–75)

One cannot help feeling that, naturally, for some of the pupils there was barely suppressed excitement at the changes ahead, if tinged with just a little sadness. Miss Fisher summed up the situation in the 1976 magazine (p. 9):

> I was appointed in January, 1976, just in time to be called Headmistress of Stourbridge Girls' High School, a title which I was pleased and proud to accept. I knew I was joining a school with high academic standards and which was respected and admired in the town. In the few months I have been in the school I have been able to appreciate how this has been achieved. Girls are given every encouragement to reach their potential by the enthusiasm of staff who believe in academic achievement; opportunities are provided individually and collectively to pursue a variety of interests including music, PE, languages and the theatre; service to the community and to those less fortunate is an important feature of the school; tradition is respected but not without thought for its current value.
>
> But what of the future? The name will change; the buildings will be extended, pupils – boys and girls – will increase in number; the Sixth Form will disappear. Changes are inevitable in any school, some by choice within, others by decree from outside. In our quest for the ideal school we hope we shall have 'Serenity to change what should be changed, and Wisdom to

distinguish the one from the other'. Redhill School will emerge with its own tradition, but something of Stourbridge High School is bound to influence its formation, We aim to see that it is the best that is kept.

Final plans for the changeover were not approved until the middle of the Spring Term 1976, leaving only six months to plan the intricate details of amalgamating Lye Secondary and the High School, to form an 11–16 co-educational comprehensive in line with government policy.

Staffing had to be finalised (Mr Harris and Dr Beal, respective heads, had done a lot of the 'spadework') and hard decisions made about staffing structure. Some staff faced losing sixth-form teaching, which was a great disappointment to them. Parents had to be reassured that the Upper Sixth would be properly taught and that pupils already in the school would be able to continue their studies.

Somehow, it all fell into place and Stourbridge Girls' High School girls broke up for the summer 1976 holidays for the very last time.

*****

It seems fitting to end this chapter with the words of Miss Butler, on the last day of term on 'breaking-up' day at SGHS during her era, after the final crashing chords of the hymn 'Jerusalem' on the piano had faded away:

'Goodbye, girls. Good luck!'

Past history? SGHS forgotten? We shall see!

Kate Worton, pupil of Redhill School in 1999, models SGHS uniform of the 1950s while Redhill School head girl Asha Omar wears the Redhill uniform.

Notes

1 DuMont, M. *et al.*, *Dudley Girls' High School: A portrait of a school*, Stourbridge, The Robinswood Press, 2002, p. 12
2 *Pear Tree* Summer Term 1976, pp. 3-4 (OGA Archives)

Appendix I
SGHS Old Girls' Association

One of the best and obvious ways of remembering a girls' school and schooldays, staff and fellow pupils is to form an old girls' association. There was no need to do this following 1976 to ensure that SGHS would not be forgotten as one had already been established many years previously. Stourbridge Girls' High School Old Girls' Association (OGA) has a history all of its own.

The first school magazine in 1926 made reference to former pupils, and members of staff who had married and produced offspring. The magazine also included a letter to the 'Dear Old Girls' asking for news of themselves and what they were doing. The 1928 magazine also contained news of marriages, births and, sadly, the death of Miss Harris 'after a lingering illness'. This practice probably continued in all subsequent magazines but, sadly, there is not a copy available until the 1932 edition. However, an all-important heading appeared in this one (p. 28): 'OLD GIRLS' ASSOCIATION'.

The article made reference to the fact that this Association had been revived by Miss Firth in July 1931 and that the inaugural meeting was attended by over 80 old girls of the school and a small committee was elected to draw up a constitution.

This rather suggests that there had been an OGA previous to 1931 but that it had probably ceased to exist for some reason. There seems to have been no lack of enthusiasm to re-form the Association and Miss Firth was elected first president, Miss Sneyd, treasurer and Miss Edwards, secretary. A committee of nine was duly elected (hopefully consisting of some of the old girls themselves) and three of these would retire every year.

The account of the first year of the OGA makes interesting reading and is in itself a social document of that particular era. Perhaps some or much of the message could be said to be true today in 2011!

> In February we invited every Old Girl, whose address was known, to a Social, which was a great success and led to a large increase in our membership. Since then there have been a Garden Party (the weather turned it into an indoor one), an evening trip to the Lickey Hills and a Social. Some of the Old Girls sing and play, sometimes there is community singing, always there is dancing; and we talk a great deal every time. The kitchen staff serves an excellent supper for sixpence a head.
>
> A Games Committee has been formed and is trying to arrange matches in tennis, netball and hockey. The great difficulty is a practice ground. If anyone can help us with this, in any way at all, we shall be most grateful.
>
> In all our meetings, we try to meet the wishes of the majority. For this reason we are arranging a Dance at the end of the term. If it is successful, we hope it will be an annual event.

> The Association has received a blow in the resignation of Miss Firth, while it is still in its first stages. Fortunately it has a solid foundation in the number of members. Any Old Girl of the School is eligible to join who has spent one year there. The subscription is 2/6 for the current year and this covers a copy of the School Magazine. The only addition is sixpence for supper at the Socials. We send an appeal to girls who will leave in the near future and to all Old Girls. The School has done much for you. It has given you a chance in life. Do not take all and give nothing in return. By joining the Association you strengthen the School, and pay back a little of the great debt you owe to it. Please do not forget.
>
> D. Edwards

The 1933 magazine reported that a very successful year had been had by the OGA with numbers increasing to 134 and that the financial position was sound! Miss Dale had been welcomed, rather nervously, as their new president (Miss Firth having retired) but she had taken such an interest in their 'doings' that they felt as if she had been their president for a long time.

The major event for that year had been a concert given in February in aid of the memorial windows to Miss Turner and Miss Harris. It seemed that nobody would ever forget the vast audience that filled the hall.

Subsequent magazines describe the OGA socials and garden parties, outings, for example to Stourport with a boating trip; drill classes and dances in the Carlisle Hall, Stourbridge.

Miss Edwards resigned the secretaryship in the 1935 magazine as she felt it would be good to have a different person and there were many other demands on her time. For that winter, the OGA would meet in the library on the second Wednesday in each month and they were 'attempting something more ambitious in the way of refreshments' at a Big Club Night 'much helped by Miss Dale's offer of her room and gas ring'. Members were requested not to touch her table and to respect the new carpet! Miss Edwards was determined, once a new secretary had been found, to obtain a piano for the library. She also remarked how good it was to welcome very 'new' old girls who had only recently left SGHS – 'girls who are just beginning to face the world'.

Theatre parties were very popular, cards, whist drives and table tennis tournaments, in addition to talks such as 'the Modern and best Way of Feathering a Fowl'. The girls of the Sixth and Upper Fifth Forms were invited to evening parties in the hopes that they would be attracted to joining the OGA when they had left school.

Not perhaps surprisingly in 1940 it was decided that, owing to the difficulties of holding meetings at school in the black-out, all activities would be suspended until the end of the war when a general meeting would be held to decide on the future of the Association. The balance in the bank was invested in National Savings Certificates.

The 1948 *Pear Tree* mentioned that during the war years the Old Girls' netball team had been playing under the title of 'Stourbridge Ladies' and had managed to play many matches in spite of difficulties regarding a 'home' court. They had managed by using the Grange School and eventually those of SGHS and the store-room attached to the gym for changing – extremely inconvenient for visitors but made the best of things.

The 1949 magazine gave numerous details about old girls but nothing about the OGA and then at long last it seemed that the Association had re-formed with a Christmas meeting. A hockey match had been played between the Old Girls and the school and there was tea, provided by the British Restaurant, followed by a beetle drive. There was an AGM and election of committee members and a proposal for a dinner in the New Year. The OGA was up and running again after the dark days of war!

The dinner was held in the January of 1950 at the Bell Hotel, Stourbridge and, after a delightful meal, entertainment was provided by members of the Association and by Form VI Upper. What a pity no photographs seem to have survived. At the AGM on Friday 14 July an American tennis tournament was held, followed by welcoming Miss D. A. Butler as the new president of the Association, Miss Dale having retired. Thus began a long association between Miss Butler and the OGA.

January 1951 saw the next dinner held at the White Horse Inn, Stourbridge and due to inclement weather neither Miss Butler nor Miss Dale was able to attend. The Association was therefore pleased to welcome Miss Sneyd to the chair. (Many of us will perhaps remember that Miss Sneyd lived quite near to the White Horse Inn and it's very likely that she donned galoshes and made her way on foot to the venue!)

The White Horse continued to be the venue for OGA dinners, dances and supper parties. Learning of Miss Dromgoole's serious illness the committee organised the sending of Elizabeth Goudge's book *And God so loved the World* to her, hoping that it would while away a few weary hours.

Sadly, the 1954 *Pear Tree* reported on the death of Miss Dromgoole and the OGA sent a letter of sympathy to Miss Wells saying that many of them would miss her as an old friend as well as a teacher.

In place of the Annual Dinner in 1953 a New Year Party was held in the school hall. It had originally been intended to hold it at the Baths' assembly rooms but there was such a good response to the invitation from Forms V Uppers and VI that the hall had to be used. The Music Group provided songs and piano solos and the Drama Group presented a mock pantomime called *Dick Riding Boots and His Flea*! Until the 1960 *Pear Tree* there is much news of the Old Girls themselves but no mention of the actual Association. However in this particular magazine there was an announcement that Miss Pat Wilkes became chairman. Although a dance had been organised in the school hall on 21 March 1959 and the committee had gone to a lot of trouble to decorate the hall and provide a dance band and delicious refreshments, the response from members was below par. A very enjoyable coffee party was held in the library in the November but it was disappointing that so few of the 1959 leavers had joined the OGA for it was felt that it was on new recruits that the life of the Association depended.

The dinner in March 1960 was held at the Talbot Hotel, Stourbridge and over 60 members were present. Miss Butler presided, supported by the chairman and Mrs Lunt, chairman of the Governors. Mrs Powell gave a very interesting account of her journey to East Berlin.

The Spring Term 1962 magazine reported that the OGA had continued its activities that year with one meeting each term and that the annual dinner was held again at the Talbot Hotel with Miss Sneyd being welcomed back for the occasion.

There was a coffee evening on 11 October when two new vice-presidents, the Mayoress Mrs Aston and Miss Moody (governor) were welcome visitors. An elegant 'Mannequin Parade' was held presented by Mrs Wooldridge of 'Margaret'. New members to the OGA would be very welcome!

At the 1962 AGM a very interesting exhibition of 'Sixty Years of Stourbridge High School' was presented, material being collected by Miss Butler and arranged by Miss Sheppard and senior girls in the school hall. One wonders whether in some cupboard or drawer there are some photographs of this event!

The annual dinner was attended by 47 members (numbers seemed to have dropped slightly) with the head girl and her deputy of SGHS representing the school. However, the 1964 *Pear Tree* reported that the many efforts of the OGA committee had been finally rewarded by a greater response to the meetings for 1963 to 1964. A cut glass vase was sent to Mrs Craddock (school secretary) in appreciation of all she had done for the Association. A bottle stall was held at the school fête in July and a dinner, held at the Talbot Hotel, was attended by 66 members. Miss Moody proposed a toast to the 'guests' and also to 'absent friends', and Miss Sneyd was called upon 'at the eleventh hour to reply to this toast, and her lively and spontaneous speech was warmly received by all present'.

Later in the year there were talks, for example Miss Scriven told of her stay in Canada where she taught at the Sir Winston Churchill High School in Vancouver, and Miss Heaton related some of her experiences during a students' exchange visit to America. These talks were illustrated with a film and colour slides.

To raise money for the swimming pool fund the OGA arranged a knitwear parade at the Old White Horse Inn where 'Ann Young' of New Road, Stourbridge presented a delightful display of Spring Fashions in Tailored Knitwear modelled, chiefly, by old girls of the school! It was estimated that about 180 old girls and their friends attended this gathering and the latest arrivals had to carry their own chairs into the room used, so it was a very popular event!

Sadly, it appeared that numbers of members of the OGA were dropping steadily and that, due to the lack of support the election of a new vice-chairman following the resignation of Mrs J. Roberts had to be postponed until a later meeting in the year 1965–6. However, there is little doubt that the people who *did* attend meetings thoroughly enjoyed them.

The report of the 1966–7 OGA year made a profound statement, in that regret was expressed by Mrs Zihni (née Moody), Mrs Wood and the president Miss Butler at the impending 'destruction' of SGHS as such, and its absorption into the system of comprehensive education.

However, on the brighter side, a fashion parade was organised by Flair Fashions to help raise money for the swimming pool with colourful and attractive clothes covering a wide range of price, age and size. An added interest was that four members of Stourbridge Ciné Society came along to shoot a film of the parade and at a future meeting would show the film to members.

At a later meeting Mrs Lunt (chairman of the Governors) was presented with a turquoise Pyrenean wool stole to mark the OGA's gratitude for her interest in the school and her support of the Old Girls' functions, on the occasion of her retirement.

The year 1967–8 saw many and varied meetings for OGA, for example hat-making, demonstrations of floral art and a talk by Mr Jack Downing on Gilbert and Sullivan, the latter tracing 'the course of their brilliant partnership in his own inimitable style'. At the annual dinner at the Old White Horse Inn profound loss was expressed at the death of Mrs Lunt, especially so soon after her retirement.

The year 1968–9 was successful for the Association with a varied programme of meetings well attended, particularly now it had become policy to invite non-members to meetings at the fee of 1s per head!

Interestingly, the last meeting before the summer interval took the form of a talk by a representative of 'Prana Wholefoods' – the wide range of health foods available in their shops and the advantages of these in relation to the functioning of a healthy body!

A new venture for the OGA in the year 1969–70 was to send, for the first time in its history, Christmas greetings cards to all members of the Association. It was hoped to continue this new idea in the future.

The New Year coffee evening was held at Stourbridge Junior Library to welcome recent school-leavers and to introduce them to the Association and its activities. In March, Mr T. H. Jarrett gave an entertaining demonstration on 'Home Wine Making' and the members tried out samples of his own sweet sherry, which was much appreciated. It was a *very* successful meeting!

The year 1972 saw the retirement of Miss Butler from SGHS and she therefore relinquished the office of president of OGA but continued to be very involved in the Association.

The year 1973–4 was a successful year for the Association with a varied programme of meetings and excellent support from members and friends. One new venture was a supper party at the Gallery Restaurant, Wollaston with the guest speaker Miss Nellie Bowater who captivated her audience with Black Country monologues.

At a meeting in November 1974 Mrs Inga Bulman, a former head girl (née Perrins), addressed the Association on 'The Social Problems in the West Midlands' which gave rise to lively discussion and opinions. A bring-and-buy sale was held at the home of Mrs Jeavons-Fellows and the proceeds of £35 were put towards buying a new electric clock for the school hall. Mr Michael Carless (husband of Susan née Plimmer) gave an interesting talk on 'Law and the Magistrates' Court'.

And so to 1976 – the last year of the 'life' of SGHS, but this certainly did *not* mean the end of the OGA. As an Association it was thriving, with well-attended meetings, social evening and outings and the Old Girls were going to continue to meet in the future. There was a presentation to Dr Beal before she left for Torquay Girls' Grammar School and at the January 1976 meeting Miss Beryl Fisher, the new head of SGHS in its final months and then of Redhill Comprehensive School, was welcomed as the OGA's new President – an association which has lasted to this day. In fact, one might say that an OGA was more necessary than ever now that SGHS was in danger of being relegated to the history books of Stourbridge (or not).

The year 1976 marked the last and final edition of the *Pear Tree* magazine, but Miss Butler rose to the occasion and it is she whom we have to thank for her many newsletters containing news of SGHS old girls and mistresses. It seemed that Miss Butler was determined that the High School was not going to be forgotten easily!

From 1977 Miss Butler compiled the News-sheets and -letters which mainly gave information regarding careers, marriages, births of offspring (and deaths) of the Old Girls in the UK and abroad. They were distributed at the OGA meetings which continued to be held on Wednesday evenings each month at Redhill School with the kind permission of Miss Fisher and subsequent heads.

The 1980 Newsletter was something of a 'special' for, on Saturday 17 May of that year a reunion to celebrate the 75th anniversary of the founding of the school was organised. It seems that Miss Butler and other retired members of staff threw themselves whole-heartedly into this occasion in addition to the OGA committee and members. There was still a 'ring' of authority in Miss Butler's Foreword – one could easily imagine her making such an announcement as headmistress from her table on the platform in the assembly hall!

FOREWORD

When I sent the preliminary notice asking for contributions for our 75th Anniversary Newsletter, I hoped to receive more than in 1977, but I certainly did not anticipate the overwhelming response which followed. Many of you kindly sent news of friends. The age range of people mentioned is from 18 to 80-plus, and they live in all parts of the world. Their occupations and activities vary from editing a journal which deals with the exploits of the rich and famous in Palm Beach, to advising on the exploration for North Sea oil and being flown by helicopter to visit the rig which was ultimately constructed, to all the usual (and often unusual) professions, and tasks, nearer home.

For the number and variety of contributions, I have to thank all of you who took the trouble to send them, and the members of staff who have collated news for me, Mr Firman, Mrs Hadley, Miss Sheppard and Miss Tolley; my thanks are also due to Miss Tolley for reading some of the proofs. Our special thanks go to members of the OGA, to Jill George (née Perry) who has typed all the script, to Margaret Acty (née Darby Rhodes) who designed the cover, and to other members of the Committee for a spending team effort in putting together the sheets after duplication. We thank Miss Fisher for allowing us to use school equipment, Mr Ryan, Editor of the *County Express*, and finally, Mark & Moody's who once again have agreed to sell the Newsletter.

D. A. Butler

Non sibi sed omnibus?

It was a marvellous occasion – I attended with my old classmate Janet Bett (née Homer), my mother, two sisters and our school friend Irene Evans (née Lear). We were not surprised to find Miss Butler in the vestibule waiting to greet people and, of course, she remembered who we were!

I was in trouble with her for leaving my ticket in the car – 'You were told to bring it with you,' she said sternly. I realised it would be no use trying to explain that it had been a stressful day organising care for my two-year-old daughter; that the train I was meeting Janet from (travelling from the south) was not the one she had intended – she had accidentally caught one that had headed towards Crewe rather than Birmingham. I almost expected to hear 'Take a B order mark'. In one minute I was back to being a naughty schoolgirl in the 1950s, regardless of the fact that I was married, with a child of my own, and had held down several responsible jobs!

Many other former members of staff came along and many will recognise faces on the photograph, looking a little older perhaps, but it was very easy to slip back into the role of pupil and teacher again when talking to them. There were displays of memorabilia; groups were divided into 'school years' in the corners of the hall and there was opportunity to go round the school buildings to see the changes that had been made and of course there were refreshments available.

Annual dinners, outings, AGMs, visiting speakers, Christmas parties and many, many more items were on the OGA programmes and continue so to this day.

Fortunately, there began to be photographic records of many of these occasions thanks to the committee members and the presence of the local newspaper reporters, and the following represent a medley of Old Girl gatherings over the years. People are not always named, nor events dated, but many of us will recognise ourselves, our friends, former members of staff and the venues!

Former staff members appeared to enjoy

Former members of staff at 75th SGHS Reunion, Saturday 17 May 1980.

Some of the Old Girls (Miss Fisher centre) with guest speaker Phil Drabble, 1981.

Some of the Old Girls meet up, 1983, ten years after their O levels.

these events every bit as much as the 'Old Girls' themselves, particularly at the Annual Dinners and Miss Sneyd was called upon on one occasion to be the visiting speaker when she reminisced about the early days of SGSS and SGHS.

Miss Fisher never seemed to lose sight of the fact that she had been the final headmistress for SGHS, albeit briefly. She attended many of the OGA meetings and events and has remained an enthusiastic member to this very day. Very appropriately she was presented with gifts by the OGA when she retired from her position as headmistress of Redhill School in 1983.

Sad news came in that Miss Anne Spencer (deputy head to Miss Fisher) and an 'old girl' of SGHS had died. She had returned to SGHS as a member of the French staff and had remained on the staff of Redhill School. Anne had always linked herself in with the OGA and will be remembered by many 'old girls' as a pupil and teacher.

Stourbridge High School Old Girls' Association held their annual dinner which was attended by over 80 members. Guests included Mr and Mrs C. T. Lacey and Miss Barbara Hadley. The chairman Mrs Anne Papworth welcomed everyone and Miss B. Fisher president commented on the absence this year of Miss Butler, due to illness. She presented a gift cheque to Mr Lacey (head of Redhill School) for the purchase of books or equipment. Mrs Lacey thanked the Association and recalled with warmth the visit to the school of Miss Sneyd last year. The chairman then introduced Miss Barbara Hadley, an ex pupil of the High School, who spoke entertainingly of school life and other experiences. She then proposed the toast to the Association. Raffle prizes were won by Mrs Merrick, Mrs Beckley, Miss Shepard, Mrs Haden, Miss Hadley and Miss Grendon.

Changes to several future meetings were announced, including the next one, which will be a demonstration of ceramic jewellery craft, by Mrs K. Kay, on Wednesday, May 20, at 7.45 at Redhill School. Mrs Kay will also bring items for sale on that night. All members and friends are welcome.

News Brief...

Old girls' meeting

Members of the High School Old Girls' Association met at Redhill School in November and were addressed by Mr Chris Bradley, who spoke on 'Deer in the Wyre Forest.' His talk was accompanied by a series of excellent slides and gave a fascinating insight on life in the Forest.

Mr Edwin George, the Forestry Commission ranger and his wife, were also on hand to answer questions, and gave details of the Deer Museum at Button Oak.

Raffle prizes were won by Mrs D. Strangewood and Miss A Strangewood.

The first meeting of 1986 will be on Wednesday, January 15, at 7.45 pm at Redhill School, when Miss J. White will talk about her recent holiday in India — illustrated with slides.

Old Girls meeting

Stourbridge High School Old Girls' Association held their last meeting of 1985 at Redhill School.

Rosemary and John Gripton provided a programme of varied music from the shows and after a selection of songs, sherry and mince pies were served.

The next meeting of the association will be held on Wednesday, January 15, 1986, at 7.45 pm at Redhill School when Miss Joan White will give an illustrated talk on her recent holiday in India.

Old Girls Assoc.

At the March meeting of the Association, held at Redhill School, Mrs Christine Round entertained members with a talk entitled "Your Character in Your Handwriting' — a fascinating insight into the art and science of graphology. Raffle prizes were won by Mrs M. Casey and Mrs S. Singleton.

Chairman Mrs Anne Papworth announced a visit to Lee Longlands (Furnishing Store) in Birmingham on May 20, and gave details about the Annual Dinner of the Association to be held on Wednesday, April 15 at the Pedmore House. All former pupils, staff and friends were welcome on that occasion — for more information please ring Stourbridge 375059.

Keeping ahead to boost charities

A Stourbridte Old Girls' Association enjoyed a display of hairdressing talents which helped raise cash for charity.

Members of the Redhill School Old Girls' Association asked Brierley Hill hairdresser Trevor Leddington to stage an evening's demonstration to raise funds for the NSPCC and Cancer Research.

Chairman Jan Lewis said the event raised £150 and 250 people turned up.

"The money will be split equally between the two charities", she said.

"We arrange a big show every two years but this is the first one solely on behalf of charity."

● Pictured are members of Redhill School Old Girls' Association with members Mrs Meg Guiness (NSPCC), Trevor Leddington and Mrs Shirley Ellison (Cancer Research).

Old girls' association

The February meeting of Stourbridge High School Old Girls' Association was held at Redhill School, when Mrs B. Deeley, of Bridge Antiques, Market Street, Stourbridge, brought along her collection of pot lids, and other small collectable items, including paperweights, silver spoons, vinaigrettes, snuff boxes, etc. Mrs Deeley gave a most interesting talk on the history of the pot lids, all made in Victorian times in Stoke-on-Trent. Members also brought along small items to display and identify.

Raffle prizes were won by Mrs Ingram and Mrs Wormington.

The next meeting will be on Wednesday, March 18—Your character in your handwriting—Mrs C. Round.

The Old Girls raise money for a good cause (1985). They have a varied and interesting programme!

Old girls' get-together

Two 'headmistresses' get together at the OGA Annual dinner.
Standing l to r: Miss D. A. Butler; Miss B. M. Fisher; Mrs J. George; Mrs K. Parkes (1983).
Sitting: Mrs M. Acty.

Miss Sneyd returns as visiting speaker (Miss Butler sitting next to her).

Miss Voyce in relaxed mood at an OGA social event.

The Old Girls make a surprise presentation to Miss Fisher on her retirement from Redhill School: an encyclopaedia of flowers and garden plants, a garden centre token and a miniature cricket bat (she had an interest in Worcestershire County Cricket Club) signed by WCCC players! L to r: Miss Butler; Mrs K. Parkes; Miss Fisher; Miss A. Spencer.

```
        R E D H I L L    S C H O O L


            MEMORIAL   SERVICE

                  for

    MISS ANNE SPENCER  (1939 - 1984)

                   on

            MONDAY 16th JULY 1984

                   at

               7.30 p.m.

                   in

    ST. MARY'S CHURCH, OLDSWINFORD
    (By kind permission of the Rector, Canon H.L. Davies)
```

```
              ORDER   OF   SERVICE

ORGAN VOLUNTARY                    Mr. M. Pegg
INTRODUCTION         The Rector, Canon H.L. Davies
HYMN                         'At the Name of Jesus'
LESSON             read by Mr. C.T. Lacey, Headmaster
WIND BAND              'Sheep may safely graze' (Bach)
SOLO            'Pie Jesu' by Fauré : Mrs. A. Broadbent
HYMN                  'The King of Love my Shepherd is'
APPRECIATION OF MISS SPENCER'S LIFE
                 Miss B.M. Fisher, former Head of Redhill
PRAYER AND THANKSGIVING
                     The Rector, Canon H.L. Davies
WIND BAND        'Jesu, Joy of Man's Desiring' (Bach)
HYMN                      'O Jesus, I have promised'
PRAYER AND BLESSING  The Rector, Canon H.L. Davies
ORGAN VOLUNTARY                    Mr. M. Pegg
```

Memorial Service programme for Anne Spencer.

Death of former headmistress

Former headmistress from 1950-1972 of Stourbridge Girls' High School, Miss Audrey Butler has died in Wordsley Hospital at the age of 80.

A graduate of Bedford College, London University, she held teaching posts in Winchester and at Pate's School for Girls, Cheltenham, where she was appointed to a deputy headship before gaining her first headship at Batley High School for Girls.

When she retired in 1972 her links with the school continued with the Old Girls Association, of which she was president for many years. After comprehensive re-organisation in 1976, when the High School as such ceased to exist, she was anxious that links between its former members should not be lost.

Miss Butler donated her body to the Medical Faculty of Birmingham University.

Announcement of death of Miss D. A. Butler, 1987.

Of course the inevitable had to happen one day and the OGA album contains a poignant news cutting in 1987:

In her fifteen or so years of retirement there seems very little doubt that Stourbridge High School OGA had been a lifeline to Miss Butler and a great deal of credit must go to her for ensuring that 'links between its former members should not be lost'.

It is not surprising that a Thanksgiving Service was held for our former headmistress at Oldswinford Church.

Miss Fisher's letter of tribute to Miss Butler captures entirely her character and achievements.

SGHS Old Girls' Association

Dear Member,

I know many of you are feeling that Miss Butler's death in September marked the end of an era, and this is natural since she had been associated with the school and O.G.A. for 37 years.

Before coming to Stourbridge Miss Butler taught in Winchester, was a Deputy Head in Cheltenham, and Head of Batley High School. On hearing of her death a Head under whom she worked wrote 'I was always fond of her, respected her high standards of scholarship, her integrity, her capacity for hard work, and enjoyed her sense of fun! No doubt the Governors recognised these qualities when they appointed her to the Headship of S.G.H.S. in 1950 with a brief to expand the VIth Form. When she retired in 1972 she had certainly carried this out for the VIth Form had risen from 30 to over 130, and the school numbers from 400 to 600. With this increase had come steadily rising academic standards, a wider curriculum and more girls were going on to Higher Education. Miss Butler was also interested in other aspects of personal development and did much to encourage extra-curricular activities. She often recalled the time when parents and school were working for the swimming pool, and her interest and enjoyment of school musical and dramatic productions continued after re-organisation and she rarely missed one.

The O.G.A. was an important part of the school and Miss Butler herself was anxious not to lose touch with girls when they left school. I don't think she relished the idea of retirement because the school had become the centre of her life. However she soon found that helping with the Duke of Edinburgh Award Scheme at the Y.W.C.A. was an enjoyable way of keeping in touch with High School pupils and her desire to see the O.G.A. continue after re-organisation proved to be the tonic she needed. She had a phenomenal memory for names and never appeared to have the slightest difficulty in remembering any of the 2000 or so girls who had passed through the school in her day. We shall always remember her frequent requests for news and the ways in which she sought out news of careers, current whereabouts, marriages and families. It was a mammoth task to turn the scraps of paper we gave her into the interesting newsletter which must have been read in most parts of the world. When her health necessitated her giving up her home earlier in the year, the one consolation was the fact that the home for the elderly was run by an Old Girl and therefore would 'be all right'! Messages from Old Girls did much in her last months to make her still feel part of the O.G.A.

In a letter like this it is impossible for me to include all that you would wish to be written about Miss Butler, but you must add your own memories......... Those of you who were at the Thanksgiving Service will recall the Rector of Oldswinford referring to Miss Butler as 'one of Stourbridge's characters'. Yes, a character recognised by many as she cycled round the town; respected by those who knew of her contribution to education in the town; remembered with affection by those who knew her as 'my Headmistress'.

The most fitting memorial to Miss Butler is a thriving O.G.A., and I hope you will help to make it so by coming to meetings and letting the secretary have your news. As a more tangible memorial the Committee are consulting the Rector and hope to provide something for the church. If you would like to contribute please contact Kate Parkes, our Treasurer, at the address given above.

With all good wishes for Christmas and 1988,

Yours sincerely,

Beryl Fisher,
President.

Letter of tribute by Miss B. Fisher to Miss D. A. Butler, 1987.

The Old Girls meet and 'make merry', usually on the third Wednesday in the month.

The Old Girls enjoy looking through the OGA photo album.

An Old Girls line-up: they haven't changed much, have they?

The 100th anniversary celebration 2005, where the cake was cut by 'old girl' Beryl Bloomfield.

And so we fast-forward to 2005 when a very special event was held – complete with a cake depicting the school badge and colours to mark the 100th anniversary of the founding of the school. The cake was white with 100 on it and the badge and ribbon in, of course, school colours of gold, green and navy.

The OGA continues to thrive, with meetings held, by tradition, on one Wednesday evening of each month – the only exception being the month of August. An excellent programme is planned for each year – the one below is for 2011 and gives name and contact details of chairman and treasurer (Pat Grainger (née Seabury) for people interested in joining. Thanks to Pat and Kate Parkes (secretary) and their hard-working committee, there is no danger of Stourbridge Girls' High School and the OGA being forgotten. (Chairman/Treasurer/Membership: Mrs P. Grainger, Email: pandrgrainger@hotmail.com)

In addition to the monthly Old Girl meetings various reunions are frequently held (for example, an annual dinner), often organised

Pat Grainger (née Seabury) Chairman/ Treasurer of SGHS OGA.

Stourbridge High School Old Girl's Association

Programme 2011

Meetings are held at 7.45 pm
at Redhill School
Junction Road
STOURBRIDGE

By kind permission of the Headmaster

Programme 2011

Jan 19   **Stourbridge Street Pastors**
         Mrs. C. Hall

Feb 16   **A Book about The High School**
         Mrs. M. Brettle

Mar 16   **The Work of Mother Teresa**
         Mrs. M. Bose

Apr 20   **ANNUAL DINNER at the Granary**

May 18   **The Hazards of Entertaining**
         Mrs. C. Paterson

Jun 15   **Summer Outing**
         Halfpenny Green Vineyard

Jul 20   **Black Country Murders**
         Mr. I. Bott

August   Holiday – no meeting

Sep 21   **Annual General Meeting . . . . . plus**

Oct 19   **A Talk on Badgers**
         Mr. E. Amess

Nov 16   **Worcester Cathedral**
         Mr. J. Bailey

Dec 7   **Christmas Meeting plus Flower Demo**
         Mrs. S. Munden

OGA programme for 2011.

'The best hockey team ever!' said the 'Golden Girls'.

by different 'groups' or 'eras' of OGA and other 'old girls'. On occasions enjoyable social functions are arranged between SGHS 'old girls' and KEGS 'old boys'! One such function (admirably organised by Adrian Clark ('old boy') is a regular reunion between those 'boys' and 'girls' (with Mr Dennis Waters) who acted in the joint plays together!

I think it is fitting to conclude this section of the book with mention of a Stourbridge Girls' High School 'Golden Girls' 50-year Reunion held at Grafton Manor Hotel, Bromsgrove on Friday 3 April 2009, organised in the main by Gill Onslow (née Balderstone); Jackie Jeavons-Fellows (née Harris) and Vivienne Mason (née Rushton). (It only seems like yesterday that Gill and Viv were school prefects.)

This event was to mark the occasion of it being 50 years since many of the 'girls' had left the High School and a marvellous programme

'Golden Girls' Reunion 2009.

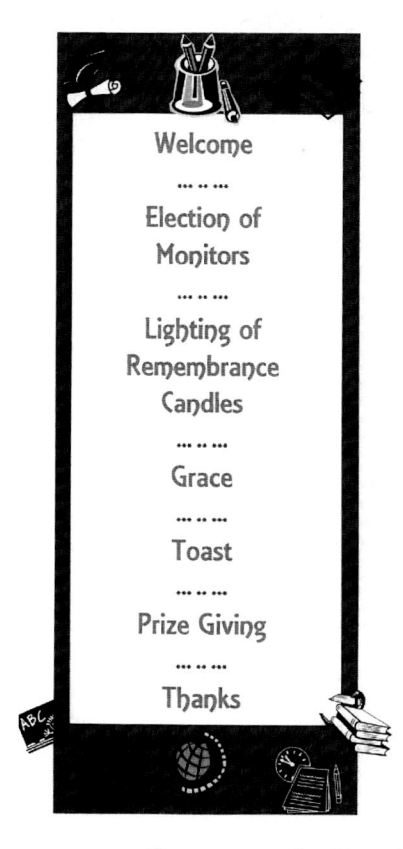

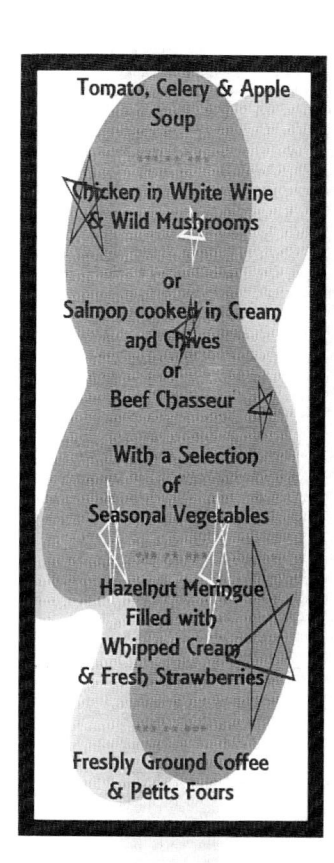

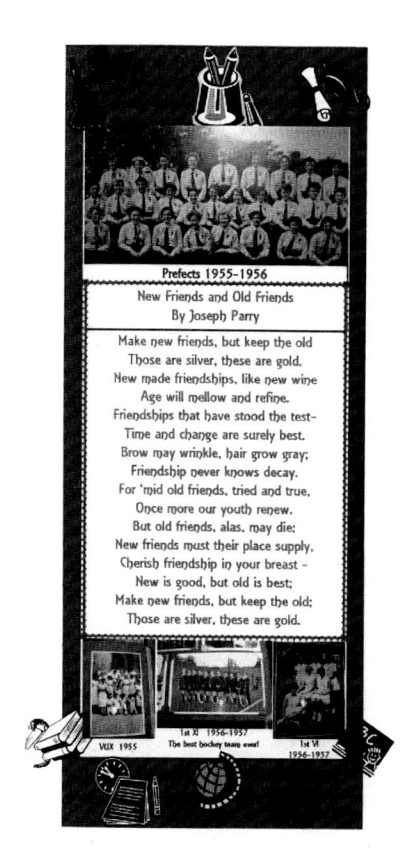

Programme for Reunion, April 2009, for leavers 50 years ago. How time flies!

Marjorie Davies née Bird, aged 96, and Ivy Freemantle, aged 97, probably the two longest surviving 'old girls' of SGSS and SGHS.

was produced, again in school colours, complete with a selection of school photographs in miniature.

It's difficult to think of a more appropriate *raison d'être* for the OGA than the poem 'New Friends and Old Friends' by Joseph Parry which was included in the programme for that occasion:

New Friends and Old Friends
by Joseph Parry

Make new friends, but keep the old
Those are silver, these are gold.
New made friendships, like new wine
Age will mellow and refine.
Friendships that have stood the test –
Time and change are surely best.
Brow may wrinkle, hair grow gray:
Friendship never knows decay.
For 'mid old friends, tried and true,
Once more our youth renew.
But old friends, alas, may die;
New friends must their place supply,
Cherish friendship in your breast –
New is good, but old is best;
Make new friends, but keep the old;
Those are silver, these are gold.

(Well, our schooldays *were* our happiest days. Weren't they?)

Appendix II
Whatever became of the staff?

Thanks to Miss Butler's Newsletters it is possible to obtain news of the staff of SGHS and their whereabouts up until 1986. It becomes rather more difficult after that, but, with the help of 'old girls' and former members of staff, a bit of detective work and consultation of the website for Ancestry.co.uk, etc. it has been possible to find up-to-date information for some of them. Unfortunately it cannot be a complete list by any means. Where news is 'hot off the latest press' it is indicated by (2011). Alphabetical order rather than 'hierarchical' order has been used, and names are included, even if they are already mentioned in the text, as it seemed the 'right' thing to do.

Hopefully, readers will not regard this merely as a list of retirements and deaths but rather as a chance to remember the *lives* of those who undoubtedly influenced our daily lives and achievements when we were SGHS girls!

ADAMS, Mrs	Retired in 1971 and continued to live in Stourbridge.
BACHE, Mrs (née WELLS)	Went to live in Bourneheath near Bromsgrove after retirement.
BACON, Mrs	Stayed on as a member of Redhill School staff.
BANNER, Miss	Left SGHS to teach French at St Mary's Convent, Folkestone.
BARGEMAN, Mrs	Stayed on as a member of Redhill School staff.
BARNES, Mrs E. (née NAGLE)	Left SGHS and went to live in Hertfordshire.
BARTLETT, Mrs	Took a post in a consortium in Birmingham – appointed to try to raise the standard of Maths teaching in the city.
BARTON, Mrs	Died in 2000.
BEAL, Dr M.	After leaving SGHS went as headmistress of Torquay Girls' Grammar School which had no plans to become comprehensive. Retired and enjoyed learning Spanish and exploring Exmoor. It was the custom at the Torquay school to name Houses after headmistresses – thus there was a Beal House there some time after she retired.
BEST, Mrs	Transferred to King Edward Sixth Form College staff. Became joint head of Music Dept. and conductor of the Choral Society and String Orchestra.
BOWEN, Mrs	Went to live in Stroud, teaching at a local secondary modern school and enjoying having a first-year tutor group.

BRADLEY, Mrs (née ELLIOTT)	Retired and lived in Stourbridge.
BRAITHWAITE, Mrs (née MOODY)	Lived in the south after 1948. Great interest was sailing.
BUCK, Mrs	Went to live in Bradford, looking after her young children and no longer teaching.
BURKE, Mrs (née COLLETT)	Went to work in the Education Dept. of the Middlesex Polytechnic, although her home was in St Albans.
BUTLER, Miss Doris Audrey	After retirement in 1972 she continued to live locally, taking a keen interest in the OGA. She died in Wordsley Hospital in 1987 at the age of 80, leaving her body to medical research.
BUTTER, Miss	Went to teach on the staff of independent school Alice Ottley in Worcester.
COBOURNE, Mrs C. (née PARRY)	Transferred to staff of King Edward Sixth Form College and was staff rep. on governing body and liaison tutor.
COGHLAN, Mrs E. (née FLETCHER)	Went to live in Wargrave near Reading and taught Spanish part-time at the Holt School, Wokingham.
COOPER, Miss D.	Retired from SGHS and went to live in Hagley.
COTTON, Dr	Transferred to staff of King Edward Sixth Form College.
DALE, Miss Beatrice May	She came back to Stourbridge very little after her retirement in 1950. Had more than 20 years of very happy retirement in her Cotswold house at Guiting Power, involving herself in gardening, landscaping and being vigorously active in village affairs. When her health failed she went to live near her sister in Cambridge. She died on 26 January 1980.
DAVIES, Mrs (née GRANT)	Went to West Horsley, near Leatherhead – no longer teaching and has a young daughter and a son.
DAY, Mrs	Stayed on after 1976 to teach at Redhill School.
DRANE, Mrs P.	After retirement in she went to live in Bexhill. After her husband died she frequently visited her son in Germany.
DREW, Mrs (née DYKINS)	Taught Biology in early 1950s at SGHS and still taught in the local Stourbridge area. Attended OGA dinners.
DROMGOOLE, Miss	Retired in 1948. Died in 1953.
EASTWOOD, Miss	Retired in 1950.
EDWARDS, Miss	Retired in 1942. Died in 1944.
EDWARDS, Mrs M. (née POLKINGHORNE)	When she left SGHS, she and her husband Michael (a Methodist minister) lived in rural Northamptonshire where she taught for a year in a village school. She had two children, a boy and a girl, and gave up teaching for a while whilst they were small, apart from some supply teaching. She started teaching again in 1970 when they were in the Oxford circuit and taught at Milham Ford Girls' School, which she enjoyed very much. From there they went to Kenya for seven years where she taught in a girls' high school and wrote programmes for schools' broadcasts (O and A level). Michael taught Church History in a theological college and at the University of Nairobi.

On their return to the UK Maureen decided to leave teaching and worked with the Methodist headquarters in London, sharing in the adult education programmes. This was a fascinating job, combining teaching and writing skills, and sometimes allowed her to travel overseas (the Caribbean, India, Burma, Sri Lanka) as a journalist to write up stories and information to encourage Methodists in this country to relate to and donate money for overseas projects. She met many interesting people, including many of whom she interviewed in her London office and wrote their stories.

After ten years of this work she tired of commuting and decided to go freelance as a writer and editor, which she continued for 14 years, doing as much or as little as she wanted. Again, this involved working with writers of different cultures, editing and writing Bible reading notes, mainly for the international *Bible Reading Association* and for the *Methodist Prayer Handbook* – both annual publications.

They came to Redhill, Surrey to retire in 1996, but sadly Michael died in 1997. Maureen continues to keep busy, however, in her local church which is very multicultural. She keeps in touch with Mrs Valerie Ruddle.

She remembers particularly the rules of 'silence' in the corridors of SGHS as pupils changed classrooms between lessons. Also the queuing in silence to enter the dining-room and 'no talking' until grace had been said. After lunch, girls led out in orderly lines, again in silence!

She also remembers the rules about wearing hats outside school grounds. If she met any girls in the street after 4 p.m. with their berets in their pockets they promptly retrieved them and, to avoid order marks, quickly put them on their heads. The senior members of staff were very strict, she thinks, but generally highly respected for their commitment and care of pupils. Many were prepared to spend extra time to help gifted pupils to achieve and obtain a good university entrance. She considers that the school had a good academic record and, as far as she can remember, the less bright students were encouraged to achieve their potential. She remembers a few rebels (not named!). Maureen herself received plenty of encouragement from some of the more experienced staff but lived in fear of one or two – again no names! Overall she enjoyed her six years at SGHS.

On the cultural side she remembers visits by the CBSO giving wonderful concerts in the school hall (2011).

ELDRIDGE, Miss Since 1978 was principal of the school where she had taught since 1969 – Asaba Girls' Grammar School in Western Nigeria. The school was in the process of becoming comprehensive

	and admitted its first intake of unselected pupils in December.
EMMS, Miss	Retired in 1940. Died in 1947.
FARMER, Mrs	Gave up peripatetic teaching but continued to take private pupils for piano and cello lessons.
FIRMAN, Mr	Stayed on after 1976 to teach at Redhill School.
FIRTH, Miss E. M.	Retired in 1932. Died in 1964 at Southport, aged 88.
FISHER, Miss B.	Retired from Redhill School in 1983. Has a happy and active retirement, including being involved in OGA. She was a co-author of a book about Dudley Girls' High School (2002). Lives near Stourbridge (2011).
FLAVELL, Mrs S. (née ROUND)	Transferred to staff of King Edward Sixth Form College. Later worked for the Home Tuition Service for 5 years before retiring.
FLINT, Mrs	Stayed on at Redhill School for a while and then became head of Geography at King Edward VI High School for Girls, Edgbaston.
FRANKLIN, Mrs	In 1977 was living in Stourbridge looking after her baby son.
FRAYNE, Mrs	Retired and went to live in Kidderminster. Enjoyed visits with her husband to see her married son in Canada.
GOLMAN, Mrs	Transferred to staff of King Edward Sixth Form College.
GORRINGE, Mrs	Taught at Gloucester High School and lived at Churchdown. She had a son and two daughters, the elder of whom studied Medicine at St Mary's Hospital, London.
HADEN, Mrs Joan (née MAKIN)	After retirement she became very involved in Stourbridge local affairs and was president of the Stourbridge Historical & Archaeological Society (1978–9). Died in June 1999. Her husband Jack died in 2005.
HADLEY, Mrs Elsie Freda (née SELWOOD)	Decided to take early retirement (after comprehensive education and its changes because she missed the sixth form teaching so much). Had a very busy, happy retirement with particular interest in a newly-acquired greenhouse as well as her long-standing hobbies of baking and dressmaking. Enjoyed walking and holidaying in Switzerland. Died in November 2003.
HARKNESS, Mrs (née CROFT)	Enjoyed living in Germany with her family. (Had transferred there because husband's job moved to Munich.) Learned to ski. Bought a small house in Brighton for holidays.
HART, Mr	Stayed on to teach at Redhill School after 1976.
HARTLEY, Mrs Pamela (née YATES)	Transferred to staff of King Edward Sixth Form College to teach Biology. Had two young sons.
HAYES, Mrs	Became a neighbour and colleague of Mrs Coghlan and was assistant head of the Middle School and second in the History Dept. at the Holt School, Wokingham.
HAYWARD, Mrs	Stayed on to teach at Redhill School after 1976.
HEPBURN, Miss	Stayed on to teach at Redhill School after 1976.
HEWIS, Mrs	After retirement was very involved with 'the Bench' and

	eventually retired as a JP. Was known to be living in Halesowen and enjoying a busy, active life.
HODSON, Mrs (née SKIDMORE)	On leaving SGHS she and her husband ran the well-known hotel at Alverley called The Mill.
HOLLIS, Mrs (née SHARPE)	Became superintendent physiotherapist of the Multiple Handicap Service of the Dudley Area Health Authority. Made several visits to the USA where her younger daughter taught at George Washington University. Her other daughter went to live in Worcester where she had many activities and interests.
HOSKINS, Mrs (née MORRIS)	Went to live in Edinburgh in 1977. She had come previously to SGHS for teaching practice and returned later to become a member of the French staff.
HYND, Mrs	Stayed on to teach at Redhill School after 1976. Retired and went to live in Hagley. (Her younger daughter married Kate Gingell's brother.)
INGOLDSBY, Miss E.	Retired in 1954 from SGHS.
IRONS, Miss M.	After leaving SGHS in 1953 and taking up a commission with the RAF she married Mr Richard Walton in 1956.
ISZATT, Mrs (née JACKSON)	Went to live and teach in Sheffield for 12 years but then lived in Bridlington.
JOACHIM, Mrs	Left SGHS in 1975. Gained a PhD in Geological Sciences at Birmingham Univ. in 1978. Had a baby daughter in 1977. Was Liberal candidate for West Gloucestershire in the 1979 election. Moved to London and started work in computing. In 1980 was elected as Liberal (later Alliance) prospective parliamentary candidate for Finchley and in 1983 fought the General Election against Mrs Thatcher, increasing the Liberal vote by 50 %. In 1984 she became chair of the Fawcett Society (founded 1866), the longest-established society to campaign for equality between the sexes. She also fulfilled a life-long ambition by going on a three-week trek and wildlife holiday to Nepal. Transferred to Rudolph Wolff to work with large international-accessible database of commodity trading information. In 1985 she was a panellist on BBC's *Question Time* and was selected as parliamentary prospective candidate for Epsom and Ewell. She was the British example in a *Newsweek* feature on women with careers and families. Has also been training officer for parliamentary candidates (1979–84) and helped train a group which existed to get many more women into Parliament.
JOHNSTONE, Mrs	Went to live in Stone, Staffs. Taught Classics at Clayton High School, Newcastle-Under-Lyme.
JONES, Mr	Owing to reorganisation in Taunton, moved in Sept. 1980 from Bishop Fox's Girls' Grammar School to teach Physics at the Richard Huish Sixth Form College.
KOHLASE, Mrs (née PARSONS)	Lived in Hagen, West Germany after 1969 and taught English

	and French in a large grammar school there. Had an operation but thanks to much determination and effort she recovered.
LEE, Mrs	Retired and lived in Stourbridge, taking an active interest in school and church affairs. Was the organiser in Pedmore for house-to-house collection for Christian Aid.
LEIGH, Miss M.	After retirement from SGHS in 1947 went to live near Lewes, Sussex. She died in June 1984.
LEWIS, Mrs	Stayed on to teach at Redhill School after 1976.
LLOYD, Mrs (née SMITH)	Went to teach at Leasowes School, Quinton.
LOWE, Mrs	Died in 1957 (whilst still in post at SGHS).
McCOOKE, Mrs Joan (née SHEPPARD)	As Miss Sheppard she became deputy head of SGHS and when Miss Wells retired from full-time teaching in 1969 she became head of the French Dept. and, after the change to Redhill Comp. School, she held the post of head of Languages. She retired from the staff of Redhill in July 1978 and shared a home with Miss Wells in Stourbridge. Both attended OGA functions. She enjoyed a very happy and active retirement, spending many holidays abroad with Miss Wells, chiefly in France. She married Mr John B. McCooke in December 1988 in Stourbridge. She died in October 2004 at the age of 85.

Wedding photograph of Miss Joan Sheppard and Mr John McCooke, December 1988 (her outfit was a lovely mid blue with a paler blue hat. Flowers pale pink and white).
(Photograph kindly supplied (in colour) by CJB Photography – Chris and Jenny (old girl) Bridgewater)

McLEOD, Miss	Stayed on to teach at Redhill School after 1976.
MORRIS, Mrs K.	Left SGHS in 1972 because of transport difficulties and transferred to the independent school Heathfield at Wolverley. Retired from there, but died in 1983.
MORRIS, Miss M.	Transferred to staff of King Edward Sixth Form College. Retired from her post there in 1983 and then began to take a

more active role in the Church in the parish of Kinver, eventually becoming ordained in 1994. She is still serving as Assistant Curate at the present time at the age of 83 (2011).

MOUNTFORD, Dr	Stayed on to teach at Redhill School after 1976.
NAGLE, Miss E.	Married Mr Edwin Barnes in 1956.
NIGHTINGALE, Mrs (née POPE)	Had a son and three daughters. Lived in Pedmore.
NILSSON, Miss	Went to teach at Ilkley College of Education, living in Leeds. In Jan. 1980 she had an exhibition of her wood carvings at Colwyn Bay, Wales. Her great hobby was to collect interesting shapes of wood in the forests of Sweden or by the rivers in north Wales and then to fashion them as she pleased. She retired and went to live in Wales, which she enjoyed very much.
O'KEEFE, Mrs O.	In 1977 was living in Stourbridge looking after her baby son and daughter.
PAGE, Miss	Went to live in Sudbury, Suffolk.
PAYTON, Mrs Deborah Cawthorn	Widowed in 1979, lived in West Hagley near her sister. She died in 2003, aged 96.
PEMBERTON, Mrs (née GUEST)	Went to live in Cornwall, coaching in Italian, French and Spanish, but 'retired' from teaching while her children were young.
PRESCOTT-CLARKE, Mrs Z.	After retirement became vice-chairman of her parish council. Went to live in Ockeridge in south Worcestershire. Died in 1999.
PRESLEY-JONES, Mrs Gwynneth Hilda (née PRESLEY)	After retirement she was married in Kidderminster in 1971 to Mr Alfred Jones, but was known as Mrs Presley-Jones. Lived in Chaddesley Corbett and very much enjoyed doing painting and artwork, some of which was exhibited. She died in July 1994.
PRITCHARD, Miss J. M.	Stayed on to teach at Redhill School but decided to transfer to the staff of High Arcal School, Sedgley.
RUDD, Mr	After leaving SGHS returned to further education. Lectured in Applied Science at the Dept. of Graphic Communication and Printing Technology, an outpost of the Matthew Boulton Tech. College on the campus of Aston University. In 1983 he stood for Parliament as an Ecology candidate and also set up a branch of the Friends of the Earth in Stourbridge and Halesowen. His other activities included singing with the Brierley Hill Choral Soc.; Nature Conservation with Worcs. Nature Conservation Trust and support for mentally handicapped adults through the Camphill Houses movement.
RUDDLE, Mrs Valerie (née HILL)	Left SGHS in 1958 to take up a music teaching post in Jamaica, where she also met and married an Englishman working for Barclays Bank. They returned to England in 1973 and she did a little teaching, but then became increasingly involved in church music, leading 'music in worship' workshops in many places as well as being director of music at Sevenoaks

Methodist Church which she attends now. She keeps in touch with Maureen Edwards (née Polkinghorne).

She remembers in her first week of teaching at SGHS that she had the entire Sixth Form, all 90 of them, for class singing, which was somewhat daunting and a little ridiculous. She also remembers Bettine Rogers (remembered by many old girls, especially those who sang with her in New Road Methodist Church choir) had lessons alone for O level Music in Valerie's first year at SGHS and again in her second year for A level, getting through the two-year syllabus in one in each case, which was quite a challenge and delight. Apparently nobody had taken O level Music as a GCE subject before, so Valerie felt privileged to be responsible for its introduction. She says that her own diaries make several references to her work with the junior and senior choirs, which she felt was a great joy (2011).

SCARRATT, Miss	Worked at Chorley Wood College for the Blind. Lived in Stourbridge and worked at Wolverhampton Poly. in an administrative capacity.
SHAFEE, Miss	Stayed on to teach at Redhill School after 1976.
SHAND, Miss	Went to teach in Germany but regularly visited England to see her mother in Bexhill.
SHOTBOLT, Mr	Stayed on to teach at Redhill School after 1976.
SMITH, Mrs (née COOK)	Went to live in Loughborough. Taught Physics part-time at Loughborough High School (independent). Had two daughters.
SNEYD, Miss Dorothy Naomi	Lived (after retirement in 1960) in Barcombe in Sussex with Miss Leigh. She missed the friendship of Jane Staples (née Green and an old girl of SGHS), whose husband was Rector of Barcombe but who moved to Old Windsor. Miss Sneyd continued to return to Stourbridge and spoke at an OGA dinner. Also officiated at the unveiling of Miss Firth's memorial window. She died in August 1990 in Lewes, Sussex at the age of 89.
SPENCER, Miss Anne	Stayed on to teach at Redhill School after 1976 and was deputy head. (She was an 'old girl' of SGHS.) She died in May 1984.
TAYLOR, Mr	After the closure of Bangor College where he had transferred as a lecturer he returned to teaching in the Hemel Hempstead area.
TILLEY, Miss	Retired in 1947. Died in 1968.
TOLLEY, Miss	After retirement, she continued to live in Red Hill, working hard to maintain her garden to its usual standard of excellence.
TURNER, Miss Claire	Remained on the staff of Redhill School after 1976. Retired in July 1985 after being on the staff of SGHS and Redhill for a total of 29 years and had worked with four heads. Enjoyed doing more skiing after retirement. Lives in Worcestershire (2011).

VINCENT, Miss Flora May	Retired in 1955. Died in Malvern in 1966.
VOYCE, Miss Constance Joan	Stayed living in Stourbridge after her retirement and attended OGA functions. My mother, working for WVS, remembers taking Miss Voyce Meals on Wheels and she told my mother that she remembered me! Ominous? Helped to transcribe the parish registers of Oldswinford during her retirement. She died in 1993, aged 88.
WALL, Miss Z.	Having left SGHS in 1955 to return to her native county of Northumberland for another teaching post, she married Mr R. Murray in 1958.
WELLS, Miss E. M.	Finally retired at the end of Summer Term 1977 after she had been teaching at SGHS for 48 years and this set up a record. She had given up full-time teaching in 1969 but after that had been taking Oxford Entrance and Scholarship work. Died in November 1986.
WOODALL, Miss Lorna Ruby	After retiring from SGHS she stayed living in Hagley and did a lot of voluntary work for Hagley Free Church. She said that her years of retirement were some of the happiest ones of her life. She died in 1978 after an illness that necessitated a long stay in Bromsgrove Hospital. Former pupils and colleagues attended her funeral, and the church was full.
WYLDE, Miss	Transferred to staff of King Edward Sixth Form College and became one of their vice-principals.

Appendix III

The 'Old Girls' remember ...

(Only space for just a few)

ADAMS, Linda (née LEMON) 1953–8 ...*Miss Sneyd...(always reminded me of Queen Victoria), History, sweet lady...actually listened to her in class. Miss Pritchard - the only teacher who I felt a connection with...whilst others gave up she supported and encouraged me in a kind, caring, dedicated way. Miss Woodall - I think she was a little puzzled by me but was a quiet 'nice' lady. Mrs Hodson - Art, she actually looked like a 'real' woman! No offence intended but the other teachers were just a little, well if you were there at the time you know just what I mean! Miss Nagle - French...enjoyed learning the basic language with her. Later I was transferred to a higher group and Miss Wells (educated at the Sorbonne no less) was charged with furthering my French education. Sadly the enjoyment waned.*

BAMBER, Viv (née MARTIN) 1958–63 ...*the hats, the order marks (no I don't think I got many, but the threat was always there), the prefects who were scary, the uniform, and the strict discipline. Oh how I wish the schools these days had half the discipline which we had then. We respected most of the teachers - there were one or two who scared us and one or two who we despised - and we behaved ourselves in class. We had assembly every day, and although at the time a school of 650 or so seemed very big, especially on the first day there, nowadays it seems positively cosy in size.*

Living in Kinver I did not have much chance to join in after school activities as there was always the school bus to catch, even during the journey keeping our hats on until we got home, and never never eating in the street...I left at 16 despite having very good exam results, but the value of study and academic knowledge was well installed into my personality, I just needed to make the choice myself, rather than follow the set path which was expected of me. Now I am a Church of England Reader at the same church - Kinver St Peter's - as Mary Morris, then my RE teacher, now my priest and honorary curate, and I wear a uniform again - although not a hat!

BAXTER, Megan (née ROUND) 1950–8 ...*playing 'steps' on the quad. steps. Miss Pritchard falling down the platform steps following assembly and nobody moving a muscle because Miss Voyce turned round and glared at us, to see if she could catch anyone daring to laugh.*

BETT, Janet (née HOMER) 1953–60 ...*'scrumping' little apple-like fruit from off the trees in the school garden - delicious. Miss Nilsson saying in a strong Swedish accent - 'rart side against rart side' - referring to crossway strips in needlework. Every time I thread my own sewing machine to make curtains for myself or my children I remember Miss N. and her instructions. Also, Mrs Peyton tapping the side of her desk and calling for quiet in a ladylike way...Lyn Flavell and Pat Charles bursting the new pipe of the very new spin dryer by putting it through the rollers...it makes me giggle even now, over 50 years later!*

BLOOMFIELD, Beryl (née SMITH) 1939–46 ...*diving under the desks (during War time) at the teachers' command 'Take cover!' to practice taking cover from possible falling bombs. (fortunately it was never for real!). Knitting squares for blankets for troops in France and, under Miss Wells's instruction pinning small notes to those destined for the French soldiers...'Que Dieu vous bénisse' (May God keep you safe). Wearing black overalls for Chemistry and white ones for Cookery. Miss Wells telling them that if they ever had the opportunity to get married - take it!*

BRETTLE, Marion (née DAVIES) 1953–60 ...*being enthralled by a performance of 'Macbeth' in the school hall by a visiting theatrical group - we all fancied Banquo - finding out later much to our surprise that it was an all-female group with very gruff voices! Getting a 'B' order mark in my first Term for leaving my purse in the cloakroom (temptation for thieves!) Getting another 'B' order mark during my first Term (throwing somebody's beret down the road, to defend a friend from attack but not listened to). The consequence of this was that I had to hand my Form Prefect's badge to Miss Vincent for 2 weeks, i.e. publicly 'dishonoured'! Feet dragging up the hill after lunch at home to face 'double Chemistry' with dread. Eating cherries (from home) with friends across the games field in Summer and feeling that all was right with my world - Sixth Form.*

BRIDGEWATER, Jenny (née CARTWRIGHT) 1960–7 *Miss Woodall - gave me a love of Eng. Lit. and even grammar. Remember a lesson in the Library, when some of us caught sight of a mouse coming out of the waste paper basket. She never turned a hair! She was such a lovely elderly lady even then. Miss Woodman (?) - she taught us Latin and also played the piano on occasions during school assembly. Some of the pupils made her life hell, I felt so sorry for her, as looking back she was just a young and inexperienced teacher who was doing her best.*

Miss Presley - lurking in the Chemistry Lab. put the fear of God into all of us! Woe betide you if you spilt anything on her work benches. I still remember her instruction that if this happened, you were to flood the surface with water, trouble is we were all totally paralysed with fear when it happened. And why would my equations never balance? Miss Butler - knew the name of every girl in the school. Miss Makin - Geography, put the fear of God into us, woe betide you if you were caught running along the corridor or were inside when you should have been out. Instant order mark. Miss Eldridge - exceptionally tall French teacher. Remember one April Fool's Day we had hung a spider over the door. She just reached up and took it down. She inspired my love of French language, together with Miss Parsons and later Miss Sheppard and Miss Wells. 'Bonjour mes élèves, comment allez-vous?' Mrs Hewiss, for Maths; remember how shocked we all were when told by our form teacher that her husband had been killed in a freak accident. We all behaved extra well for the next few days. All credit to her, she did not take time off.

Our form rooms - how we would groan if we were allocated one of the 'travelling' ones...it meant that you had virtually no lesson in your own form room, and consequently had to carry all your books around for lessons. So easy to forget something and get a 'C' order mark.

BUTLER, Ann (née DAVIES) 1949–54 ...finding a stick insect and taking it to the Staffroom at break time to show Miss Vincent who showed great interest and absolutely no anger at having her precious break interrupted. (Devotion to duty!)

CLEWLEY, Rachel (née ROBINS) 1957–64 ...I submitted my college applications to Miss Butler for approval. I had chosen all mixed-sex colleges. Miss Butler sent them back with my choices crossed out and had substituted them with all-female colleges! I duly went to an all-female college...

COBOURNE, Carole (née PARRY) Miss Butler being kind to her because she had transferred to SGHS from another school at the time of mock 'O' levels and the syllabus had changed. Miss B persuaded Carole's peers to copy out their notes for her so she would have some idea of what to revise.

DAVIES, Kay (Professor Dame) (née PARTRIDGE) 1962–9 The person I remember best is Miss Presley who was an inspirational chemistry teacher. She was an enthusiastic communicator and encouraged us to do practical work first hand which sometimes led to exciting fires! This would not be allowed today.

I remember having a difficult time in my first year because I was not very good at languages and there was a science bias. However, I found the staff supportive and I eventually settled. Mr. Cameron had to get me an O level in Latin in 2 years which he did in an inspiring way. I had a *good time in the school and remember also enjoying the hockey. I was a bit geeky but I made good friends that I am still in touch with.*

DAVIES, Marjorie (née BIRD) 1926–30 ...*Miss Leigh used to 'borrow' girls' handkerchiefs with which to clean the blackboard.*

At break time at the 'old library' building someone came up from the basement with trays of cut up fruit cake and cups of milk - the girls could buy them for a halfpenny.

DAVIES, Pat (née DAVIES) 1947–53 ...*Miss Selwood in Biology saying to her: 'You know, Pat, it's like extracting a tooth to get an answer out of you!'*

EDWARDS, Chris (née WILLIS) 1959–64 ...*Miss Makin falling over backwards off her chair at the beginning of a Geography lesson. Uninjured but nobody dared to laugh at the time.*

Eventually Miss M. picked herself up and told the class that she had been told that theirs was a 'bad' class but that she could see that this was not true, at which she smiled and the class could let out its pent-up hysterical laughter.

EVANS, Irene (née LEAR) 1949–56 *Miss Eastwood (Music) swooping around the corridors wearing a dramatic purple cloak and getting the girls to sing about '<u>naice</u> mince pies'.*

FREEMANTLE, Ivy 1925–32 ...*the walks after lunch, (SGSS days) in a crocodile, wearing hats and gloves of course. There was a New Road/Worcester Street/Love Lane route.*

The original SGSS hats resembled a nurse's cap in navy, turned up at the front and back and sides. Cream panamas in Summer. No ties. Miss Leigh (Geography) taking a class outside on the balcony of the 'old' Library building - very exciting if dangerous.

GEORGE, Linda (née HARPER) 1964–70 *I think it was in my Fifth year at SGHS and Mrs Hewis was our Form Teacher but we seemed to have an arrangement where Mrs Haden (Miss Makin) would step in if Mrs Hewis wasn't there. This would usually be due to her Magisterial Duties as a JP. One morning Mrs Hewis wasn't there to take the Register, she turned up later in the morning, all in a flap. (If you knew her, you would remember her flaps, she was delightful but dotty) 'GIRLS!!' she said. 'Girls! I called into Market Street, on the way to school and when I went back to my car, it wasn't there!!! It's been STOLEN!' Of course we were all righteously indignant on Mrs Hewis's behalf.*

Later in the day, Mrs Hewis came in, all shame-faced. 'Girls!! They found my car. I didn't park it where I thought I had!' We all laughed with her, not at her, she was a delightful Form Teacher.

The 'Old Girls' remember ...

I remember Miss Makin, shyly telling us that she was to be married. I think she was almost 50 but as 13-year-olds we all thought she was incredibly old to be getting married for the first time. I thought it was lovely, as she was clearly very much in love and liked to tell us tales about her husband, who I think was known as Jack, a local journalist, historian and eccentric.

HUGHES, Diane (née HAINES) 1955-60 ...*being late back to school after lunchtime and hiding with a friend behind a car so that Miss Sneyd wouldn't see us. We forgot that our feet showed underneath the car and we heard the dreaded words 'I can see you both' from Miss Sneyd! Caught red-handed - we weren't wearing our hats!*

KEIGHTLEY, Madeleine (née JOHNSON) 1960-5 ...*wearing navy blue knickers for PE and having to go across the road to the playing fields in them in full view of passers-by. Having to keep to the left-hand side in the corridors like traffic.*

LAU, Juanita (née YOUNG) 1966-73 ...*going to Gwyneth Postlethwaite's very proudly to buy my new SGHS uniform; my new shiny satchel; having to wear my hair in pigtails because not allowed to be long and loose. Indoor and outdoor shoes!*
Being STCF Monitor and collecting the money from people every week on Wednesdays. Being very embarrassed running through the showers - a friend slipped and broke her wrist doing this.

MERRICK, Sue (née RYDER) 1955-60 ...*hiding with friends in the toilets from Miss Makin...we shouldn't have been there!*
We were considered by the Staff as the naughtiest/worst form in the history of SGHS!

ONSLOW, Gill (née BALDERSTONE) 1950-7 ...*my memories are all happy ones because of the sport as much as anything. Used to play in hockey, tennis and cricket teams, which helped a lot with Physics (Yuk!) and Chemistry (likewise). Doing a lot of family history these days makes me wish I had paid more attention to History though. Being told off as one of a group of girls for picking raspberries off the allotment alongside the hockey pitch! I was normally a law-abiding person and tended never to rock the boat too much and feared the backlash of my parents (particularly my Father who disciplined us with a mere look!) more than the school.*

TROTMAN, Margaret (née ORFORD) 1941-7...*my Grandfather and Great Uncle used to rent the fields where the High School was built, on which they ran a dairy farm. The fields were referred to, locally, as 'Orfords' fields.*

WILKES, Hilary 1955–60 ...*that I was the friend hiding behind the car from Miss Sneyd with Diane Haines!*

WORTON, Jane (later MACDONALD) 1963–8 ...*being one of a group of about 25 SGHS girls who went by coach to London for the Centenary celebrations of Dr. Barnardo's Homes, held at the Royal Albert Hall. It was a very exciting day and in the morning we were driven round the sights of London. At the Albert Hall, my friend Susan Newey presented our purse of money to Princess Margaret. It was a very proud moment. The only downside was that we had to wear our school uniform all day, but, thankfully, no hats. We were really impressed with 'swingin' sixties' London, and it seemed a long way from Stourbridge! A truly memorable day.*

Were they the naughtiest form in the school? Surely not!

Acknowledgements

I would like to thank the following people without whose help this book could not have been a realistic portrayal of life at Stourbridge Girls' High School, and of its pupils and staff. I am indebted to them for providing me readily and willingly with help and support, information, original photographs, memorabilia, and/or their own unique memories; also for their enthusiasm for a book about SGHS.

SGHS 'Old Girls' and Former Members of Staff

Linda Adams (née Lemon); Viv Bamber (née Martin); Megan Baxter (née Round); Janet Bett (née Homer); Zeldah Bishop (née Lock); Beryl Bloomfield (née Smith); Barbara Bolter (née Hall); Ann Butler (née Davies); Jenny Bridgewater (née Cartwright); Carole Cobourne (née Parry); Kay Davies (Professor Dame) (née Partridge); Marjorie Davies (née Bird); Pat Davies (née Davies); Chris Edwards (née Willis); Maureen Edwards (née Polkinghorne); Irene Evans (née Lear); Beryl Fisher (for providing the Foreword); Ann Fox (née Cartwright); Ivy Freemantle; Linda George (née Harper); Pat Grainger (née Seabury); Velda Hampton (née Skelding); Madeleine Homer; Diane Hughes (née Haines); Madeleine Keightley (née Johnson); Annette Kyte; Juanita Lau (née Young); Jane Macdonald (née Worton); Viv Mason (née Rushton); Sue Merrick (née Ryder); Mary Morris; Gill Onslow (née Balderstone); Kate Parkes (née Fisher); Valerie Ruddle (née Hill); Marjorie Webb (née Lowe); Hilary Wilkes.

People Other Than 'Old Girls'

Richard and Alison Brettle (my husband and daughter) for their unfailing support and encouragement (yet again) throughout the research and writing of this book.

Mr S. Dunster (headmaster, Redhill School) and his predecessors for allowing the 'old girls' to meet in the school premises and for his interest and enthusiasm for the book. Also for allowing me (via a member of his staff) a nostalgic view of the Honours Board and stained glass windows in the Hall.

David Hickman for alerting me to the vital, all-important fact that the OGA existed and was 'alive and well'. Also for liaison on my behalf with the Stourbridge Historical Society and for support and interest generally.

Colin Macdonald for help and support via his Stourbridge website.

David Quinton (Dudley Architects' Department) for a copy of A. Vernon Rowe's 'Elevation' for the proposed new Stourbridge High School building.

Businesses & Organisations

Black Country Bugle newspaper.

CJB Photography (Hagley: Chris and Jenny Bridgewater) for so promptly and willingly providing me with a copy in colour of Miss Sheppard's wedding day photograph.

Dudley Archives staff for help and advice.

Ellingham Press (publishers) for their professionalism at all times and for guiding me through the process of writing and publishing this book.

Stepalong, Wollaston for their interest and support.

Stourbridge Girls' High School Old Girls' Association members generally, for all their support and encouragement.

Stourbridge Library staff for archive material and help generally.

Worcester County Archives staff for help and advice.

Illustrations

I am grateful to the following people for the loan of their personal photographs and documents:

Linda Adams (née Lemon) SGHS badge on front cover, 91 top left

Janet Bett (née Homer) 111

Chris and Jenny Bridgewater (CJB photography, Hagley) 196

Robert Butler 189 bottom left

Irene Evans (née Lear) 90, 91 bottom left + right, 92 top right, 93 top + bottom right, 94 top right and bottom, 95 top

Ann Fox (née Cartwright) 94 top left, 102

Ivy Freemantle SGSS badge on back cover, 31, 32 top left, 45, 46 top, 47 bottom, 48, 189 bottom right

Pat Grainger (née Seabury) 187, 189 top

Annette Kyte 156-7

Sue Merrick (née Ryder) 206

Gill Onslow (née Balderstone) 89, 91 top right, 92 bottom, 93 bottom left, 104, 105 bottom, 106 bottom, 188 top + bottom

Marjorie Webb (née Lowe) 97 top right + bottom

All remaining illustrations were from Stourbridge High School Old Girls' Association archives and were kindly loaned to me by Kate Parkes (née Fisher), the secretary of the Association, and Pat Grainger (née Seabury), chairman and treasurer.

Bibliography

Chambers, R. L.	*King Edward VI School Stourbridge:the story of a school,* Stourbridge, Mark & Moody Ltd, 1988
DuMont, M. *et al.*	*Dudley Girls' High School: a portrait of a School 1881–1975,* Stourbridge, The Robinswood Press, 2002
Edrich, R.	*Bayley's Children: a history of Wrekin College 1880–2005,* Shrewsbury, Ellingham Press, 2005
Haden, H. J.	*The Stourbridge Scene 1851–1951,* Dudley Teachers' Centre, 1976
Haden, H. J.	*Stourbridge in Times Past,* Chorley, Lancs., Countryside Publications Ltd., 1980
Marshall, A.	*Girls Will Be Girls,* London, Hamish Hamilton, 1974
Perry, N.	*A History of Stourbridge,* Chichester, Phillimore & Co. Ltd, 2001
Redhill School	*Redhill School Summer Garden Party 1999,* Stourbridge, Redhill School, 1999

DVDs

Heritage Media	*Looking Back At Stourbridge*
Heritage Media	*The Stourbridge Story*

Websites

www.ancestry.co.uk
www.friendsreunited.co.uk
www.google.co.uk
www.stourbridge.com
www.thisiswherearetheynow.co.uk

Index

NOTE: Page numbers in *italic type* refer to illustrations.

11-plus examination, 69, 98
50-year 'Golden Girls' Reunion, 188-90
75th SGHS Reunion, 179-80
100th anniversary celebrations, *186*, 187

Acty, Mrs M., *183*
Adams, Linda (née Lemon), 89, 201
Adams, Mr, 170
Adams, Mrs, *76*, *87*, 149, 150, 159, 191
Albright Medal, 45, 49
Allen, J., *58*
Allen, Miss, 122
Allman, Mrs, 116, 122
Allott, Miss, *87*, 100
Andrews, Mrs, 115
art, 13
art and technical school, 8
Ashmore, Mrs, 142
assembly, 88, 143, 145
athletics, 128
Atholl, Duchess of, 42-4
Atkins, Mrs, 115

Bache, Mrs E.N. (née Wells), *24*, *27*, 33-4, 191
Bacon, Mrs, 159, 170, 191
badges, 105-6
    school badge, *9*, *42*, 45
badminton, 160
Balderstone, Gill (later Onslow), *97*, *105*, 188, 206
Bamber, Viv (née Martin), 201
Banner, Miss, 122, 159, 191
Barbara Price Medal, *28*, 45, 49, 79
Bargeman, Mrs, 191
Barlow, F. (née Hughes), 38-9
Barnes, Mrs E. (née Nagle), 191, 197

Barritt, Olive (née Clare), 52, 79
Bartlett, Mrs, 159, 191
Barton, Mrs, 124, 168, 191
Baxter, Megan (née Round), 202
Beal, Dr Mavis, 155, *162*, 164-5, 191
Beale, Brenda, *111*
Bendall, Mr, 142, 158
Besso, Miss Ruth, 122
Best, Mrs, 116, 168, 172, 191
Bett, Janet (née Homer), 108, *111*, 202
bicycles, 21
Bird, Marjorie (later Davies), 30, 31, 45-7, *189*, 204
Bird, Norma, 92
Bishop, Barbara, 97, 108, *111*
Blakeway, Dorothy, 133
Bloomfield, Beryl (née Smith), *186*, 202
Bloor, Hilary, 145, *160*
Bowen, Mrs, 122, 191
Boys' Grammar School *see* King Edward's Grammar
    School for Boys
Boyt, Mr, 21, 62
Bradley, Mrs (née Elliott), 120, 192
Braithwaite, Mrs (née Moody), 192
Brander, Miss, 68
Brazier, B., *58*
Brettle, Marion (née Davies), *111*, 202
Bridge, Catherine, 46
Bridge, M., *58*
Bridgewater, Jenny (née Cartwright), 202-3
Brodie, Pandy, 152
Brookes, Margaret, 126
Brown, Joyce, *93*
Brown, Katherine, *111*
Brown, May, *47*
Brown, Richenda, 108
Bryan, Miss, 116

Buck, Mrs, 159, 170, 192
Bullock, Gill, *91*, 95
Burke, Mrs (née Collett), *86, 92, 97, 104,* 109-10, 192
bursars, 10, 12
bus/coach journeys, 31, 161
Butler, Ann (née Davies), 203
Butler, Miss Doris Audrey, 85, 101, 104, 192
    death of, 184-5
    on grammar/comprehensive education, 98, 108, 163
    headmistress's report (1957), 98
    and Old Girls' Association, *147,* 177, 178-80, *183,* 184
    photographs of, *86, 87, 147, 151, 162, 183*
    praise for, 88, 148-9, 184-5
    on public-spiritedness, 109
    retirement of, 148-9, 150-1
    tributes to others by, 129-30
Butler, Molly, *92*
Butter, Miss J., 120, 162, 192

Cameron, Jane, *91, 94, 96,* 122
Cameron, Mr, 122, 158, 159
careers advice, 99, 113, 117
careers on leaving school, 12, 99, 104, 113
Carnegie, Andrew, 7, 9
Cartwright, Mrs, 170
Case, Olive, *47,* 58
catchment area, 7, 10, 85, 89
Chambers, Mr, 103
Chambers, Priscilla, 106
Chance, Miss, *24, 39, 45,* 70
charity work, 66, 127-8, 133, 147
    see also community work
Charles, Mrs, 130
Cheshire, Gill, *92,* 95
chess club, 128
choir, 101, *107,* 108, 129
Christmas Carol Service, 146
Christmas performance (1963), 116
Clark, Adrian, 188
Clark, Miss Margot, *77, 91, 94,* 95
Clewley, Rachel (née Robins), 203
cloakroom, 36, 39
Cobourne, Mrs Carole (née Parry), 168, 192, 203
Coghlan, Mrs Elizabeth (née Fletcher), 67, 80-1, 161, 162, 192
Collett, Miss A. (later Mrs Burke), *86, 92, 97, 104,* 109-10, 192
Collins, Alison, 126
'Colours' and games girdles, 20, *29,* 47, 106
commemoration service (1954), 101
committee minutes, 68-9
community work, 45, 109, 126-7, 148, 160
    see also charity work

comprehensive school system, 98
    move to, 123-4, 163-5, 170, 173
Cook, Miss (later Mrs Smith), 137, 198
Cook, Mrs P., *162*
Cooke, Miss, *17, 24, 27,* 37, *39, 45,* 51-2, *57, 64, 65,* 67
Cooke, Mrs E.J., *147, 151*
Cooper, Miss D., *76, 87,* 133, 143-4, 145, 192
Cooper, Mrs, 142
Corcoran, Josephine, *47*
Coronation of King George VI, 62
Costain, Miss, *76*
Cotton, Dr, 170, 192
Cotton, Miss, 168
County Coat of Arms, *42*
Cox, Mrs, 122
Craddock, Mrs, *86,* 101, 155-8, 177
Crawford, Elizabeth, 133
cricket team (1959), *106*
Croft, Miss R. (later Mrs Harkness), 121, 133, 194
Cromack, Mr, 39
CSE examinations, 128, 146
cultural activities, 89
    see also choir; plays; societies and clubs; trips and visits
curriculum
    1909 HMI report, 13
    1950 HMI report, 88
    sixth form, 35, 99, 146
Curry, Pat, *96, 97*

Dale, Miss Beatrice M., 55-9, 63, 176, 192
    photographs of, *56, 57, 59, 60, 64, 65, 76, 77*
    reminiscences by, 78-9
    resignation, 75
Darby, Helen, 95
Davies, Mrs, 108
Davies, Mrs (née Grant), 192
Davies, Cissy, *46*
Davies, Kay (Professor Dame) (née Partridge), 203-4
Davies, Marion (later Brettle), *111,* 202
Davies, Marjorie (née Bird), 30, 31, 45-7, *189,* 204
Davies, Pat (née Davies), 204
Davis, M., 61-2
Davis, Mrs, 115
Day, Mrs, 170, 192
detention, 34
dining room
    in new school, *43,* 51, 114, 121
    in old school, 33, 34, 36, 39, 40
discipline, 31, 34, 80, 171, 193
Dodd, Audrey, *47*
Doley, Jennifer, *96*
domestic science, 81, 125
Downing, Patricia, 142
Dr Barnardo's, 66, 127-8

Index

drama, 150, 160
  see also plays
dramatic societies, 130-1, 160
Drane, Mrs P., 100, 102-3, 158-9, 192
Drew, Mrs (née Dykins), 192
Dromgoole, Miss E., *24, 26,* 39, *45, 57, 65,* 68, 74, 99-100, 177, 192
Dutton, I., *58*
Duvignère, Mlle, 100

Eastwood, Miss, *24, 28,* 38, 39, *45, 56, 65,* 75, 82, 169, 192
Eaton, Miss, 148
Education Act (1902), 8
Education Act (1918), 22
Education Act (1944), 69-70
education policy, 8, 22, 69, 163
  see also comprehensive school system
Edwards, Chris (née Willis), 204
Edwards, Mary, 142-3
Edwards, Miss, 39, 66, 67, 175, 176, 192
  photographs of, *24, 25, 45, 56, 57, 64*
Edwards, Mrs M. (née Polkinghorne), *87,* 100, 103, 192-3
Eldridge, Miss, 103, 115, 193-4
eleven-plus examination, 69, 98
Elliott, Miss (later Mrs Bradley), 120, 192
Elwell, Carmel, 171
Emms, Miss L.M., *17, 24, 26,* 38, 39, 40, *65,* 70-1, 78, 194
English, 13, 79-80, 131, 137, 138
entrance examinations, 69, 98
equipment
  HMI reports on, 12, 14
  science laboratory, 19, *20*
Evans, Irene (née Lear), *91, 92, 94,* 204
Evans, Mr, 110, 120
Eveson, Mrs (Mayoress), 62
examination paper (1933), *48*
examination results, 21, 128, 146
examinations, 35, 102
  CSE, 128, 146
  entrance exams, 69, 98
  GCE, 74-5, 99, 146
exchange visits, 89, 128, 139
expulsion, 22, 34

Fanshaw, Miss, *45*
Farmer, Mrs, 162, 194
Faulkner, Elizabeth, *111*
fees, 9, 10, 12, 21, 69
  see also scholarships
fire watching, 67
Firman, Mr, 194

Firth, Miss Ethel M., 9, 175, 194
  1909 HMI report, 12-13
  death of, 120, *121*
  photographs of, *8, 10, 19, 24, 45*
  praise for, 33, 122-3
  pupil recollections of, 31, 36-7
  resignation, 49-50
  strength/ingenuity of, 15, 19
Fisher, Miss Beryl M., 167, 169, 172-3, 194
  and Old Girls' Association, 179, 181, *183,* 185
Flavell, Mrs S. (née Round), 109, 142, 168, 194
Flint, Mrs, 194
Folk Group, 127
forms, renaming of, 120
Forrest, Janet, 95
Forrest, Nicola, 148
Forsythe, Christine, 162
Francis, Ms Emily, 68
Franklin, Mrs, 170, 194
Frayne, Mrs, 133, 194
Freemantle, Ivy, 30-1, 45, *46,* 47-9, 120, *189,* 204
French, 13, 81, 139, 161
French examination, author's late arrival for, 102
fundraising, 115, 161, 169, 178, *182*
  see also charity work
funeral of Priscilla Chambers, 106
further education, 12
  see also higher education

Games Committee (OGA), 175
games girdles, 20, *29,* 47, 106
games lessons, 34, 36, 38, 81
  uniform for, 90, *91*-7
  see also gymnasium; playing fields; sports; sports teams
GCEs (General Certificate of Education), 74-5, 99, 146
George, Linda (née Harper), 204-5
George, Mrs J., *183*
Gibson, Miss, 44
Girl Guides, 22, 24, 29, 30, 63, 68
girls, secondary education for, 8
'Golden Girls' 50-year Reunion, 188-90
Golman, Mrs, 194
Goodman, Mrs, 168
Goodwin, Miss, *86*
Gorringe, Mrs, 103, 194
Gougs' cafe, 45-7
governors, 49, 62, 70, 120, 129-30, 169, 178
governors' minutes, 20-2
Grainger, Pat (née Seabury), *187*
grammar schools
  Miss Butler's opinion of, 98, 108
  see also King Edward's Grammar School for Boys
Grant, Miss S., 122, 137

'great gale', 78
Green, Brenda, *111*
Green, Susan, *92*, *95*, *97*
Grémy, Mlle, 148
Griffiths, Pauline, *111*
Guest, Miss M. (later Mrs Pemberton), 122, 197
Gunn, Miss, 87, 102
Gunn, Mrs, 120
Guttery, Helen, *92*, *94*
gym lessons, 36
    see also games lessons
gymnasium
    new school, *46*, *47*, 114
    old school, 34, 39

Haden, Mr Jack, 122
Haden, Mrs Joan (née Makin), 77, 87, *102*, 122, 136, 139-40, 194
Hadley, Gaynor (née Beauchamp), 139-40
Hadley, Mrs Elsie Freda (née Selwood), 103, 139-40, 194
Hadley, Mrs G., *147*
Haig, Miss, *86*, 100, 115, 120
Hale, Mrs, *147*
Hand, F., *58*
Handley, Mr, 122, 133
Hanke, Maureen, 171
Harkness, Mrs (née Croft), 121, 133, 194
Harris, Miss, *10*, *15*, *20*, 44, 49, 61
Hart, Mr, 194
Hartley, Mrs Pamela (née Yates), 142, 168, 194
Hayes, Mrs, 162, 194
Hayward, Mrs, 162-3, 194
head girl, 80
headmistress's report (1957), 98
Hepburn, Miss, 170, 194
Hewis, Mrs, *86*, 143, 145, 159, 194-5
Higgins, Mrs J., *151*
higher education, 12, 35, 99, 104, 108, 112, 123, 128, 149
    fund for university students, 66, 67
Hill, Barbara, *46*
Hill, Janice, 148
Hill, Miss (later Mrs Ruddle), 87, 103, 197-8
Hinchley, Jennifer, *96*, *97*, *111*
Hinchley, Josephine, *111*
Hindle, Ann, 125
Hingley, Clare, 172
history, 132, 133
HMI inspections, 9-15, 88
hockey teams, *18*, *29*, *47*, *89*, *92*, *97*, *143*, 176
Hodson, Mrs (née Skidmore), 77, *86*, 124, 126, 195
Hollis, Mrs (née Sharpe), 195
Homer, Janet, 108, *111*, 202

homework book, 38, 55, 59
Hopkins, Ruth, *160*
Horridge, Ann, 95
Hoskins, Mrs (née Morris), 195
house captains, 109
House system, 13, 44-5, 51, 66, 105, 162, 171
housecraft see domestic science
Housecraft Society, 128
Hughes, Diane (née Haines), 205
Hunter, H., 62-3
Hurley, Canon A.V., 101
Hutchins, Miss, 44
Hynd, Mrs, 142, 195

Ingoldsby, Miss E., 100, 195
Irmela Filz, 128
Irons, Miss M., 100, 103, 195
Iszatt, Mrs (née Jackson), 195

James, Lesley, 171
Jeavons, I., *58*
Jeavons-Fellows, Jackie (née Harris), 188
Joachim, Mrs, 158, 170, 195
Johnson, Hilary, *91*
Johnson, Karen, 162
Johnson, Madeleine, 100
Johnson, Mrs P., *151*, *162*
Johnstone, Mrs, 115, 159, 195
Jones, Hilary, 108
Jones, Margaret, *111*
Jones, Mr, 195
Jones, R., *58*

Kay, Angela, *109*
Keightley, Madeleine (née Johnson), 205
Kelly, Philippa, 126
Killon, M.R., *58*
Killon, Ruth, 130
King Edward's Grammar School for Boys (KEGS), 21, 31, 63, 126
    joint choir with, 108, 129
    joint plays with, 103, 116, 126, *127*, 160, 188
    reunions with, 188
King Edward's Sixth Form College, 163, 167, 168
Kirton, Gloria, *111*
'Knit-In', 147
Kohlase, Mrs (née Parsons), 116, 122, 195-6

'late transfer' girls, 85
Latin, 13
Lau, Juanita (née Young), 205-6
Lawton, Darrylyn, *91*, *94*, *96*
Lea, Margaret, *111*
Lear, Irene (later Evans), *91*, *92*, *94*, 204

Index

Leather, Mr, 129
Lee, Mrs, 142, 161, 196
Lefrere, Mrs, 160, 163
Leigh, Miss M., 37-8, 39, 51, 71, 81, 82, 196
    photographs of, *24, 26, 56, 57, 64, 65*
Lester, Mrs, 124
Lewis, Miss (later Mrs Payton), *57, 64, 76, 77, 86,* 121, 124-5, 132, 197
Lewis, Mrs, 170, 196
library *see* public library; school library
Lloyd, Louise, *111*
Lloyd, Mrs (née Smith), *77, 93,* 116, 196
Local Education Authorities (LEAs), 8, 14
Lofthouse, Mrs, 137
Love, Mr, 110
Lowe, Maureen, *97*
Lowe, Mrs, *86,* 102, 196
lunches, 21, 36, 40, 51, 121, 160
    see also dining room
Lunt, Mrs M., 129-30, 178
Lye Secondary School, 163, 173

McCooke, Mrs Joan (née Sheppard), *86,* 121, 128, 138-9, 196
McDonald, Miss W.M., *45,* 116
McKnight, Miss, 100
McLeod, Miss, 170, 196
Makin, Miss Joan (later Mrs Haden), *77, 87, 102,* 122, 136, 139-40, 194
Marks, Miss, 39
Mason, Vivienne (née Rushton), *92, 94, 97,* 188
mathematics, 13, 168-9
medals, 28, 45, 49, 79
Merrick, Sue (née Ryder), 205
Methodist church circuit, 103
Millinchamp, Mrs, 142
Mills, K., *58*
Mills, Miss, 142
Mission Band, 103
Mitchell, Deborah, *160*
Mobberley, Ena, *97*
Moody, Miss Eileen, 70, 178
Morfey, Kathryn (née Waterton), 112-13
Morgan, Mrs, 101
Morris, Miss M., 167, 168, 196-7
Morris, Mrs K., *87,* 121, 143, 149, 150, 196
Mountford, Dr, 197
movement performance, 115
Mumford, Miss, *86,* 116
music, 13, 168
music groups, 159-60, 172
    see also choir; orchestra
Music Society, 127
Myatt, Dorothy, 51-2, 79-80

Nagle, Miss E., (later Mrs Barnes), 191, 197
Nativity performance, 116
needlework, 100-1
netball teams, *15, 29, 58, 91, 94, 95, 96, 105, 123,* 176
Newey, Susan, 127
Newnam, Pat, *91, 96, 97*
newsletters (OGA), 179-80
Newton, Gill, *94*
Nightingale, Mrs (née Pope), 148, 170, 197
Nilsson, Miss, *87,* 100-1, 120, 197
Noott, Anne, 171
Norman, Marjorie, *94, 96*

Oakley, Miss C., *147*
O'Keefe, Mrs O., 161, 197
Old Girls' Association (OGA), 49, 125, 146-7, 150-1, 161, *162,* 169
    history of, 175-90
Oldswinford Parish Church, 101, 106
Omar, Asha, *173*
Onslow, Gill (née Balderstone), *97, 105,* 188, 205
orchestra, 117

Page, Miss, 168-9, 197
Palfrey, Mr, 120
Pankopf, Fräulein, 148
Parents' Association, 88, 136, 148, 149, 161, 163, 169
Parkes, Mrs K., *162,* 183
Parry, Joseph, 190
Parsons, Miss (later Mrs Kohlase), 116, 122, 195-6
Pattinson, Katy, *91*
Payton, Mrs Deborah Cawthorn (née Lewis), *57, 64, 76, 77, 86,* 121, 124-5, 132, 197
PE *see* games lessons
Pear Tree magazine
    articles, 61-3, 145-6, 163
    changes to, 129, *130,* 142, *144,* 155, *158*
    during World War II, 66, 67
    history of Old Girls' Association, 175-9
    memories of early years, 19, 32-40
    memories of 1930s, 51-3
    memories of 1930s-40s, 67, 78-83
    memories of 1950s, 110-14
    memories of 1960s, 142-3, 145
    memories of 1960s-70s, 151-2
    memories of 1970s, 171-3
    reviews of school, 122-4, 170
    school motto in, 108-9
    tributes to teachers
    1930s-40s, 49, 50, 67, 71
    1950s, 75, 99-100
    1960s, 110, 124-6, 130-3, 136-42
    1970s, 143-5, 148-9, 150, 158-9, 161, 164, 168, 169
    as valuable resource, 31-2, 44-5, 116

Pemberton, Mrs (née Guest), 122, 197
Petersen, Miss, 109
Platt, Ann, *111*
playing fields, 12, 21, 38
plays, 34-5, 63, 106-8
    joint with KEGS, 103, 116, 126, *127*, 160, 188
    Nativity performance, 116
    staff, 59-61, 66
Plimmer, Marjorie, *46*
Polkinghorne, Miss (later Mrs Edwards), *87*, 100, 103, 192-3
Poole, Pauline, *92, 94, 97, 105*
Pope, Miss (later Mrs Nightingale), 148, 170, 197
Powell, Janet, *111*
prefects, 13, 90, 105, 109, 122, 142
    photographs of, *25, 95, 105, 109, 123, 136*
Prescott-Clarke, Mrs Z., *86*, 120, 197
Presley, Miss, 68, *87*, 122, 137, 140-1, 143, 197
Presley-Jones, Mrs Gwynneth Hilda (née Presley), 197
Price, Barbara, 70
Price, Beryl (née Thomas), 34
Price, Ida, *28*
Price, Joan, 97, 103, *109*
Price, Mr R.H., 169
Priest, Margaret, *91, 94*
Priest, Rita, *94*
Pritchard, Miss J.M., *87*, 137, 169, 171, 197
prize-giving/speech days, 34-5, 37, 49, 78, 79, 129
prizes, 15, 70
    see also games girdles; medals
public library, 8-9
public-spiritedness, 109
pupil teacher centre, 7, 8, 9
pupil teachers, 10, 12
pupils
    background of, 10
    numbers of, 9, 10, 15, 21, 69, 85, 116, 148-9, 155
    reminiscences of, 201-6
    early years, 32-3, 34-9
    1930s-40s, 51-2, 79-83
    1950s-60s, 110-14, 142-3, 145, 151-2
    1970s, 171-2

qualifications
    of staff, 12-13, 14, 44, 88
    see also examinations

Rangers, 63
readings, in assembly, 145
Redhill School, 170, 173
Reynolds, E., *58*
Riley, Miss, *86*, 100, 102
Robins, Mr W.M., 9
Rogers, Bettine, 198

Round, Miss (later Mrs Flavell), 109, 142, 168, 194
rounders teams, *94, 96*
Rowberry, Kathleen, *111*
Rowberry, M., *58*
Rowley, Jean, *90*
Rudd, Mr, 120, 197
Ruddle, Mrs Valerie (née Hill), *87*, 103, 197-8
Rushton, Vivienne (later Mason), *92, 94, 97, 109*, 188
Russell, Sheila, 108, *111*

St Mary's Church, Oldswinford, 101, 106
salaries, 13, 14, 20
Scarratt, Miss E.M., 124, 163, 198
scholarships, 12, 30-1, 34
school badge, *9, 42*, 45
School Certificate, 35, 74
school dance, 160
school library, 40, *42*, 43, 121-2
school life
    committee minutes, 68-9
    governors' minutes, 20-2
    memories of *see Pear Tree* magazine
school motto, 108-9
school photographs, 24, 66, 116, 155
school premises
    new premises, 41-2
        extensions to, 101, 114, 146, 147, 167
        HMI report, 88
        limited space, 85-8, 98, 101-2, 112
        memories of, 52-3, 112, 113
        move to, 38
        need for, 15, 22
        official opening, 42-4
        plans, *23*
    original building, 7, 8-9
        HMI report, 12
        limited space, 21
        memories of, 33, 34, 35-6, 39
school reports, 30, *31*, 52, 55
school secretaries, 9, 101, 155-8, 170
School Training Fund, 66, 67
science, 13
science laboratory, 19, *20*
Scott, Cynthia (née Weaver), 71, 81-2
secondary education for girls, 8
Selwood, Miss (later Mrs Hadley), 103, 139-40, 194
Service of Commemoration and Dedication (1954), 101
Shafee, Miss, 159, 198
Shand, Miss, 100, 198
Sheppard, Miss J., *86*, 121, 128, 138-9, 196
Shotbolt, Mr., 198
Sixth Form
    expansion of, 85, 89, 99, 123, 148-9

Index

memories of, 35, 79, 104-5, 106-8, 113, 122
  see also prefects
Sixth Form Choir, 108
Sixth Form College, 163, 167, 168
Sixth Form Common Room, 147, 159
Skidmore, Mrs, 137
Smith, Anice (née Dewey), 131
Smith, Miss, 77, *93*, 116, 196
Smith, Mrs Margaret (née Orford), 142
Smith, Mrs (née Cook), 198
Smith, Shirley, *111*
Sneyd, Dorothy Naomi, 32-3, 67, 71, 110, 120, 159, 198
  and Old Girls' Association, 175, 177, 178, 181, *183*
  photographs of, *19, 24, 45, 56, 57, 64, 65, 76, 77, 87, 111, 183*
social class, 10
social events
  Old Girls' Association, 175, 176-8, 179-81, *185-6*, 187-90
  see also plays
societies and clubs
  1930s-40s, 45, 74, 81, 130-1
  1950s, 89
  1960s, 116-17, 126, 127, 128, 151
  1970s, 147, 160
  see also Girl Guides
Soper, Miss, 44
Southall, Edna, *46*
SPACE group, 163
speech days *see* prize-giving/speech days
Spencer, Miss Anne, 77, 122, 128, 138-9, *147*, 155, 181, *183*, *184*, 198
Spittle, Brenda, *91, 94, 96*
sports, 20, 45, *95*, 160
  see also Barbara Price Medal; games girdles; games lessons; gymnasium; playing fields
sports events, Old Girls' Association, 175, 176, 177
sports teams, 89, 106, 128
  cricket, *106*
  hockey, *18, 29, 47, 89, 92, 97,* 143
  netball, *15, 29, 58, 91, 94, 95, 96, 105, 123*
  rounders, *94, 96*
  tennis, *95, 97*
staff
  of early years, *10,* 12, 13, 14
  in HMI reports, 13, 14, 88
  living accommodation for, 22
  marriage of, 103, 161
  for new Redhill School, 173
  news of, 191-9
    1930s, 44, *45*
    1940s, 70-4, *75*
    1950s, 99-101, 102-3, 109-10
    1960s, 115-16, 120-1, 122, 124-6, 133, 136-42
    1970s, 143-5, 148-51, 158-9, 160-1, 162-3, 167-9, 170
  salaries, 13, 14, 20
  tributes to *see Pear Tree* magazine
staff plays, 59-61, 66
staff turnover, 20, 100
  see also staff (news of)
staffroom, 33, 40, 59
stained glass window memorials, 49, 61, 120, *121*
Staples, Jane (née Green), 113, 144
Stathers, Miss, 170
statues, 35, 36
Steveni, Mrs, 163, 170
Stevens, Mrs, 170
Stockley, Amanda, *160*
Stourbridge high street, as forbidden, 45, 59, 78
Strangwood, J., *58*
Streatfeild, Noel, 70
Student Christian Movement (SCM), 116-17, 127
swimming lessons, 52, 81, 114-15
swimming pool, 114-15, 122, 136, 149, 178

'T' forms, 85
Taylor, Mr, 142, 198
Taylor, Sylvia, *96*
teachers *see* staff
teaching careers, changing approach to, 100
teaching methods, 131
  HMI reports, 13, 14, 15
Telford, Muriel, *46*
tennis, *91, 93,* 177
tennis courts, 46
tennis teams, *95, 97*
Theatre Group, 126
theft, 22
Thomas, Mr, 108
Tilley, Miss A.E., 37, 39-40, 71-4, 81, 82, 130-2, 198
  photographs of, *24, 25, 45, 46, 56, 59, 60, 64*
timetable, *11,* 160
Tolley, Miss, 169, 171, 198
Torode, Mrs, 159
travel to and from school, 31, 161
'travelling form rooms', 32, 101-2, 112
tree planting ceremony, 62
trips and visits
  1920s, 33-4, 35, 37, 38
  1930s, 45, 63, 130
  1950s, 89, *94,* 100, *102,* 108, 111
  1960s, 115, *117,* 120, 126, 127-8, 151-2
  1970s, 159
  Old Girls' Association, 176
Trotman, Margaret (née Orford), 205
Turner, Jennifer, *91, 94, 95, 97*
Turner, Miss, *10, 16, 24, 25, 28,* 37, 39, 49, 61

Turner, Miss Claire, 96, 198

Uglow, Nellie, *47*
uniform
    1920s, 24, 35, 38-9
    1930s, 45, 55, 80
    1950s, 89-90, *91-7*, 111, *173*
    1960s, *136*, 142-3
    1970s, 146
    see also games girdles
universities, 35, 104, 108, 112, 123, 128, 149
university students, fund for, 66, 67

Vale, Janet, 141
Vaughan, Ann, *92*
Vincent, Miss Flora May, *76*, 126, 199
Voyce, Miss Constance Joan, 103, 116, 120-1, 124-5, 132-3, 199
    photographs of, *45, 56, 59, 64, 76, 77, 86, 89, 183*

Wadsworth, Miss, 129, 133
walks after lunch, 36, 40
Wall, Miss Z., *76*, 100, 199
Walters, Diana, *94*
war *see* World War I; World War II
War Memorial, 24, 36
Wassell, Rosemary, *160*
Waters, Bridget, 126
Waters, Mr D., 103, 188
Webster, Gaynor, *111*

Wells, Miss E.M., 68, 102, 136, 137, 138-9, 158, 161, 199
    photographs of, *45, 57, 64, 65, 68, 76, 77, 86*
Wells, Miss E.N. (later Mrs Bache), *24, 27*, 33-4, 191
West, Mrs, 115
Weston, Carol, *90*
White, Mrs, 142
Whitehouse, Susan, 126
Wilkes, Hilary, 206
Wilkes, Pat (later Wilson), 74, 82-3, *92, 95*, 110-12, 177
Williams, Miss, 70
Wilson, Miss, 44
Wilson, Pat (née Wilkes), 74, 82-3, *92, 95*, 110-12, 177
wind quintet, 159
windows (memorial), 49, 61, 120, *121*
withdrawals from school, 15, 22, 68, 69
Witherford, Mary, *96, 111*
Wood, Ann P., 152
Woodall, Miss Lorna Ruby, 62, *65*, 68, *77, 86*, 106-8, 128, 131, 136-8, 147-8, 199
Woodend, Mrs, 161
World War I, 15
World War II, 62-3, 66-9, 78-9, 80, 99, 140-1, 176
Worton, Jane, (later Macdonald), 206
Worton, Kate, *173*
Wright, Claire, 142
Wylde, Miss S.M., 103, 148-9, 164, 167-8, 199

Yates, Miss (later Mrs Hartley), 142, 168, 194

Zamir, Mr, 170